TRANSFORMING VISION

TRANSFORMING VISION

Explorations in Feminist The*logy

Elisabeth Schüssler Fiorenza

Fortress Press

Minneapolis

TRANSFORMING VISION
Explorations in Feminist The*logy

Cover image: *Hush*, Lou Wall © Lou Wall/Corbis
Cover design: Laurie Ingram
Book design: PerfecType, Nashville, TN

Library of Congress Cataloging-in-Publication Data
Schüssler Fiorenza, Elisabeth, 1938-
Transforming vision : explorations in feminist the*logy / Elisabeth Schüssler Fiorenza.
p. cm.
Includes bibliographical references.
ISBN 978-0-8006-9806-5 (alk. Paper)
1. Feminist theology. 2. Feminist theory. 3. Liberation theology. 4. Women in the Catholic Church. I. Title.
BT83.55.S39 2011
230.082—dc23   2011021847

15 14 13 12 11 1 2 3 4 5 6 7 8 9 10

To
Ivone Gebara
and
Christine Schaumberger

In celebration of their 60th birthdays
and in gratitude for their pioneering feminist work

Contents

Acknowledgments

Needless to say, the publication of a book, like all intellectual work, always owes its existence to teamwork and much unrecognized labor. Hence, it is important to make visible the people who have greatly contributed to its final embodiment. While I take all responsibility for its content and appearance (except for the cover design, which is the result of the publisher's decision), I want to thank all those who have worked on it.

I am grateful to Michal Beth Dinkler, doctoral student in New Testament/ Early Christianity, for going over the manuscript, identifying repetitions, and polishing my style. Although she did her best to mark overlaps and pages to be cut, it is in the nature of a collection of essays like this that ideas and arguments are repeated. While the individual essays are written for variegated audiences, their collection in a volume changes their context and rhetoric.

My faculty assistant Kimberly Richards O'Hagan deserves special thanks for scanning some of the articles and translating them into Word files. Her thoughtful assistance and competent help are greatly appreciated. Without her capable support I would not have found the time and energy to finish this work.

Michael West, Editor-in-chief of Fortress Press, enthusiastically supported this project and paved the way for it. I am deeply grateful for his sage counsel and sustained interest in my work over the years. With his departure, not only Fortress Press but also I have lost a trusted editor. He is a leader in the field of academic theological publishing.

I am greatly indebted, therefore, to Acquiring Editor Neil Elliott, who was willing to graciously take over the editorial work after Michael's departure to Switzerland. I have greatly appreciated Neil's willingness to work with me in order to bring the project to publication. His care and suggestions for the manuscript have significantly improved it. I am also grateful to Susan Johnson, Managing Editor at Fortress Press, for working out contractual issues and getting the project started, to Marissa Wold for coordinating all aspects of the production and manufacturing process, and to Josh Messner for his careful editing of the manuscript.

I also want to thank my colleague Dr. Linda Maloney, who consented to translate some chapters of my book *Grenzenüberschreiten: Der theoretische Anspruch feministischer Theologie: Ausgewählte Aufsätze* (Münster: LIT, 2004), which appear not only in this but also in the next two projected volumes of my selected essays. I am very grateful for her initial translation of chapters 2, 4, 6, and 11, which allowed me to work on the revision of these chapters.

Last but not least, as always I am deeply grateful to my partner Francis Schüssler Fiorenza for his unfailing companionship, love, and friendship. In particular I want to thank him for his computer help and patience with a technologically challenged scholar like me. Over the years Dr. Chris Miryam Schüssler-Fiorenza has been an inspiring presence in my life for which I am deeply grateful. I also want to thank the members of my Fall 2010 seminar on Feminist Theory and The*logy, whose spirited questions and critical challenges have greatly contributed to the conceptualization of this work.

This book is dedicated to two leading feminist the*logians, Ivone Gebara from Brazil and Christine Schaumberger from Germany, in celebration of their sixtieth birthdays and with great appreciation for their pathbreaking feminist work. Ivone is one of Latin America's leading the*logians, known for her theoretical articulation of Latin American feminist liberation the*logy in general and for the development of a planetary, eco-feminist the*logy and spirituality in particular. Christine Schaumberger's work is equally important, but unfortunately less known internationally. Over the years, she has developed and refined a critical feminist the*logy of liberation in the context of the "First World." Her work has explored political the*logy, questions of power, work, everyday life, bread and roses, racial bias, and aging. I have greatly appreciated her friendship over the years.

Both Christine and Ivone's feminist theoretical work is deeply rooted in a critical feminist the*logy of liberation and articulated in and through working with wo/men from all walks of life. I hope they will accept this dedication as a token of my great appreciation and friendship. *Ad multos annos*, Christine and Ivone!

Introduction

*A Critical Feminist The*logy of Liberation: Reality and Vision*

Almost twenty years ago, I published *Discipleship of Equals*,[1] which gathered together my work on feminist the*logy in the 1970s and 1980s. Like *Discipleship of Equals* so also the present volume circles around *power, struggle, and vision* as central topoi of my feminist the*logical work. This work is motivated by the imperative expressed by the ancient prophet Habakkuk:

> Write the vision down,
> inscribe it on tablets to be easily read.
> For there is still a vision for its own appointed time, eager for its own
>   fulfillment.
> It does not deceive!
> If it seems to tarry, wait for it;
> it will surely come, it will not delay.[2]

Contemplating the command to "write down the vision," I have decided to gather some of my essays that were written after *Discipleship of Equals* appeared and make them available to readers who do not have easy library access to the journals and collections of essays where they have first appeared. Whereas this volume gathers my feminist the*logical essays, the next book will focus on my work in feminist biblical method and hermeneutics. In a third work, I will gather essays and interviews reflecting on the experiences and social locations which have shaped my feminist the*logical voice and theoretical vision.[3]

1. Elisabeth Schüssler Fiorenza, *Discipleship of Equals: A Critical Feminist Ekklēsia-logy of Liberation* (New York: Crossroad, 1993). See also *Grenzen überschreiten: Der theoretische Anspruch feministischer Theologie* (Münster: LIT, 2004).

2. Habakkuk 2:2-3 (RSV).

3. I am grateful for the very perceptive and generous discussion of my work in *Früchte des Verstehens: Elisabeth Schüssler Fiorenza zum 60. Geburtstag* (Sonderheft der feministisch-theologischen

Originally the word *theory* was a technical term derived from ancient Greek *theoria*, meaning "looking at, viewing, beholding." Feminist theory is not so much concerned with technical precision and completeness but with generating "analyses, critiques, and political interventions and open[ing] up a political imaginary for feminism that points the way beyond some of the impasses by which it has been constrained."[4]

Vision equally has something to do with seeing and looking. I understand feminist theory to enable us to see full circle where otherwise we would see only a segment. Hence, I understand feminist the*logy and studies in religion as a vision quest, seeking to articulate the dream of justice as well as searching for transformative theories and practices of well-being in an unjust and violent world. Hence, the analysis of domination and struggle must be central to a critical feminist political the*logy of liberation.

This volume recontextualizes the individual essays in four sections that seek to reflect on sites of feminist struggles and their transforming visions. The contributions of the first section attempt to name the theoretical struggles involved in articulating a critical[5] feminist political the*logy of liberation. The chapters of the second section in turn discuss the global wo/men's movements in religion and society as sites of struggle against violence[6] and prejudice. The third section explores my own socioreligious location, Catholicism, as an institutional

---

Zeitschrift Fama, 1998); *Walk in the Ways of Wisdom: Essays in Honor of Elisabeth Schüssler Fiorenza*, ed. Cynthia Briggs Kittredge, Melanie Johnson-Debaufre, and Shelly Matthews (Harrisburg: Trinity International, 2003); *On the Cutting Edge: The Study of Women in Biblical Worlds*, ed. Jane Schaberg, Alice Bach, and Esther Fuchs (New York: Continuum, 2003); *Toward a New Heaven and a New Earth: Essays in Honor of Elisabeth Schüssler Fiorenza*, ed. Fernando F. Segovia (Maryknoll: Orbis, 2003); *Vermessen! Globale Visionen konkrete Schritte*, ed. Andrea Eickmeier und Jutta Flatters (Bonn: Schlangenbrut, 2003); Glenn Enander, *Spiritual Leaders: Elisabeth Schüssler Fiorenza* (Philadelphia: Chelsea, 2005); Elizabeth Green, *Elisabeth Schüssler Fiorenza* (Brescia: Morcelliana, 2005), and especially Nam Kim and Deborah Whitehead, eds., *Journal of Feminist Studies in Religion*, Special Issue in Honor of Elisabeth Schüssler Fiorenza, 25/1 (2009).

4. Judith Butler and Joan W. Scott, eds., *Feminists Theorize the Political* (New York: Routledge, 1992), xiii.

5. For the discussion of the relation of my work to the critical theory of the Frankfurt School, see Marsha Aileen Hewitt, *Critical Theory of Religion* (Minneapolis: Fortress Press, 1995).

6. Cf. Shawn M. Copeland and Elisabeth Schüssler Fiorenza, eds., *Violence against Women* (Maryknoll: Orbis, 1994); Carol J. Adams and Marie Fortune, eds., *Violence against Women and Children: A Christian Theological Sourcebook* (New York: Continuum, 1998); Nantawan Boonprasat Lewis and Marie M. Fortune, eds., *Remembering Conquest: Feminist/Womanist Perspectives on Religion, Colonization, and Sexual Violence* (Binghamton: Haworth Pastoral, 1999); Leela Fernandez, *Transforming Feminist Practice: Non-Violence, Social Justice, and the Possibilities of a Spiritual Feminism* (San Francisco: Aunt Lut, 2003); Joy A. Schroeder, *Dinah's Lament: The Biblical Legacy of Sexual Violence in Christian Interpretation* (Minneapolis: Fortress Press, 2007); Elizabeth A. Castelli and Janet R. Jakobsen, eds., *Interventions: Activists and Academics Respond to Violence* (New York: Palgrave Macmillan, 2004), and Daniel C. Maguire and Sa'diyya Shaikh, *Violence against Women in Contemporary World Religion: Roots and Cures* (Cleveland: Pilgrim, 2007).

site of struggle.[7] The volume ends by looking at the*logy proper, our speaking about the divine, as a site of struggle for naming the fullness of feminist religious vision.[8]

All of the chapters seek to present aspects of a critical feminist political the*logy of liberation. Nancy A. Dalavalle has criticized Catholic feminist the*logy as being too closely aligned with liberation the*logy. She argues that

> the assumption that the important cry for justice and liberation provides an exhaustive framework for feminist theology forecloses a thorough examination of the possibilities raised at the intersection of feminism and Catholic theology. Indeed, reducing either the insights of feminism or the complexities of Catholic theology to justice concerns ignores the fact that some feminist theories reflect exclusively on being female and the fact that the object of Christian theology, and the ground of the Catholic tradition's catholicity, is God, not human concerns for justice.[9]

While I can not speak in the name of all Catholic feminist the*logians who are indicted here for being too much concerned with human worries about justice rather than catholicity and the divine, I hope that these chapters convince readers that the concern for justice is not only essential to catholicity and G*d, but also fundamental to feminist the*logy, that is to feminist *the*-legein* which means *speaking about the divine,* since justice is the prerequisite for such feminist *the*-legein.*

The Power of Naming

Around forty years ago, Mary Daly wrote in *Beyond God the Father* that "under patriarchy wo/men have had the power of naming stolen from us." Daly directs our attention to the second creation story of the book of Genesis in which Adam names all the animals as well as the woman who names no one and nothing. Daly draws the conclusion: "Wo/men are now realizing that the universal imposing of names by men has been false or partial because to exist humanly is to name the self, the world, and God."[10]

---

7. Cf. Mary J. Henold, *Catholic and Feminist: The Surprising History of the American Catholic Feminist Movement* (Chapel Hill: University of North Carolina Press, 2008); Susan Abraham and Elena Procario-Foley, eds., *Frontiers in Catholic Feminist Theology: Shoulder to Shoulder* (Minneapolis: Fortress Press, 2009).

8. Cf. Carol Christ, *She Who Changes: Re-Imagining the Divine in the World* (New York: Palgrave, 2004), Melissa Raphael, *The Female Face of God in Auschwitz: A Jewish Feminist Theology of the Holocaust* (London: Routledge, 2003), and Elizabeth A. Johnson, *She Who Is: The Mystery of God in Feminist Theological Discourse* (New York: Crossroads, 1992).

9. Nancy A. Dalavalle, "Toward a Theology That Is Catholic and Feminist: Some Basic Issues," *Modern Theology* 4/4 (1998), 535.

10. Mary Daly, *Beyond God the Father* (Boston: Beacon, 1968), 8.

However, wo/men did not simply lack the sacred power of naming.[11] Rather, we were actively prohibited from exercising it. After centuries of silencing and exclusion from the*logical studies and religious leadership, wo/men have moved into the academy, assumed religious leadership, and claimed their religious agency and heritage.[12] The second wave of the feminist movement has not only engendered a wo/men's rights movement in religion resulting in wo/men's admission to ordination and academic faculty status. It also has created new areas of research.

In the context of the second wave of the wo/men's movement, research in wo/men, gender, and feminist studies in religion and the*logy has exploded.[13] Nevertheless, just as in other academic disciplines, the knowledge produced by feminist studies in religion remains marginal to the overall the*logical or religious studies curriculum and the self-identity of the disciplines. It appears as a "special interest" topic and often remains restricted to those who are already "converted." Feminist students still have to do "double" or even "triple duty" if they belong to a minority group. They study feminist or black or Asian the*logy because these forms of the*logy speak to their own experience, but in order to be judged professionally competent, they still have to know the hegemonic intellectual work of "the*logy" as such.

Feminist theories and the*logies have emerged from wo/men's participation in emancipatory movements such as the struggles for full democratic citizenship, religious freedom, abolition of slavery, civil rights, national and cultural independence as well as those for democratic, ecological, labor, peace, or gay rights. In these struggles for religious, civil and human rights which are going on in the Middle East and in Wisconsin at the writing of this introduction, feminists have learned that words such as "human" or "worker" or "civil society" are gender typed and often do not include the rights and interests of wo/men. Hence, I do

---

11. Cf. Elisabeth Schüssler Fiorenza, ed., *The Power of Naming: A Concilium Reader in Feminist Liberation Theology* (Maryknoll: Orbis, 1996).

12. Cf. Ann Braude, ed., *Transforming the Faith of Our Fathers: Women Who Changed American Religion* (New York: Palgrave, 2004), which seeks to dispel the myth that feminism and religion are "inherently incompatible."

13. See among many others Melissa Raphael, *Introducing Thealogy: Discourse on the Goddess* (Cleveland: Pilgrim, 2000); Darlene M. Juschka, *Feminism in the Study of Religion: A Reader* (New York: Continuum, 2001); Musimbi R. A. Kanyoro, *Introducing Feminist Cultural Hermeneutics: An African Perspective* (Cleveland: Pilgrim, 2002); Rebecca S. Chopp and Sheila Greeve Davaney, *Horizons in Feminist Theology: Identity, Tradition, and Norms* (Minneapolis: Fortress Press, 1997); Serene Jones, *Feminist Theory and Christian Theology: Cartographies of Grace, Guides to Theological Inquiry* (Minneapolis: Fortress Press, 2000); Rita M. Gross and Rosemary Radford Ruether, *Religious Feminism and the Future of the Planet: A Buddhist-Christian Conversation* (New York: Continuum, 2001); Anne M. Clifford, *Introducing Feminist Theology* (Maryknoll: Orbis, 2001); Susan Frank Parsons, *The Cambridge Companion to Feminist Theology* (Cambridge: Cambridge University Press, 2002); Stephanie Y. Mitchem, *Introducing Womanist Theology* (Maryknoll: Orbis, 2002); Rosemary Radford Ruether, ed., *Feminist Theologies: Legacy and Prospect* (Minneapolis: Fortress Press, 2007); Marcella Althaus-Reid and Lisa Isherwood, *Controversies in Feminist Theology* (London: SCM, 2007); Margaret D. Kamitsuka, *Feminist Theology and the Challenge of Difference* (New York: Oxford, 2007); María Pilar Aquino and Maria José Rosado-Nunes, eds., *Feminist Intercultural Theology: Latina Explorations for a Just World* (Maryknoll: Orbis, 2007).

not see feminist the*logy primarily as a philosophical inquiry concerned with ontological and metaphysical questions but as a cultural, sociopolitical one concerned with power in general and the power of naming in particular.

The story of feminist the*logy and studies in religion is generally told either in progressivist-temporal or in descriptive-definitional terms. I want to tell it here with reference to its analytical categories and feminist practices. As far as I can see, the field of feminist studies in religion and the*logy is presently construed in four divergent methodological ways: Firstly as women studies, secondly as gender studies, thirdly as intersectional-cultural feminist studies, and fourthly as critical political-liberationist feminist studies.[14] These different approaches are distinctive but not necessarily exclusive of each other. They all have developed feminist practices that reclaim the "power of naming."

By claiming the power of naming, feminist scholars are in the process of reforming malestream[15] the*logies and religious practices, a process that seeks to correct and complete the one-dimensional tunnel vision of the world and of organized religions. They seek to rectify gendered knowledges and spiritual perceptions of the world and the divine, which are still one-sided to the extent that they continue to be articulated in the interest of elite white western men. A different feminist understanding of religion in turn will lead to the articulation of a feminist politics and spirituality that can empower wo/men to bring about further change in society and culture. Although it often remains part of the problem, religion too plays an important role in emancipatory radical democratic struggles. Feminist the*logy therefore needs to discuss critically the theoretical frame and perspective of its approach to religion.

My own theoretical approach is firmly rooted in the decolonizing[16] liberationist paradigm of feminist studies in religion, although it also owes much of its theoretical articulation to other approaches. If I qualify my own theoretical approach as political and liberationist, I hasten to stress that it is first of all critical and feminist. My work cannot uncritically align itself with either political or liberation the*logies, since on the one hand political and liberation the*logies have not made the struggles of wo/men focal points of their theoretical articulations and on the other hand, women/or gender studies have not sufficiently interrogated the sociopolitical function of the category *woman* and the *feminine*.

Such a clarification of a critical feminist political liberationist approach is still necessary because many continue to identify feminist studies with woman or

---

14. See my article, "Sprache und Herrschaft: Feministische The*logie als Kyriarchatsforschung," in Renate Jost and Klaus Raschzok, eds., *Gender, Religion, und Kultur: Biblische, interreligiöse, und ethische Aspekte* (Stuttgart: Kohlhammer, 2010), 17-35.

15. I owe this expression to the feminist sociologist Dorothy Smith.

16. For my argument to qualify my feminist approach as *decolonizing* rather than as *postcolonial*, see my book *The Power of the Word: Scripture and the Rhetoric of Empire* (Minneapolis: Fortress Press, 2007).

gender studies, which supposedly are the domain of wo/men. While in my understanding feminist the*logy engages both women and gender studies for its work, it is not identical with and cannot be limited to them. In other words, religion is not primarily seen as a woman or gender problem. Rather, both feminist political theory and the*logy focus on issues of power and structures of domination in light of wo/men's struggles against kyriarchal relations. Thus I understand feminist the*logy and studies in religion as social-cultural-political studies.

However, the object of feminist studies as well as the subject of the feminist movement and its identity has been hotly debated in feminist theory and the*logy. Is woman/women the subject or object of investigation? How to define the subject of feminist movements? This discussion has shown that wo/men do not have an essence in common. Rather than understanding "woman" as a unitary feminine ontological entity, "woman" must be seen as a social gender construct that stamps people as belonging to either a feminine or a masculine group category. Femininity and masculinity[17] are thus sociopolitical constructs and not essences. Hence a critical feminist theory articulates the subject of feminist struggles not on the basis of essential difference but in the interest of naming subjects who struggle against structures of domination.

Like those of gender, the social relations that give rise to theories of race, class, or ethnic differences are also socioculturally constructed as relations of domination and not simply biological givens. Nineteenth-century scientists constructed the so-called lower races, wo/men, the sexually deviant, the criminal, the urban poor, and the insane as biological "races apart." Their differences from the white male, and their likeness to each other "explained" their lower position in the social hierarchy. In this scheme the lower races represent the "feminine" aspect of the human species, and wo/men represent the "lower race" of gender. In other words, relations of domination determine academic as well as religious institutions. Thus wo/men do not share an unitary essence but are multiple and fractured in many different ways by race, class, age, sexuality, and gender. To indicate this fracturedness linguistically, I have introduced the writing of "wo/man" in a fragmented way. This mode of writing wo/men seeks to signify an intersectional definition of the feminist subject.

An Analytic of Domination

Early second-wave theorizing "placed patriarchal power relations—the system of male domination and women's subordination—at the center of analysis."[18] Since such an understanding of patriarchy assumes a unitary concept of wo/man,

---

17. See Judith Kegan Gardiner, ed., *Masculinity Studies and Feminist Theory: New Directions* (New York: Columbia University Press, 2002).

18. Jennifer Einspahr, "Structural Domination and Structural Freedom: A Feminist Perspective," *Feminist Review* 94/1 (2010): 1-19.

it has been problematized by African American, postcolonial, and two-thirds-world feminists as the primary form of oppression. Moreover, poststructuralist, psychoanalytic, and constructivist feminist theorists have sought to show "how patriarchal power comes to be installed in our very subjectivities."[19] In the process the feminist theoretical focus has shifted from structural domination to the process of "subjectivation."[20] With this theoretical shift the notion of patriarchy as a central structure of domination has been relegated to the historical dustbin rather than critically investigated and reformulated on the one hand and differently theorized on the other.

The term *intersectionality* was coined by the legal scholar Kimberly Crenshaw and entails "the notion that subjectivity is constituted by mutually multiplicative vectors of race, gender, class, sexuality, and imperialism." Intersectional analysis[21] has emerged in critical feminist and race studies as a key theoretical tool for subverting race/gender and other binaries of domination. Some have also criticized "identity politics" for eliding intragroup differences. Intersectionality seeks to address such criticisms while still recognizing the necessity of group politics. Finally, "intersectionality invites scholars to come to terms with the legacy of the exclusions of multiply marginalized subjects from feminist and antiracist work," and "to draw on the ostensibly unique epistemological position of marginalized subjects to fashion a vision of equality."[22]

In a critical assessment of intersectionality, Kathy Davis[23] has pointed out that the meaning of the term is far from being clear: does it designate individual experience, theorize identity, or is it a property of social structures and cultural discourses? Similarly, its conceptualizations "as a crossroad (Crenshaw, 1991), as 'axes' of difference (Yuval-Davis, 2006) or as a dynamic process (Staunaes, 2003)"[24] differ.

Despite its theoretical fuzziness, Davis argues, the theory of intersectionality is attractive and useful because it "brings together two of the most important strands of contemporary feminist thought that have been in different ways concerned with the issue of difference. The first strand has been devoted to understanding the effects of race, class and gender on wo/men's identity, experience and struggles for empowerment."[25] The second important strand within feminist theory, Davis argues, welcomed intersectionality because it fits

---

19. Ibid., 2.

20. Judith Butler, *The Psychic Life of Power: Theories in Subjection* (Stanford: Stanford University Press, 1997)

21. Cf. Marcia Texler Segal and Theresa A. Martinez, eds., *Intersections of Gender, Race, and Class: Readings for a Changing Landscape* (Los Angeles: Roxbury, 2007).

22. Jennifer C. Nash, "Rethinking Intersectionality," *Feminist Review* 89/1 (2008): 3.

23. Kathy Davis, "Intersectionality as Buzzword: A Sociology of Science Perspective on What Makes a Feminist Theory Successful," *Feminist Theory* 9/1 (2008): 67-85.

24. Ibid., 68.

25. Ibid., 68.

"neatly into the postmodern project of conceptualizing multiple and shifting identities. It coincided with Foucauldian perspectives on power that focused on dynamic processes and the deconstruction of normalizing and homogenizing categories."[26]

Most importantly, intersectionality provides a shared theoretical and normative platform for a mutually beneficial collaboration between disparate feminist theoretical projects and approaches. It is able to focus on questions of identity as well as on social structures.

However, if intersectionality should hold together and integrate both strands of feminist theory, it needs to be spelled out not only in terms of circulating power but also in terms of structures of domination. Structure is best understood "as a set of socially constructed frameworks, patterns, and material conditions that frame our collective lives and that can be understood only in relation to 'agency,' or a human being's socioculturally mediated capacity to act."[27] Gender as well as race, class, heteronormativity, age, or colonialism are such structures of domination that intersect with each other in a "hierarchal," or better, kyriarchal fashion.

If the analytic object of feminist theory and the*logy is not simply wo/man or gender but intersectionality, it needs to be also understood in terms of the ontology of kyriarchal power. Kyriarchy[28]—a neologism coined by me—is best understood as a sociopolitical and cultural-religious system of domination that structures the identity slots open to members of society in terms of race, gender, nation, age, economy, and sexuality and configures them in terms of pyramidal relations of domination and submission, profit and exploitation. The Western kyriarchal system works simultaneously on four levels: first, on the sociopolitical level; second on the ethical-cultural level; third, on the biological-natural level;

---

26. Ibid., 71.

27. Jennifer Einspahr, ibid., 5 However, I do not think that patriarchy as a analytic concept should be "resurrected," since it has been replaced by gender.

28. The notion of kyriarchy seems to have arrived in the blogosphere. I am grateful to Elizabeth Gish who forwarded some examples and links to feminist blogs that use *kyriarchy*: First, www.raisingmyboychick.com/2009/08/kyriarchy. This is the link to her glossary, but she uses the word regularly in her posts. Here www.raisingmyboychick.com/category/kyriarchy you can see her posts where kyriarchy is a central theme of the post, including this one called "This Is Kyriarchy in Action": www.raisingmyboychick.com/2010/03/this-is-kyriarchy-in-action-the-new-york-times-on-mommy-bloggers/

Here is a post at Authentic Parenting: www.authenticparenting.info/2011/02/on-feminism-religion-superiority.html.

Here is a post at feminist philosophers: feministphilosophers.wordpress.com/2008/05/01/word-of-the-day-kyriarchy/

Here is a post at the feminist caterpillar (http://www.myecdysis.com/2010/11/truthout-about-kyriarchy-an-open-letter-to-feminist-writers-bloggers-and-journalists/) whose original post on the term garnered a lot of attention in the feminist blogosphere including this post at one of the top-two major third-wave feminist blogs: www.feministe.us/blog/archives/2008/05/01/i-blame-the-kyriarchy/

and fourth, on the linguistic-symbolic level. These four levels are interrelated and strengthen each other's power of domination.

Diverse feminist approaches such as womanist, queer, latina, or postcolonial the*logies work on different nodal sites of the intersecting discourse levels of kyriarchy and hence emphasize different aspects of the kyriarchal system. Kyriarchal power is both repressive and productive: "According to Foucault power subjects individuals in both senses of the term: Individuals are both subject to the constraints of social relations of power and simultaneously enabled to take up the position of a *subject* in and through those very constraints . . . a uniquely modern modality of power, one that differs from previous modalities, is that it is capillary, local, and spread throughout the social body, rather than concentrated in the center of the state in the person of the sovereign."[29] While it is true that democratic power is not concentrated in the person of the sovereign, such power still needs to be spelled out also in political terms of domination.

Kyriarchy (from the Greek *kyrios* for "lord, master, father" and *archein* for "to rule, dominate") is best theorized as a complex pyramidal system of intersecting multiplicative social and religious relations of superordination and subordination, of ruling and exploitation. Kyriarchal relations of domination are built on elite male property rights as well as on the exploitation, dependency, inferiority, and obedience of wo/men who signify all those subordinated. Such kyriarchal relations are still today at work in the multiplicative intersectionalities of class, race, gender, ethnicity, empire, and other structures of discrimination.

Since I have developed the genealogy of the concept in my writings, I want to summarize here the structural intersectional aspects of kyriarchy and its shaping of religion:

- Feminist the*logians have greatly valorized relations and relationality but overlooked that such relations are kyriarchally typed.[30] Kyriarchy is a complex pyramidal system of *relations* of domination that works through the violence of economic exploitation and lived subordination. However, this kyriarchal pyramid must not be seen as static, but as an always-changing net of relations of domination.
- Kyriarchy is realized differently in different historical contexts. Democratic kyriarchy, or kyriarchal democracy, has been articulated differently in antiquity than in modernity. It is different in Greece, Hellenism, Rome, Asia Minor, Europe, America, Japan, or India; it is different in Judaism, Islam, or Catholicism.

---

29. Amy Allen, *The Power of Feminist Theory: Domination, Resistance, Solidarity* (Boulder: Westview, 1999), 33.

30. See Katherine Keller, "Seeking and Sucking: On Relation and Essence in Feminist Theology," in Rebecca S. Chopp and Sheila Greeve Davaney, eds., *Horizons in Feminist Theology: Identity, Tradition, and Norms* (Minneapolis: Fortress Press, 1997), 54-78, esp. 69-76, who caricaturizes my position in defense of relation/relationality.

- Not only the gender system but also the stratification systems of race, class, colonialism, and heterosexism structure and determine the system of kyriarchal relations. These structures intersect with each other in a pyramidal fashion; they are not parallel but multiplicative. The full power of kyriarchal oppression comes to the fore in the lives of wo/men living on the bottom of the kyriarchal pyramid.

- In order to function, kyriarchal cultures need a servant class, a servant race, a servant gender, a *servant people*. Such a servant class is maintained through the ideologies of kyriocentrism, which are internalized through education, socialization, and brute violence, as well as rationalized by malestream scholarship. Kyriarchy is sustained by the belief that members of a servant class of people are naturally or by divine decree inferior to those whom they serve.

- Both in Western modernity and in Greco-Roman antiquity, kyriarchy stands in tension with a democratic ethos and social system of equality and freedom. In a radical democratic system, power is not exercised through "power over" or through violence and subordination, but through the human capacities for respect, responsibility, self-determination, and self-esteem. This radical democratic ethos has repeatedly engendered emancipatory movements that insisted on equal freedom, dignity, and justice for all.

- Feminist political theorists have shown that the classical Greek philosophers Aristotle and Plato have articulated a theory of kyriarchal democracy in different ways, in order to justify the exclusion of certain people, such as freeborn wo/men or slave wo/men and men, from participating in democratic government. These people were not fit to govern, the philosophers argued, because of their deficient natural powers of reasoning. Such explicit ideological justifications need always to be developed at a point in history when it becomes increasingly obvious that those who are excluded from the political life of the *polis*, such as freeborn wo/men, educated slaves, wealthy *metics* (alien residents), and traveling mercenaries, are actually indispensable to it. Philosophical rationalizations of the exclusion of diverse people from citizenship and government are engendered by the contradiction between the democratic vision of the city-state and its actual practices.

- This contradiction between the logic of democracy and historical sociopolitical kyriarchal practices has produced the kyriocentric logic of identity as the assertion of "natural differences" between elite men and wo/men, freeborn and slaves, property owners and farmers or artisans, Athenian-born citizens and other residents, Greeks and Barbarians, the civilized and uncivilized world. A similar process of ideological kyriocentrism is inscribed in Christian Scriptures and traditions in and through the so-called codes of submission (Household Codes). It is found in modern societies in the form of the patriarchal family understood as the heart of the kyriarchal state.[31]

Finally, it must not be overlooked that the kyriarchal pyramid spells out not only the power of domination over humans, societies, and religions but also over nature, the earth, and the whole cosmos. Global capitalist domination jeopardizes not only the well-being of people but also that of nature and the ecology of the earth.

Religion and Feminist Theory

Such a kyriarchal analytic compels feminist the*logy and studies in religion to make sure that they critically analyze and do not promote or legitimate kyriarchal structurers of domination. They also need to articulate alternative religious visions for bringing about the wellbeing of all the inhabitants of the earth and for inspiring planetary justice. Feminism is not and never has been just a theoretical world-view and political movement for change. It has also always articulated itself as a spiritual vision and religious optic insofar as it has sought to bring about a "coming-into a different consciousness." However, this religious dimension of feminism is barely recognized in feminist theory. The reasons for this are manifold. Let me just point to one.

In modernity "religion" was feminized insofar as European Christianity was dislodged from its hegemonic role and restricted to the private sphere. At the same time religion became a civilizing project of colonialism, the cultural feminization of religion has led both to the societal emasculation of the*logy and clergy and to the reassertion of their masculine roles in the*logy, church, and the home. Feminist research and education in the*logy and religion has brought to consciousness the complicity of religion in wo/men's low self-esteem, economic exploitation, societal marginalization, and sexual victimization.

Like the "White Lady," Christianity[32] had the function of ameliorating the horrors of rampant capitalism and colonial imperialism. Moreover, the study of religion has turned other people's religions into an object of the western colonial kyriocentric gaze. Feminist scholars question this modern colonialized and feminized conception of religion and refuse to engage in its further objectification. Consequently, feminist post-colonial studies in religion have become increasingly important in the last ten years or more.

---

31. See the excellent intersectional analysis of Patricia Hill Collins, "It's All in the Family: Intersections of Gender, Race, and Nation," *Hypatia* 13/3 (1998): 62–82.

32. For such a focus on Christianity see my article "Critical Feminist Biblical Studies: Remembering the Struggles-Envisioning the Future," in Mary E. Hunt and Diann L. Neu, eds., *New Feminist Christianity: Many Voices, Many Views* (Woodstock: Skylightpath, 2010), 86-99.

Moreover, in modernity "religion" was rejected as biased because it does not operate within the limits of reason alone. In consequence, many progressive feminists do not distinguish between emancipatory and reactionary forms of religion but take biblical religions' oppressive character for granted. Hence they do not see biblical religions as a feminist site of struggle for change. Feminist studies in religion in turn have pointed to religion's ability to articulate liberating visions that can authorize and empower wo/men in our struggles for survival, dignity and self-determination. While feminist scholars in religion carefully discuss and confront feminist research and theories in other fields,[33] our own scholarship and struggle remains mostly unrecognized by feminists in other disciplines. The wealth and importance of scholarship in diverse religions[34] is thereby often neglected in feminist studies and global women's struggles.

Yet this disinterest of academic feminism in religion seems to be in the process of changing insofar as the binary *secularism-religion* and therefore also the dichotomy between secular feminism and religious feminism is theoretically more and more questioned. Niam Reilly has pointed out that most Anglo-American feminist political theorizing seems to assume that secularization has diminished the societal import of religion. However, this assumption is being increasingly challenged in two key ways: *first*, the coherence of the secular-religious binary is questioned on postmodern theoretical grounds and *second*—viewed from a global sociological perspective—"the presumption of secularization as an inevitable and uniform process" in modernity is no longer tenable.[35] These feminist debates that challenge the equation of modernity with secularization open up a dialogical space for secular and religious feminist theorists. Different approaches in feminist political theory "emphasize 'democracy' and the values that underpin it as the larger discursive frame in which the principle of secularism can be redefined with emancipatory intent in a neo-secular age."[36]

---

33. See especially the variegated contributions in *The Journal of Feminist Studies in Religion* (Bloomington: Indiana University Press), which for more than twenty-five years has published scholarship in religion.

34. Paula M. Cooey, William R. Eakin, and Jay B. McDaniel, *After Patriarchy: Feminist Transformations of the World Religions, Faith Meets Faith* (Maryknoll: Orbis, 1991); Rachel Adler, *Engendering Judaism: An Inclusive Theology and Ethics* (Philadelphia: Jewish Publication Society, 1998); Mahnaz Afkhami, ed., *Faith and Freedom: Women's Human Rights in the Muslim World* (Syracuse: Syracuse University Press, 1995); Jane H. Bayes and Nayereh Tohidi, eds., *Globalization, Gender, and Religion: The Politics of Women's Rights in Catholic and Muslim Contexts* (New York: Palgrave Macmillan, 2001); Irshad Manji, *The Trouble with Islam: A Muslim's Call for Reform* (New York: St. Martin's, 2004); Judith Plaskow with Donna Beerman, *The Coming of Lilith: Essays on Feminism, Judaism, and Sexual Ethics, 1972–2003* (Boston: Beacon, 2005).

35. Niam Reilly, "Rethinking the Interplay of Feminism and Secularism in a Neo-Secular Age," *Feminist Review* 97 (2011), 5-31.

36. Ibid., 5.

For instance, in a constructive article entitled "Mapping the Feminist Imagination," the feminist political theorist Nancy Fraser[37] is beginning to take religion and intersectionality seriously into account as central to feminist political theory. She seeks to correct the standard feminist narrative of theoretical progress according to which feminism has developed from an exclusionary white, middle class, heterosexual woman-dominated movement to a broader movement that allows for the inclusion of the needs of wo/men of color, lesbians, working class, migrant, and poor wo/men.

Fraser is critical of this framework not only because it is modernist-progressivist but also because it tells the story of feminist theory and movement as internal development. Hence it is not able to make the connections to the broader sociopolitical developments as sites of struggle for feminism. She in turn reconstructs three phases in the trajectory of second wave feminism. Feminism in its *first* phase, which Fraser characterizes as "redistribution," began its life as one of the New Left and civil rights social movements that sought to engender the "socialist imaginary" and an "expanded idea of social equality," arguing for justice and equal rights and presupposing the welfare state and social democracy.

The *second* phase, which coincided with postcommunism and postcolonialism, was dedicated to bringing about cultural change and transformation that were always an important project of feminism but were now decoupled from the project of distributive justice and political-economic transformation.

The *third* emerging phase of the feminist imaginary is that of the transnational politics of *representation*[38] that seek to link and integrate the economic politics of redistribution and the cultural politics of recognition within a transnational frame that is also determined by fundamentalist religions. Since transnational maldistribution, misrecognition, and misrepresentation cannot adequately be addressed in a state-territorial frame, transnational feminist theory seeks to reframe the problem of meta-injustice in a global context.

Moreover, Fraser understands *representation* as "claims-making" in political terms not only as ensuring equal political voice for wo/men in national communities but also as a reframing of disputes about injustice. Transnational feminism is in the process "of reconfiguring gender justice as a three-dimensional problem,

---

37. Nancy Fraser "Mapping the Feminist Imagination: From Redistribution to Recognition to Representation," *Constellations* 12/3 (2005): 295-307.

38. Since Fraser is concerned with political misrepresentation but not *representation as "representing" wo/men in writing and research*, she does not refer to the intense discussions on the "politics of representation" of white, Western feminists who represent third-world wo/men as passive victims in cultural studies. For this discussion see especially Gyatri Chakravorty Spivak, "Can the Subaltern Speak?" in Cary Nelson and Lawrence Grossberg, eds., *Marxism and the Interpretation of Culture* (Urbana: University of Illinois Press, 1988), 271-97, and Chandra Talpade Mohanti, "Under Western Eyes" in Chandra Talpade Mohanti, Ann Russo, and Lourdes Torres, eds., *Third World Wo/men and the Politics of Feminism* (Bloomington: Indiana University Press, 1991), 51-80. It is clear, however, that Fraser's concern is with "challenging the state-territorial framing of political claims making" (Nancy Fraser, "Mapping the Feminist Imagination," 304).

in which redistribution, recognition, and representation must be integrated in a balanced way . . . so as to challenge the full range of gender injustices in a globalized world."[39] In order to do so, one needs to resort also to the language of religion.

The post-9/11 political situation in the United States, which has far-reaching implications for global capitalism, is characterized according to Fraser by the strategy of a "gender-coded politics of recognition" that is invoked to "hide a regressive politics of economic redistribution." Both the rhetoric of the "war on terror" as well as the so-called "family-values" campaign are sustained by reactionary religions. In the cultural-values campaign pertaining particularly to abortion rights and gay marriage, the manipulation of gender, she argues, has been "a crucial instrument of Bush's victory" in the 2004 election. This victory was achieved through the alliance of "free-marketeers with Christian fundamentalism."

In a time when people experience real economic and social insecurities, religious fundamentalisms in general and Christian evangelicalism in particular address this real insecurity. However, they do not actually give people security but provide means to manage such insecurity. With Foucault, Fraser understands evangelicalism "as a care-of-self-technology that is especially suited to neo-liberalism, insofar as the latter is always generating insecurity." However, she sees that religion as "care of self" can be seen also in positive feminist terms. She concludes that many working-class wo/men "are deriving something significant from Evangelicalism, something that confers meaning on their lives."[40]

Fraser's mapping of the "feminist imagination" also opens up a theoretical space for mapping transnational feminist studies in religion. With her I suggest that a transnational decolonizing feminist the*logy also needs to articulate three dimensions: historical redistribution, ideological deconstruction and religious-the*logical re-presentation. This requires a reframing of feminist studies in religion and the*logy so that they can "challenge the full range of injustices in the world" while at the same time articulating "technologies of the care of self" (Foucault) that inspire wo/men to struggle for justice and well-being rather than to adapt to kyriarchal domination.

Like Fraser, I thus understand this third mode of feminist studies as reframing *representation,* not so much in cultural as in political terms. To operate in the third mode, we need at one and the same time to reframe feminist the*logy and studies in religion in such a way that we can analyze not only the struggles of wo/men in religion but also and equally importantly, make the political-religious

---

39. Nancy Fraser "Mapping the Feminist Imagination," 305.
40. Ibid.," 303. However, she concludes that feminists have not yet "figured out how to talk to them or what feminism can offer them in its place." This remark reveals not only the ignorance of the feminist work done in religion and the*logy by a leading feminist theorist but also the assumption that feminism can be substituted for religion.

connections to the struggles, interests, and aspirations of wo/men for survival and justice today in global capitalism that makes life increasingly more poor and insecure for the majority of people. We can do so, I suggest, by constructing an imaginative space for articulating an alternative radical egalitarian discourse.

Religious Optic, Struggle, and Spiritual Vision

An intersectional kyriarchal analytic compels feminist the*logy and studies in religion to articulate not only an analytic of domination but also alternative religious visions for bringing about the wellbeing of all the inhabitants of the earth and for inspiring planetary justice. Religious feminism is not and never has been just a theoretical worldview and political movement for change. It has also always articulated itself as a spiritual vision and religious optic insofar as it has sought to bring about a "coming-into a different consciousness." Four vision practices seem crucial.

First, religious optic: Such a religious optic facing the devastations of kyriarchy is first of all a call to *metanoia,* to a turning around for engaging in a different mindset and way of life. It becomes realized again and again in wo/men's struggles to change relations of inequity and marginalization. Therefore it becomes necessary to focus specifically on wo/men's struggles for self-determination in society and religion that lead to a different self-understanding and vision of the world. To quote the nineteenth-century African American educator Anna Julia Cooper:

> Woman . . . daring to think and move and speak—to undertake to help shape, mold, and direct the thought of her age, is merely completing the circle of the world's vision. . . . The world has had to limp along with the wobbling gait and one-sided hesitancy of a man with one eye. Suddenly the bandage is removed from the other eye and the whole body is filled with light. It sees a circle where before it saw a segment. The darkened eye restored, every member rejoices with it. [41]

Feminist studies in religion and the*logy seek to correct the one-sided vision of G*d and the world and to articulate a different the*-ethical optics and religious imagination. How then can feminist studies in religion restore the world's full spiritual vision? How can we correct the fragmentary circle of religious understanding and change its narrow and biased perception of the world and of G*d? These are central questions for feminist the*logy and studies in religion that call for theory and vision. Such a theory needs to take into account how gender discourses have shaped religion and how religion has engendered and authorized prejudices against wo/men.

---

41. Anna Julia Cooper, *A Voice From the South*, 1892; republished in the Schomburg Library of Nineteenth-Century Black Women Writers (New York: Oxford University Press), 134.

To again quote Anna Julia Cooper, who has underscored the key position of wo/men of color for articulating such a feminist theory and the*logy: "The colored woman of today occupies, one may say, a unique position in this country. . . . She is confronted by both a woman question and a race problem and is as yet an unknown or an unacknowledged factor in both."[42]

In other words, the struggle of feminist intersectional studies in religion and their ability to challenge inscribed, religiously justified power relations of domination must be located at the juncture of racial, sexual, colonial class politics. Only when the unique hermeneutical viewpoint of multiply oppressed wo/men comes into focus will the "darkened eye" be restored. Only then can feminist studies in religion begin to "see a circle rather than just a segment."

Second, struggle:[43] Like *Discipleship of Equals,* so also the present collection of essays understands feminism in terms of struggle against kyriarchy and for the transformation of sociopolitical and internalized cultural-religious structures of domination. The following chapters seek to present integral aspects of such a critical[44] feminist-political the*logy of liberation in terms of *struggle,* a term at home in Latin American liberation the*logies.

According to the Encarta Dictionary, the word *struggle* has multifaceted meanings. It means to make a great effort to deal with a challenge or to achieve or obtain something, to fight by grappling and wrestling, to move forcefully in an attempt to escape, or to move with great effort. The noun in turn expresses similar meanings: struggle is a great effort made over a period of time to overcome difficulties or achieve something, a prolonged fight or conflict, a strenuous physical or mental effort, or something requiring such. All these meanings of struggle circumscribe the difficulties to change and transform structures of domination and violence.

I understand struggle therefore not in the restricted sense of resistance. Struggle includes the power to resist but it also seeks the power to change. Amy Allen[45] offers an analysis of power that proves adequate to feminist theorists who analyze, critique, and seek to transform relations of domination. She insists that feminists need a complex notion of power understood as *power over,* as *power to,* and as *power with.* She characterizes the two analytic perspectives from which feminists view power as the *foreground perspective* and as *the background perspective.* The first investigates the power relations between individuals or discrete groups of individuals. However, such an approach does not take into account the institutional-structural contexts of such power relations. Hence a second strategy

---

42. Anna Julia Cooper, *A Voice from the South,* 134.
43. See especially also Ada María Isasi-Díaz, *En La Lucha/In the Struggle: Elaborating a Mujerista Theology* (Minneapolis: Fortress Press, 2004).
44. The qualifier "critical" belongs to European political the*logies.
45. Amy Allen, *The Power of Feminist Theory: Domination, Resistance, Solidarity* (Boulder: Westview, 1999), 119-38.

of inquiry is necessary. The *background perspective* is concerned with *situated power*. It can be differentiated into five distinct aspects that need to be analyzed and discussed: *subject-positions, cultural meanings, social practices, institutions, and structures*. She concludes: "Taken together, this definition of power and these methodological considerations provide a feminist conception of power that can illuminate the complex multifarious relations of domination, resistance and solidarity with which feminism is concerned."[46]

While fully agreeing with her, I would want to modify her conclusion somewhat. In my view it is important to name domination as *kyriarchal*, to articulate resistance as *struggle* and to empower solidarity with creative vision and imagination. Hence, the four sections of this book explore and reflect on such sites of struggles and their transforming visions.

Third, vision: However, in order to struggle against the variegated kyriarchal structures of domination, one needs both a different vision of the world and a site or location alternative to kyriarchy from which to see the world. Feminist theorists for instance have named as such a site the "standpoint of wo/men." According to standpoint theory, a standpoint is a place from which one looks at the world and that influences how people socially construct it.[47] Christian feminists have suggested religion and church as homeland or insisted on the exodus from patriarchal religion to the margins as such alternative feminist strategic sites. In light of my theoretical historical-political analysis of kyriarchy, I have suggested the notion of the *ekklēsia* of wo/men[48] as such an imagined alternative space and community of struggle.

However, it must be understood that the word *ekklēsia* does not mean in the first place "church." Rather, it means "congress," or the democratic assembly of full citizens who come together to decide issues pertaining to their rights and well-being. It is moreover important to qualify *ekklēsia* with wo/men, since democracy has been kyriarchally deformed insofar as throughout the centuries wo/men and other non-people have been excluded from democratic rights and decision-making powers. For instance, the ongoing struggles around the right to birth control and the termination of pregnancy document that wo/men still have to struggle for their full citizenship and

---

46. Ibid., 135.

47. See especially Nancy Hartsock, *The Feminist Standpoint Revisited* (Boulder: Westview, 1999).

48. Elizabeth A. Castelli, "The Ekklesia of Women and/as Utopian Space: Locating the Work of Elisabeth Schüssler Fiorenza in Feminist Utopian Thought," in *On The Cutting Edge: The Study of Wo/men in Biblical Worlds* (New York: Continuum, 2004), 36-52. In *Feminist Biblical Interpretation in Theological Context: Restless Readings* (Burlington: Ashgate, 2002), 32-59, 142-62. Jánnine Jobling discusses the concept of the *ekklēsia* of wo/men but chooses *ekklēsia* without the qualification of *wo/men* as her hermeneutical key concept in order to restrict the concept to the Christian feminist movement (143). In so doing she re-inscribes the division between the Christian and the so-called secular women's movements that I sought to overcome with this radical, democratic, counter-kyriarchal image.

decision making democratic rights in kyriarchal democracies and religious communities. This struggle is not a question of choice but a claiming of our right to decide. Hence, the radical democratic *ekklēsia* of wo/men is already an alternative reality to kyriarchy and at the same time a not yet realized imaginary space.

However, it has been correctly objected[49] that the term *ekklēsia* is too Christian typed and therefore cannot function in different cultural and religious contexts as such an alternative site to kyriarchy. While I first introduced this term in the context of the Catholic wo/men's movement,[50] I have sought to develop the political aspect of *ekklēsia* in my subsequent work. To avoid narrowing the meaning of *ekklēsia* to church, I have found Kwame Anthony Appiah's notion of cosmopolitanism helpful.[51]

Cosmopolitanism is derived from the Greek word *kosmos* ("world") and the political term *polis* ("city state"). A *cosmopolis* is then a world city-state. The cosmopolitan tradition combines two strands of thought, one stressing global visions and obligations and the other celebrating local differences. The connection between the two is made through the imagination. To quote Appiah elaborating our connection to art:

> One connection—the one neglected in cultural patrimony—not through identity but *despite* difference. . . . But equally important is the human connection. My people—human beings—made the Great Wall of China . . . the Sistine Chapel: these things were made by creatures like me. . . . The connection through a local identity is as imaginary as the connection to humanity . . . [it] is a connection made in the imagination; but to say this isn't to pronounce either of them unreal. They are among the realest connections that we have.[52]

In this cosmopolitan imaginary the *ekklēsia of* wo/men is the decision-making assembly that seeks to create the connection between the local/particular struggles of wo/men and the vision of a *cosmopolis* of justice and well-being that no longer can be imagined without wo/men. However, as Christine Delphy so forcefully has pointed out: "We do not know what the values, individual personality traits, and culture of a non-hierarchical society would be like and we have

---

49. See, for example, Musa W. Dube, *Postcolonial Feminist Interpretation of the Bible* (Saint Louis: Chalice, 2000); and Dube, "Villagizing, Globalizing, and Biblical Studies," in Justin S. Upkong, et al., eds., *Reading the Bible in the Global Village: Cape Town* (Atlanta: Scholars, 2002), 41-64.

50. See Elisabeth Schüssler Fiorenza, *In Memory of Her: A Feminist Theological Reconstruction of Christian Origins*, Tenth Anniversary Edition (New York: Crossroad, 1994).

51. Kwame Anthony Appiah, *Cosmopolitanism: Ethics in a World of Strangers* (New York: Norton, 2006).

52. Ibid., 135.

great difficulty in imagining it. But to imagine it we must think that it is possible. Practices produce values: other practices produce other values."[53]

The same can be said about religion. My hope is that the religious practices of the cosmopolis of the *ekklēsia* of wo/men also can produce egalitarian values and visions of justice and well-being for everyone without exceptions. It is the imaginary site of feminist religious "world-making."

Fourth, religious "world making": Such religious "world-making"[54] is difficult but possible. I suggest that feminist the*logy has the means to imagine and to articulate the "not yet" of a domination-free, violence-free, and just world. The*logy is usually understood as the science of faith. As such it attempts to adhere to historically congealed experience and thought, to scripture and tradition, which seek to preserve traditional thought as the truth of faith and to explore its efficacious power for today. In so doing, it overlooks that traditional truth not only already speaks the language of kyriarchy, but also continues to inscribe historical structures of domination.

Thus, it becomes necessary that a critical political feminist the*logy of liberation articulate *the*-legein* not only as science of faith but also as science of hope, which seeks to realize change and transformation through critique and new perspectives. The*logy as science of hope seeks to imagine the domination- and violence-free world intended by G*d and to envision it anew with the help of religious traditions and language as an alternative to kyriarchy.

Whereas *faith* often is understood as believing in something as true that excludes other religious perspectives, *hope* refers to the desire for something that we lack, to the longing for justice, happiness, life and well-being, to the yearning for a different more just world and future. The words of the Jewish-German poet Hilde Domin express that hope is something delicate and fragile, something that can vanish and succumb to despair: "The longing for justice does not decrease, but hope does. The yearning for peace does not, but hope does" (my translation).[55]

Hope needs strength, defiance, it needs—I would say—religion, in order to remain alive. Religion is a slippery concept, which is differently defined und understood. No generally accepted definition of religion exists. In my view the understanding of religion as "world making," as "world creating," is important for a critical feminist the*logy. Religion and the*logy rely on existing symbol systems and myths for such a process of "world making." In and through symbolic

---

53. Christine Delphy, "Rethinking Sex and Gender," in Darlene Juschka, ed., *Feminism in the Study of Religion: A Reader* (New York: Continuum, 2001), 422.

54. Cf. Darlene M. Juschka, "General Introduction," in Delphy, ed., *Feminism in the Study of Religion*, 18; and William E. Paden, *Religious Worlds: The Comparative Study of Religion* (Boston: Beacon, 1994).

55. Die Sehnsucht nach Gerechtigkeit nimmt nicht ab, aber die Hoffnung. Die Sensucht nach Frieden nicht, aber die Hoffnung.

actions and imagination, religion creates again and again a world of grace different from our present world of injustice and violence.

Such an understanding of religion does not conceive of transcendence as "hereafter," but envisions it as the alternative world of G*d that radically questions and challenges the systems of domination and the injustices of our present world. The means to realize such a radical different imagination are language, ritual and art. However, it must not be overlooked that religious language, as all other language, has a double-effect: It can either mirror our historical-kyriarchal world and legitimate the status quo religiously, or it can articulate G*d's intended world as an alternative world of justice and love.

The imagery of both worlds, that of the kyriarchal world of domination, violence, and injustice on the one hand and that of the gender-free divine world of wellbeing, justice, and love on the other, is linguistically inscribed in holy scriptures and formative traditions. Hence, Christian the*logy must develop a the*logical hermeneutics that is able to differentiate between and critically evaluate these two very different worlds. It must ask again and again what kind of G*d Christian religion proclaims, how the divine is imagined, to what ends the name of G*d is (mis)used, and what its accountability is for the kyriarchal exploitation and colonial injustices of our world.

Such critical querying and imagining is necessary so that Christian the*logy, liturgy, and ethics are able to annunciate the non-violent divine world of justice, wellbeing, and love that was proclaimed by Jesus of Nazareth and Mary of Magdala.

All religious discourses, not just Christian the*logy, I argue, have to learn how to understand critique as a science of hope. If Christian the*logy wants to proclaim the *domination-free alternative world of G*d* effectively and to continue such proclamation in the future, it has to engage intentionally in the process of religious and ethical "world making." I hope that these essays will convince readers to develop such an imagination and science of hope in struggle.

PART I

Feminist Theory
and Feminist The*logy

1

Religion, Gender, and Change

A Critical Feminist Exploration[1]

In this chapter I discuss the encoding of gender discourses and their religious legitimizations. I argue that a critical academic analysis of gender need to remain rooted in the variegated social wo/men's movements for change. Critical liberationist feminist studies in religion and Christian the*logy therefore may not only focus on a critical deconstructive gender[2] analysis but may also seek to develop religious and spiritual resources and visions that empower wo/men in religion for change and transformation.

In a global situation of venture capitalism, poverty, and information highways, all religions are challenged to articulate a liberating spiritual vision of justice and well-being for everyone. In order to speak to this global situation of increasing insecurity and exploitation that challenges all universal claims to justice and liberation we need to recognize and affirm that we all are in the same fragile global "life-boat" called earth. In attempting to articulate a spiritual vision of well-being for all, it is especially necessary to focus on the struggles of wo/men at the bottom of the global pyramids of domination and to unearth the subjugated knowledges of every woman around the globe.

---

1. This chapter has appeared only in Chinese in *The Dance of Interpretation*, ed. Yeh Pao-Kuei (Taipei: Yeon Wang, 2007).

2. Elisabeth Schüssler Fiorenza, "Gender," in *The Encyclopedia of Politics and Religion*, ed. Robert Wuthnow (Washington, D.C.: Congressional Quarterly Books, 1998), 290-94. See also Hadumod Bussman and Renate Hof, eds., *Genus: Zur Geschlechterdifferenz in den Kulturwissenschaften* (Stuttgart: Kröner, 1995); Linda Nicholson, "Interpreting Gender," in *Social Postmodernism: Beyond Identity Politics*, ed. Linda Nicholson and Steven Seidman (New York: Cambridge University Press, 1995), 39-67. See also the work of Judith Butler.

Feminist liberation theologies and movements therefore seek to weave together the heterogeneous strands of emancipatory visions of the world's religions into the multicolored tapestry of ethical-religious spiritual vision. They invite religious people to rediscover and affirm spiritual traditions of human dignity, justice, inclusivity, diversity, and the richness of creation. In my reflections I will attempt to address some of these questions not just from a feminist perspective but from a Christian feminist the*logical[3] perspective. I explore the topic as a Catholic feminist the*logian[4] from an Euro-American social location who understands the specific struggles of Christian wo/men as similar to those in other religions. If I focus on Christian religion and the*logy as sites of feminist struggles, I do not mean to suggest that only Christian churches and the*logies are such sites of feminist ideology critique and transformation. To the contrary, similar issues are raised by feminists in Judaism and Islam, the other two biblical religions.[5] Moreover, other major world religions also are undergoing intense feminist scrutiny and re-visioning of their belief systems and institutional practices.[6]

The second wave of the feminist movement has not only engendered a wo/men's rights movement in religion. It has also inaugurated feminist studies in religion and the*logy as new academic areas of research and inquiry.[7] Feminist studies in religion and the*logy have broken through the silencing of centuries and have begun to reclaim the sacred power of naming. They have begun to name the divine, the world, and the Self anew.[8]

In short, I approach the topic from a critical feminist perspective and practice that seeks to change Christian religion. I will argue first that the problem of religious culture and gender ethics needs to be negotiated within a critical feminist framework that is rooted in feminist movements for change, because feminists have

---

3. In order to indicate the brokenness and inadequacy of human language to name the divine, I have switched in my book *Jesus: Miriam's Child, Sophia's Prophet: Critical Issues in Feminist Christology* (New York: Continuum, 1994) from the orthodox Jewish writing of G-d, which I had adopted in *But She Said* and *Discipleship of Equals*, to this spelling of G*d, which seeks to avoid the conservative malestream association that the writing of G-d has for Jewish feminists. Since the*logy means speaking about G*d or G*d-talk, I write it in the same way.

4. See my book *Grenzen überschreiten: Der theoretische Anspruch feministischer Theologie* (Münster: LIT, 2004).

5. For a widely-discussed example of such a dialogue between wo/men in the three biblical religions, see Ranya Idliby, Suzanne Oliver, and Priscilla Warner, *The Faith Club: A Muslim, A Christian, A Jew—Three Women's Search for Understanding* (New York: Free, 2006). For a more scholarly dialogue, see Rita M. Gross and Rosemary Radford Ruether, *Religious Feminism and the Future of the Planet: A Buddhist-Christian Conversation* (New York: Continuum, 2001).

6. See the excellent contributions in Paula M. Cooey, William R. Eakin, and Jay B. McDaniel, eds., *After Patriarchy: Feminist Transformations of the World Religions* (Maryknoll: Orbis, 1991).

7. *The Journal of Feminist Studies in Religion*, which I cofounded with the Jewish feminist Judith Plaskow, has provided a forum for such interreligious and interdisciplinary work and discussion over the past twenty-six years.

8. See Darlene M. Juschka, ed., *Feminism in the Study of Religion: A Reader* (New York: Continuum 2001) and Elizabeth A. Castelli, ed., *Women, Gender, and Religion* (New York: Palgrave, 2001).

always linked gender to "power over" and understood gender "as a central dynamic through which power is exercised."[9] Then, in a second step, I will maintain that such gender[10] analysis must be situated within a feminist kyriarchal analytic. Because the sex-gender system intersects with other structures of domination such as race, class, ethnicity, age, culture and religion, it is necessary to develop a complex kyriarchal sociopolitical analytic of domination.

Finally, I will propose three ethical criteria, articulated by the black feminist scholar Patricia Hill Collins, for evaluating a feminist intersectional gender analysis[11] at work not only in Christian but in all religious feminist discourses. I thereby hope to contribute some critical concepts for a variegated feminist discussion across religious and cultural boundaries.

Feminism and Gender

I will first discuss gender within a critical feminist framework, although "feminist" is a much disputed and multifaceted concept. Not only is feminism often rejected as a Western colonialist term, it is also shunned in the academy as too ideological and as non-scientific. Moreover, in both the United States and all over the world, audiences still react negatively when they hear the word *feminist*. While many agree with the goals of feminism, they do not want to be labeled feminist, because they associate the f-word *feminism* with either lesbian, bra-burning, men-hating, crazy wo/men, or Western colonialism. The press reinforces this prejudice when it asks, "Is feminism dead?" and always answers with a resounding yes. For these reasons, I hasten to explain how I understand the f-word *feminist*.

To my mind, the best definition of feminism is expressed by a popular bumper sticker which, tongue-in-cheek, declares: "Feminism is the radical notion that wo/men are people." This definition reminds us of the centuries of democratic struggles for equal rights and full citizenship. It asserts that wo/men are not beasts of burden, sex-objects, temptresses, or goddesses. Rather, all wo/men without any exceptions are fully entitled citizens in society and religion who should have equal power, rights and responsibilities. Yet Christian wo/men have not been accorded such citizen-rights in religion and society throughout the centuries.

Although there are many divergent forms and even contradictory articulations of feminism today, such that it is appropriate to speak of "feminisms" in

---

9. Lynne Segal, *Why Feminism? Gender, Psychology, Politics* (New York: Columbia University Press, 1999), 42.

10. For the argument that gender is a Western invention, see Oyeronke Oyewumi, *The Invention of Women: Making an African Sense of Western Gender Discourses* (Minneapolis: University of Minnesota Press, 1977).

11. Patricia Hill Collins, *Fighting Words: Black Women and the Search for Justice* (Minneapolis: University of Minnesota Press, 1998).

the plural,[12] most feminists nevertheless agree that contemporary feminism is not just a political movement which is akin to other emancipatory movements. It also is an intellectual methodology for investigating and theorizing the experience and structures of wo/men's dehumanization. I suggest that the diverse theoretical articulations of feminism come together in their critique of elite, male, white, Western supremacy and in their assertion that gender is socially constructed rather than innate or ordained by G*d.

Feminism—as I understand it—is not just concerned with gender inequities and female marginalization. Rather, feminism is first of all a multi-various social, political, and religious movement that seeks to transform kyriarchy, which means the domination of the emperor, lord, slave-master, father, husband—the elite propertied male head of household. I have coined the word *kyriarchy,* an analogy to the German term *Herrschaft,* in order to distinguish a critical feminist intersectional analytic from the prevalent dualistic feminist understanding of patriarchy as the domination of all men over all wo/men. This understanding of patriarchy is inadequate, because many men are dominated while many elite wo/men have had power over men and other wo/men.

Moreover, the neologism *kyriarchy,* I submit, is historically more accurate and the*logically more appropriate than the term *hierarchy,* which is commonly used in English to designate a pyramidal system of power relations. Whereas much of feminist thought still locates the root of misogyny and patriarchal oppression in gender dualism, I argue to the contrary that the sociopolitical, pyramidal system of exploitation produces such ideological gender constructions. I understand kyriarchy as a pyramidal system of dominations that are inter-structured and multiplied through racism, heterosexism, classism, ethnocentrism, colonialism, ageism and other structures of exploitation. Gender is inflected by race, class, age, culture, and religion.[13] Although kyriarchy has changed throughout history, its Greek Aristotelian articulation is still powerful in Western culture and Christian religion today. It would therefore be interesting to study how kyriarchy has been articulated in other cultures and religions.[14]

Feminism always has expressed itself also as an intellectual and a spiritual movement insofar as it is seeking to come into a different consciousness and hence is struggling to change relations of inequity and dehumanization. Participation in social movements for change has often led to different self-understandings and different visions of the world. Such different understandings in turn lead to the

---

12. See Sandra Kemp and Judith Squires, eds., *Feminisms* (Oxford: Oxford University Press, 1997).

13. See Everett Yuehong Zhang, "Goudui and the State: Constructing Enterpreneurial Masculinity in Two Cosmopolitan Areas of Post-Socialist China," in *Gendered Modernities: Ethnographic Perspectives,* ed. Dorothy L. Hodgson (New York: Palgrave, 2001).

14. For instance, the Japanese feminist theologian Hisako Kinukawa, in *Wo/men and Jesus in Mark: A Japanese Feminist Perspective* (Maryknoll: Orbis, 1994), 15-22, points to the "emperor system" as a similar system to that of classical Greek kyriarchy.

articulation of a feminist politics and spirituality that can empower wo/men to bring about further change in society and religion.

In the past as in the present, feminist movements have emerged from wo/men's participation in emancipatory struggles, such as the struggles for full democratic citizenship, religious freedom, abolition of slavery, civil rights, national and cultural independence, as well as the struggles of the labor, peace, or GLBT movements. In these struggles for civil and human rights, feminists have learned that the terms "human" or "workers" or "civil rights" often do not include the rights and interests of wo/men. Therefore, it is necessary to struggle specifically for "wo/men's rights, well-being and self-determination."

In the past four decades, feminists also have been and remain engaged in multiple and variegated struggles to change religion, struggles over: equal rights in religion; access to sacred power; centuries of exclusion from ordination; reproductive rights and the rights of differently abled wo/men; wo/men's bodily integrity on religious grounds; moral agency and personal authority to determine their own lives; violence against wo/men in the home and the imperialist exploitation of wo/men around the world; abolishing death-dealing structures and the languages of hate; combating exploitative, sacral powers of domination and reconstructing a radical, democratic church and society that repents of and undoes the horrors of colonialism and other forms of wo/men's oppression; wo/men's the*logical education and teaching authority, seeking to overcome the centuries of silencing in the*logy, church, and society; a new sacred language that reclaims the power of word and ritual as well as the authority of religious naming; and last but not least, in struggles for a different kind of spirituality and liberating the*logy that seek to envision and name the divine and sacred anew. Presently, the struggles against wo/men's second-class citizenship center on the question of the non-ordination of wo/men in Roman Catholicism and on that of same sex marriage or the ordination of gay and transgendered people in Protestant churches.

I do not want to suggest, however, that only Christian religion and the*logy are such sites of feminist struggles. To the contrary, feminists in Judaism, Islam, Buddhism,[15] Sikhism, Hinduism, Chinese religions, or Indigenous religions around the world raise both similar and different issues. In consequence, not only biblical religions but also other major world religions are undergoing intense critical scrutiny by feminists. All religious belief systems and institutional practices are experiencing the growing pains of feminist re-visions.

Religion has not only been used throughout the centuries to oppress wo/men. It also has found its most faithful adherents among wo/men. Hence, no serious reform of society in the interest of wo/men's emancipation will be

---

15. See, for example, Simone Heidegger, *Buddhismus, Geschlechterverhältnis, und Diskriminierung: Die gegenwärtige Diskussion im Shin-Buddhismus Japans* (Münster: LIT, 2004).

successful if it does not seek to also advance the reform of religion. Moreover, since all reforms are interdependent, one cannot change the law, education, or other cultural institutions without also attempting to transform religion. Feminists who believe that we can neglect the re-vision of religion because there are more pressing political issues at stake do not recognize the impact of religion on society, and especially on the lives of women.[16]

Millions of women around the world actively participate in religious practices and institutions. They derive their self-identity, self-respect, sense of worth, dignity, courage, and vision from their religious engagement. Consequently one cannot simply relegate wo/men's religious commitments to "false consciousness." This not only overlooks wo/men's active participation in all religions, it also disregards the fact that religion still provides a framework of meaning that is not just alienating and oppressive but also self-affirming and liberating for millions of women.

To reject religion as totally oppressive or to neglect it as a positive source of empowerment and hope in creating a better future for wo/men would be to relinquish religion to the ownership claims of reactionary, rightwing fundamentalisms.[17] The resurgence of such global anti-feminist dogmatism and its success not only among men but also among women exploits people's fears, alienation, deep anxieties and feeling of loss concerning the world as they have known it. The experience of losing cultural, social, and religious roots coupled with the sense of personal isolation and social marginalization leads to a desire for assured certainty, definite security, fixed truth, and a stable picture of the world that is guaranteed by G*d. With this desire comes a longing for great leaders and father figures who will take care of everything and therefore rightfully require submission.

Wo/men's traditional cultural and religious socialization toward feminine passivity, subordination, and self-sacrificing love for a man conditions them to be lured by the appeal of such religious fundamentalist promises. Since the fundamentalist religious ethos of submission addresses wo/men's personal, economic, and political insecurities, it can harness these insecurities for rightwing, antidemocratic ends. Therefore, the maxim that the progress of a society can be judged by the progress of its wo/men must be applied also to the progress of wo/men in Christian and all other religions.

---

16. Elizabeth Cady Stanton, *The Original Feminist Attack on the Bible: The Woman's Bible*, ed. Barbara Welter (New York: Arno, 1974). See also the collection of essays *Searching the Scriptures: A Feminist Introduction* (New York: Crossroad, 1993), which I initiated and edited in celebration of the centennial anniversary of the *Woman's Bible*.

17. See Shirley Rogers Radl, *The Invisible Woman: Target of the Religious New Right* (New York: Dell, 1981); Sara Diamond, *Spiritual Warfare: The Politics of the Christian Right* (Boston: South End, 1989); Hans Küng and Jürgen Moltmann, *Fundamentalism as an Ecumenical Challenge* (London: SCM, 1992); "Fundamentalismen," *Beiträge zur feministischen Theorie und Praxis* 32 (1992); Margaret Lamberts Bendroth, *Fundamentalism and Gender: 1875 to the Present* (New Haven: Yale University Press, 1993); and Elizabeth A. Castelli and Janet R. Jakobsen, eds., *Interventions: Activists and Academics Respond to Violence* (New York: Palgrave, 2004).

Throughout the centuries religion has been used both as a weapon against and as a defense for subjugated wo/men. Religion has been invoked in wo/men's struggles for access to citizenship, public speaking, reproductive rights, the*logical education or ordained ministry. In these often bitter debates, the opposing parties continue to cite religion not only for and against wo/men's full participation and religious leadership, but also for and against the full citizenship of freeborn wo/men, the emancipation of slave wo/men, colonized wo/men, the rights of GLBT people, and, finally, for and against economic equity for poor wo/men and their children.

In sum, I argue here that it is necessary to contextualize the ethics of gender in feminist movements that seek to transform kyriarchal religious structures which not only perpetuate dehumanizing heterosexism and gender stereotypes, but also perpetuate other forms of wo/men's oppression, such as racism, poverty, religious exclusivism and colonialism.[18] Therefore, it is important to adopt a feminist decolonizing analysis[19] of the kyriarchal sex-gender system in which religious discourses are embedded and which in turn shape and sustain this kyriarchal system and its discourses. This kyriarchal sex-gender system is articulated differently in different religions and cultures, but it still seems to be at work in all of them.

The Kyriarchal Sex-Gender System as a Discursive Frame of Meaning

The assumption of "natural" sex-gender differences informs everyday experience and turns it into "common sense" knowledge, making gender difference appear to be "commonplace" and "G*d-given." The kyriarchal sex-gender system[20] serves as a pre-constructed frame of thinking and meaning. It constructs masculine and feminine difference in positivistic terms either as a natural-historical fact or as a metaphysical essence that is revealed rather than socially constructed. By presenting the sex-gender system of male/female or masculine/feminine as universal and "common sense," this pre-constructed frame of meaning obscures and mystifies the reality that the very notion of two sexes is a sociocultural construct for maintaining kyriarchal domination rather than a biological "given" or innate essence. This gender-frame religiously legitimates the kyriarchal disciplines of

---

18. For the implication of such intersectional studies for feminist theory and pedagogy, see Laura Gray-Rosendale and Gil Harootunian, eds., *Fractured Feminisms: Rhetoric, Context, and Contestation* (New York: SUNY Press, 2003). See also Elizabeth Abel, Barbara Christian, and Helene Moglen, eds., *Female Subjects in Black and White: Race, Psychoanalysis, Feminism* (Berkeley: University of California Press, 1997); Ruth Frankenberg, ed., *Displacing Whiteness: Essays in Social and Cultural Criticism* (Durham: Duke University Press, 1997); and Joan Acker, *Class Questions: Feminist Answers* (New York: Rowman and Littlefield, 2006).

19. See my book *The Power of the Word: Scripture and the Rhetoric of Empire* (Minneapolis: Fortress Press, 2007). See also Kwok Pui-lan, *Postcolonial Imagination and Feminist Theology* (Louisville: WJK, 2005).

20. For the elaboration of this notion and discussion of the literature on this concept, see my book *But She Said: Feminist Practices of Biblical Interpretation* (Boston: Beacon, 1992), 105-14.

the body and destroys the creative and unique self as the image of the divine which each of us is called to become.

Feminist theory has elaborated that the kyriarchal sex-gender system operates simultaneously on four discursive levels: first on the *social-political* level; second, on the *ethical-symbolic* level; third, on the *biological-natural* level; and finally, on the *linguistic-grammatical* level. These levels are interactive and mutually reinforce each other. Different feminist approaches enter their critical analysis at different nodal points of these interlocking discursive levels and hence emphasize different aspects of the sex-gender system. They generally distinguish the following terms: *male/female*, which classify human beings on the basis of anatomical differences; *man/woman*, which are based on social relations; and *masculine/feminine*, which are seen as the cultural-religious ideals, norms, values, and standards appropriate to one's gender position.

Feminist liberationist and postcolonial the*logies and studies in religion adopt a social analytic that can break through the kyriarchal sex-gender system's totalizing dualistic frame of reference. Such an analytic enables one not only to interpret religious texts and traditions as socioreligious constructions, but also to see how gender, race, class and colonialist structures are multiplicative and interdependent. This can be shown with respect to all four levels of the kyriarchal sex-gender system.

The Sociopolitical Level

A critical feminist inquiry begins its analytic work with the sociopolitical level of the kyriarchal sex-gender system. If one conceptualizes reality not in terms of gender dualism, but rather as a socially constructed web of interactive structures of dehumanization, one is able to problematize dichotomies such as world-church, human-divine, profane-sacred, politics-religion, orthodox-heretic, earth-heaven, male-female. If oppression is understood not in terms of dualistic opposites but as variegated kyriarchal social, interactive, and multiplicative structures of power, it becomes apparent that social location determines cultural-religious positions and intellectual perspectives. In such an analysis, the categories male/female, masculine/feminine, or man/woman do not signify dualistic opposites or fixed gender slots but sociopolitical and socioreligious discursive practices that are defined not only by sex, but also by race, class, age and culture. The social relations that give rise to gender differences are socioculturally and religiously constructed as relations of domination; they are not simply biological givens. In other words, the world is determined by relations of domination. Sex-gender is a part of such relations of ruling which also ground other divisions such as class, ethnicity or race.

Although maleness and femaleness are supposedly natural—biological "givens"—they are cultural norms that are backed by social and religious sanctions. Since sex-gender differences are grounded in social kyriarchal arrangements, they are articulated differently in different historical periods and religions.

Nonetheless, they are taken to be "commonplace" universals, natural "givens," that are ordained by G*d. Whereas in Greco-Roman antiquity, for instance, menial service was seen as appropriate to the nature of slaves and serfs, in modernity it is construed as a "feminine" ideal appropriate to the nature of wo/men. Public political service in turn is conceptualized as "masculine," appropriate to the nature of men. This modern separation between the public male sphere and the private female domain has generated a separate system of economics for wo/men[21] which has resulted in the increasing feminization of poverty and the destitution of female-headed households[22]—a development with devastating effects especially on wo/men of the "two-thirds world" and their children.

Consequently, the modern kyriarchal sex-gender system must be scrutinized not only for its economic-cultural heterosexist biases. It must also be analyzed with respect to its classist, racist, and colonialist underpinnings. Hundreds of years ago, Aristotle had argued that the freeborn, propertied, educated Greek male is the highest of moral beings and that all other members of the human race are deficient by nature in the interest of his service.[23] Modern political philosophy continues to assume that the propertied, educated elite Western man is defined by reason, self-determination, and full citizenship whereas wo/men and other subordinated peoples are characterized by emotion, service and dependence.[24] They are seen in colonialist discourses not as rational and responsible adult subjects, but as emotional, helpless and child-like objects. In short, kyriarchal societies, cultures and religions need for their functioning a "servant class," a "servant race," or a "servant people," be they slaves, serfs, maids, coolies, or mammies. The existence of such a "servant class" is maintained through religion, law, education, socialization, and brute violence. It is sustained by the belief that members of a "servant class" of people are by nature, or by divine decree, inferior to those whom they are destined to serve.[25]

The Ethical-Symbolic Level

Western political kyriarchal relations of domination and subordination are explicitly formulated in the context of Greek kyriarchal democracy. They have been

---

21. See Maria Mies, *Patriarchy and Accumulation on a World Scale: Women in the International Division of Labor* (London: Zed, 1986).

22. See the systemic analyses in Elisabeth Schüssler Fiorenza and Anne Carr, eds., *Wo/men Work and Poverty* (Edinburgh: T and T Clark, 1987).

23. Susan Moller Okin, *Women in Western Political Thought* (Princeton: Princeton University Press, 1979), 73-96.

24. See Elisabeth List, "Homo Politicus—Femina Privata: Thesen zur Kritik der politischen Anthropologie," in *Weiblichkeit in der Moderne: Ansätze feministischer Vernunftkritik*, ed. J. Conrad and U. Konnertz (Tübingen: Diskord, 1986), 75-95.

25. For example, the biographical reflection and analysis of apartheid as an ideology and institution to maintain a "servant people" by Mark Mathabene, *Kaffir Boy: The True Story of a Black Youth's Coming of Age in Apartheid South Africa* (New York: Macmillan, 1986).

mediated by Christian scriptural-the*logical traditions and have decisively deter-mined modern forms and ideologies of democracy. Feminist political philoso-phers have documented that modern (and postmodern) understandings of both rationality and the world have been articulated by white, Western, elite, educated men.[26] These men have not only defined white wo/men as "others," but also all other non-persons as "others" who lack human—that is, masculine—qualities. The definition of other races and peoples as "feminine Other" has enabled colo-nial Western powers to exploit and utilize religion in the colonial capitalist quest for identity and property.

The modern bourgeois ethos of "femininity" prescribes that "good" wo/men perform unpaid services in and outside the family with self-less love, nurturing care, and patient loving kindness. The ethos of "true womanhood," romantic love, and domesticity defines wo/men's nature as "being for others" in actual or spiritual motherhood. Whereas men are measured by the masculine standards of self-assertion, independence, power and control, wo/men are called to fulfill their G*d-given true nature and destiny by self-sacrificing service and loving self-effacement. The Christian preaching of self-sacrificing love and humble service reinforces and perpetuates the cultural socialization of wo/men to self-less femi-ninity and altruistic behavior.

Moreover, since the industrial revolution in Europe and America, church and religion have been pushed out of the public realm and relegated to the private sphere of individualistic piety, charitable work, and the cultivation of home and family. Nevertheless, both religion and wo/men were also crucial in maintaining public interests in the antithetical "other" and in shaping Western colonialism.[27] Like the "White Lady," Christianity as a "missionary religion" also had the func-tion to "civilize" the savages, who were understood as "untamed nature." Here, the Western discourses on femininity and female nature are grounded in in the colonial exercise of power.[28]

---

26. Genevieve Lloyd, *Man of Reason: Male and Female in Western Philosophy* (Minneapolis: University of Minnesota Press, 1984). See also her chapter, "The Man of Reason," in *Women, Knowledge, and Reality: Explorations in Feminist Philosophy*, ed. Ann Garry and Marilyn Pearsall (New York: Routledge, 1992), 111: "By the Man of Reason I mean the ideal of rationality associ-ated with the rational philosophers of the seventeenth century. And, secondly, something more nebulous—the residue of that ideal in our contemporary consciousness. . . . The main feature of the Man of Reason that I am concerned to bring into focus is his maleness." See also Sarah Coakley, "Gender and Knowledge in Western Philosophy: The 'Man of Reason' and the 'Feminine Other' in Enlightenment Thought," in *The Special Nature of Women?* ed. Anne Carr and Elisabeth Schüssler Fiorenza (London: SCM, 1991), 75-84.

27. See, for example, Joan Jacobs Brumberg, "The Ethnological Mirror: American Women and Their Heathen Sisters, 1870-1910," in *Women and the Structure of Society. Selected Research from the Fifth Berkshire Conference on the History of Women*, ed. Barbara J. Harris and JoAnn K. McNamara (Durham: Duke University Press, 1984), 108-28.

28. See my article, "The Politics of Otherness: Biblical Interpretation as a Critical Praxis for Liberation," in *The Future of Liberation Theology: Essays in Honor of Gustavo Gutiérrez*, ed. Marc H. Ellis and Otto Maduro (Maryknoll: Orbis, 1989), 311-25, and Kwok Pui-Lan, "The Image of the

In the process of religious privatization and cultural "feminization," the clergy lost their privileged status and came to be treated like "woman" in polite society. This feminization of Christian religion has led both to the emasculation of the clergy in society[29] and to the reasserting of their masculine roles in the*logy, church, and the home. Here, the debates on wo/men's ordination have their "setting in life."[30] Wo/men's recent access to professional ministry and the*logy is resisted by male clerics who fear that the church will be totally feminized if wo/men join the ranks of the male church leadership.

The Biological-Natural Level

Like "white and black," both "maleness and femaleness" and "man and woman" are discursive categories and symbolic constructs of the kyriarchal sex-gender system. They *appear*, however, to be *"natural" or "factual" sex differences* in everyday understanding. Hence, the second-class citizenship of wo/men is not primarily achieved by brute force but in and through individual cultural-religious socialization into the naturalized kyriarchal sex-gender system and the public discourses that reinforce it. Like education, religion also has a major role in the discursive construction and symbolic legitimization of naturalized, heterosexual sex-gender relations. For instance, biblical religion has applied the metaphor of patriarchal marriage-relationships to the relation between G*d and the individual soul as well as to the relationship between Christ and the community. Early Christian the*logy continued the rhetoric of Hebrew prophetic discourses that understood God as the groom/husband of his bride/wife Israel. In Western mysticism and piety, men, like wo/men, have taken up the "feminine" position of receptivity and surrender with respect to G*d, conforming to a masculine G*d's desire for the feminine, while at the same time sustaining his masculine practices of control and superiority with respect to the world.

This analogy between G*d-Christ-husband-male, on the one hand, and soul-bride-female, on the other, has become "naturalized" and biologized in modern the*logical discourses.[31] Christian churches have excluded wo/men from ordination on grounds of anatomical sex until very recently, and my own church still does so today. Female sex-gender disqualifies one from representing Christ.

'White Lady': Gender and Race in Christian Mission," in *The Special Nature of Women?* ed. Anne Carr and Elisabeth Schüssler Fiorenza (Philadelphia: Trinity International, 1991), 19-27. See also Kwok Pui-lan, *Chinese Women and Christianity 1860–1927* (Atlanta: Scholars, 1992).

29. Rosemary Radford Ruether, "Male Clericalism and the Dread of Women," *The Ecumenist* 11 (1973): 65-69.

30. See the analysis of this situation in my keynote address at the Second Ordination Conference in 1978, reprinted in *Discipleship of Equals*, 129-50, especially 140-44. For a comparative ecumenical view, see also Jacqueline Field Bibb, *Women toward Priesthood: Ministerial Politics and Feminist Practice* (New York: Cambridge University Press, 1991).

31. For the right wing, conservative tendencies of such a "biologization" process, see Renate Bridenthal, Atina Grossmann, and Marion Kaplan, eds., *When Biology Became Destiny: Women in Weimar and Nazi Germany* (New York: Monthly Review Press, 1984).

Whereas traditional the*logy had rationalized the exclusion of wo/men on Aristotelian and scriptural grounds of subordination, modern the*logy argues either that wo/men cannot physically resemble Christ, the bridegroom of the church, or they maintain wo/men's essential difference and complementarity of role.

In order to undo such kyriarchal "naturalizing" sex-gender tendencies, some feminist the*logians have insisted that religious discourses must distinguish between biological sex and kyriarchal symbolic gender constructions. Although attempts to separate biological sex from gender are common in the*logical discourses, they are nevertheless problematic since they do not sufficiently reflect that the cultural sex-gender system "naturalizes" the category of "sex" as biologically given rather than as discursively constructed—just as it has done with regard to race and colonized people. For instance, common sense holds that facial hair is a physical male characteristic. This commonplace assumption conceals, however, that it is discursively constructed. In order to uphold this ostensibly male sex standard, a multi-billion-dollar cosmetic industry strives to eradicate all facial hair in wo/men. Anatomical physical differences are discursively constructed and socially maintained as cultural sex differences. Moreover, varying cultures construct the meaning of anatomical distinctions differently. For instance, one could argue that boy and girl children are physically more alike than girls and nursing mothers. In addition, biological differences receive different significance if they are discursively constructed on a continuum rather than in terms of dualistic oppositional classification.[32]

Finally, the religious naturalization of gender and its reduction to anatomical sex conceals its social location in a modern bio-social science of human variation. For, according to nineteenth-century scientists

> lower races represented the "female" type of the human species, and females the "lower race" of gender. . . . By analogy with the so-called lower races, women, the sexually deviant, the criminal, the urban poor, and the insane were in one way or another constructed as biological "races apart" whose differences from the white male, and likeness to each other, "explained" their different and lower position in the social hierarchy.[33]

The Linguistic-Grammatical Level

A religion that upholds kyriarchal sex-gender differences as natural or G*d-given can do so because its readings of Scriptures and traditions engage in a linguistic-

---

32. As Ann Oakley in *Sex, Gender, and Society* (New York: Harper and Row, 1972), 191, already observed in 1972: "One expert on intersexuality has said that it is impossible to define male and female genital morphologies as distinct: they exist as a continuum of possible developments and are thus a constant reminder, not of biological polarity of male and female but of their biological identity."

33. N. Leys Stepan, "Race and Gender," in *The "Racial" Economy of Science: Toward a Democratic Future*, ed. Sandra Harding (Bloomington: Indiana University Press, 1993), 361.

symbolic process of "naturalizing" grammatical gender. Not only religious, but also kyriocentric cultural language in general repeatedly re-inscribes the cultural-religious prejudices and socio-kyriarchal relations which in turn undergird their disciplinary practices. While many studies have been done with regard to Western grammatically androcentric languages, research is needed as to how languages that are structured according to status construct gender. However, I am aware only of Japanese the*logian Satoko Yamaguchi's work in this regard.[34]

The term *gender* derives from Latin *genus*, which means "class, kind, or category in general." The Western grammatical masculine/feminine noun-classification system is said to have been introduced by the fifth-century B.C.E. Sophist Protagoras. If Protagoras had used a different classification system such as, for instance, long/short, the devastating conflation of grammatical gender with biological sex in Western symbolic discourses might have been avoided.

According to the grammarian Dennis Baron,[35] the association of grammatical gender with human generation was developed by medieval grammarians into Latin [*species*], an association which later grammarians imposed on Old English by arguing for it in cultural-religious terms. For instance, in his *Theory of Language* published in 1788, James Beattie argues for the distinction of biological sex as the primary basis for noun-classification on the*logical grounds: "Beings superior to man, although we conceive them to be of no sex, are spoken of as masculine in most of the modern tongues of Europe, on account of their dignity; the male being according to our ideas, the nobler sex. But idolatrous nations acknowledge both male and female deities; and some of them have even given to the Supreme Being a name of the feminine gender."[36]

How much language and social structures are intertwined becomes evident in the fact that in 1850 the British Parliament passed an act declaring that henceforth the pronoun *he* would be used as an inclusive reference to wo/men as well as to men, thereby replacing the use of "they" as generic with the pseudo-generic "he."[37] The Western linguistic sex-gender system that uses gender classifications as rooted in biological sex cannot help but reify and naturalize sociopolitical and cultural-religious gender constructs. In such a linguistic system, masculine terms function as "generic" language in which *man/male/masculine/he* stands for human *and* male, while *woman/female/feminine/she* connotes only femaleness. Grammatically androcentric "generic" Western languages that are based on the classical grammatical systems of Greek and Latin explicitly mention wo/men

---

34. Satoko Yamaguchi, "Father Image of God and Inclusive Language: A Reflection in Japan," in *Toward a New Heaven and a New Earth: Essays in Honor of Elisabeth Schüssler Fiorenza*, ed. Fernando F. Segovia (Maryknoll: Orbis, 2003), 199-224.

35. Dennis Baron, *Grammar and Gender* (New Haven: Yale University Press, 1986).

36. Robert H. Robins, *A Short History of Linguistics* (London: Longmans, 1979), 137.

37. See Casey Miller and Kate Swift, *Words and Women: New Language in New Times* (Doubleday: Anchor, 1977).

only as the exception to the rule, as problematic, or specifically as particular individuals. In all other cases one has to adjudicate in light of contextual linguistic markers whether wo/men are meant or not.

Moreover, Western androcentric languages and discourses do not just marginalize wo/men or eliminate them from the historical cultural-religious record. As kyriocentric languages, they also construct the meaning of being "wo/men" or being "men" differently. What it means to be female/woman/feminine does not so much depend on one's sex but rather on one's location in the socio-symbolic kyriarchal system of multiplicative superordinations and subordinations. The meaning of "woman" is unstable and ever shifting[38] depending not so much on its sex-gender relation, but on its socio-systemic kyriarchal contextualization.[39]

The category "woman" today has become a "naturalized," generic, sex-based term, although until very recently it referred to lower class females only. A statement such as "slaves were not wo/men" offends "commonsense" understandings, whereas a statement such as "slaves were not ladies" makes perfect sense. One can perceive the slippages, the cultural constructedness, and the historical ambiguity of the meaning of "woman" much more easily in the term "lady," because this discursive appellation readily "reveals" its race, class, and colonial bias. "Lady," until very recently, not only was restricted to wo/men of higher status or educational refinement, it also functioned to symbolize "true womanhood" and femininity.

Such a cursory discussion of the Western kyriarchal sex-gender system explains why critical feminist explorations of religious symbol systems usually raise great, albeit often repressed, anxieties among religious wo/men. Since colonized religious men are culturally stereotyped as "feminine," they need to establish their cultural-religious self-identity by professing and maintaining masculine standards. Wo/men in turn are upholding the ideal of femininity which in modernity means that men are to be educated to be *their own man*, whereas wo/men are to be educated to be *women for men* (Rousseau).[40] Accordingly, Christian wo/men understandably fear a loss of their cultural-religious feminine self-identity and prestige if they no longer can model their relations to men on the paradigm of their relation with Jesus, the perfect man for whom they live.[41] As long as this fear is not addressed the*logically, Christian wo/men and men will remain entrenched in the kyriarchal sex-gender system.

---

38. See Denise Riley, *"Am I That Name?": Feminism and the Category of "Women" in History* (Minneapolis: University of Minnesota Press, 1988).

39. The same can be said for race classifications. Cf. Gloria A. Marshall, "Racial Classifications: Popular and Scientific," in *The "Racial" Economy of Science*, ed. Sandra Harding (Bloomington: Indiana University Press, 1993), 116-27.

40. Susan Moller Okin, ibid., 135.

41. For a feminist discussion of the interplay between language and identity see, for instance, the contributions in Joyce Penfield, ed., *Women and Language in Transition* (Albany: SUNY Press, 1987).

Conclusion

To sum up and conclude my argument: Feminist the*logies and studies in religion explore the religious–cultural kyriarchal sex-gender system in order to understand the societal and religious second class citizenship status of wo/men. By situating a critical gender analysis in the diverse struggles for changing religious kyriarchal structures and mindsets of domination and subordination, we are able to articulate the differences between and within wo/men. By deconstructing religious kyriarchal discourses, we are able not only to overcome the the*logical silencing and marginalization of wo/men in religion, but also to identify the resources in religious discourses and traditions that empower wo/men to surmount the discursive inculcations of the kyriarchal sex-gender system.

From such a critical feminist vantage point, scholars in religion are also able to formulate alternative religious visions and strategies for undoing the religious legitimizations of the kyriarchal sex-gender system. Such alternative discourses need to be articulated at all four levels: the sociopolitical, the cultural-symbolic, the biological-natural, and the linguistic-grammatical levels. In so doing, feminist the*logies and studies in religion can articulate a spiritual-religious vision that is able to inspire diverse movements of liberation with a spiritual ethos of equality and well-being for everywoman and everyone.

Such critical feminist analyses and visions must be evaluated in terms of their effective power for change. Patricia Hill Collins has suggested three interdependent questions for the assessment of a social theory. These criteria can also be applied to the discourses of religious and the*logical studies.

- Does a social or religious theory speak the truth to wo/men about the reality of their lives? Whose knowledge counts, whose standards are used, and who is discredited? Who decides what counts as knowledge, and how knowledge and truth are validated?
- What is the stance of a social or religious theory towards freedom, and what pragmatic strategies does it suggest to achieve its vision of emancipation? What is its theory of emancipation and does it facilitate political action for change?
- Does a critical social or religious theory move wo/men to struggle against dehumanization, and how effectively does it provide moral authority for emancipatory praxis? Does it engender the search for justice as an ongoing principled struggle that resists disciplinary power relations and gives meaning to everyday life?

If vision and knowledge are determined by their sociopolitical location and function, then knowledge and vision for the future must remain situated within the diverse feminist struggles which seek to overcome kyriarchal mindsets and exploitations. Feminists in religion are especially positioned to articulate spiritualities of struggle that enable and defend life that is threatened or destroyed by hunger, destitution, sexual violence, torture and dehumanization. Such feminist spiritualities of struggle seek to give dignity and value to the life of the social non-person as the presence and image of the divine or sacred in our midst. To that end, feminist scholars in religion and the*logy continue to seek not only to produce a different body of knowledge, but also to inspire people for engaging in the variegated feminist struggles around the world to change kyriarchal structures and to transform discourses of dehumanization. To be able to do so in the creative power of Wisdom/wisdom,[42] we need to remain rooted in wo/men's movements for social and religious change.

---

42. See my books *Wisdom Ways: Introducing Feminist Biblical Interpretation* (Maryknoll: Orbis, 2001) and *The Open House of Wisdom: Critical Feminist Theological Explorations* (Tokyo: Shinkyo Shuppansha, 2005; only in Japanese).

2

Feminist The*logy between Modernity and Postmodernity

"M odernity" and "Postmodernity" are ambiguous, shifting concepts that are often set over against each other as dichotomous.[1] For example, it is not clear when modernity begins and when it ends, whereas postmodernity is said to have reached its high point in the 1980s, so that today one speaks of late postmodernity.[2] While the notion of the "modern" is characterized by sociopolitical developments such as capitalism, industrialization, liberal democracy, colonialism, and globalization,[3] the understanding of postmodernity is determined by language and symbols.[4]

As feminist and postcolonial discourses have shown, modernity did not realize its promise of liberty, justice, and equality for most people but instead excluded them from democracy through kyriarchal discourses of dominance and

---

1. This is a revised text of a chapter that has appeared in my book *Grenzen überschreiten*, and I want to thank Linda Maloney for the translation on which my revision here is based. I also want to express my sincere thanks to Prof. Herta Nagl-Docekal and Dr. Friedrich Wolfram of the Catholic Academy Association of the Archdiocese of Vienna as well as the interfaculty working group on philosophy of religion for the invitation to participate in the lecture series on "Religion, Theology, and Churches under the Conditions of the Modern/Postmodern."

2. For a discussion of the critical interrelation between postmodernity, psychoanalysis, and feminism, see Jane Flax, *Thinking Fragments: Psychoanalysis, Feminism, and Postmodernism in the Contemporary West* (Berkeley: University of California Press, 1990).

3. See Saskia Sassen, "The Excess of Globalisation and the Feminization of Survival," *Parallax* 7/1 (2001): 100-110; Diane Austin-Broos, "Globalisation and the Genesis of Values," *Australian Journal of Anthropology* 14/1 (2003): 1-18.

4. See also Hedwig Meyer-Wilmes, "Tirzia oder—durch einen Spiegel in einem erzählten Wort . . . Zur Entfaltung Gottes in einer gottlosen Zeit," in *Die widerspenstige Religion: Orientierung für eine Kultur der Autonomie?*, ed. van den Hoogen, Küng, Wills, Baumann, et al. (Kampen: Kok Pharos, 1997), 249-67.

submission.[5] Postmodernity, on the other hand, suppresses feminist critiques of existing sociopolitical structures of domination by understanding power as diffuse, productive, local, multiple, and fragmentary, by locating it on the level of representation and the symbolic, and by emptying concepts such as oppression, marginalization, and equality of their oppositional expressive power, whereby social movements for emancipation lose their language of protest and their vision of justice.[6]

Moreover, the "post" in "postmodern" is disputed. Does *postmodern* mean that modernity has been overtaken and superseded by postmodernity, or does it mean that the *postmodern* critically examines the *modern* in order to change it? Whereas *modern* and *postmodern* are often understood as mutually exclusive, and the playful-aesthetic *postmodern* tends to fall back into the premodern,[7] I want here to relate modernity and postmodernity as political enlightenment discourses correctively to each other in a critical feminist way.

If it is not clear how modernity and postmodernity and their "in-between" are to be defined, it is even less clear how the notion of "feminist," which modifies the word "the*logy," is to be understood. In postmodernity the term "feminist" has been qualified with a great variety of meanings, all of which have developed different theoretical frameworks: Latina,[8] womanist, mujerista, Africana,[9] sexual-difference, queer, third-world, Western, equal-rights, multicultural, inter-religious, Christian, Jewish, Muslim, Buddhist, Black, critical, postmodern—to mention only a few.

In light of this plurivocity of feminist the*logy it is necessary to begin by first briefly characterizing my own theoretical-feminist approach. In a second step I will look more closely at the debate on whether feminist the*logical discourses should be assigned either to modernity or to postmodernity, and I want to do so by critically reflecting on the discussion of equality and difference. In a third step I will argue that the anthropologically defined theory and the*logy of gender difference must be seen as multiply interwoven with other sociopolitical structures of domination such as race, class, colonialism or age.

Finally, I want to address briefly the uniqueness of a feminist political the*logy. My own theoretical approach of a critical feminist the*logy of libera-

---

5. Wendy Brown, "Women's Studies Unbound: Revolution, Mourning, Politics," *Parallax* 9/2 (2003): 3-16.

6. For the discussion of the postmodern from a "black feminist" perspective, see Patricia Hill Collins, *Fighting Words: Black Women and the Search for Justice* (Minneapolis: University of Minnesota Press, 1998), 124-54, and the literature cited there.

7. See Graham Ward, ed., *The Postmodern God: A Theological Reader* (Malden: Blackwell, 1997).

8. See Maria Pilar Aquino, Daisy L. Machado, and Jeanette Rodrigues, eds., *A Reader in Latina Feminist Theology: Religion and Justice* (Austin: University of Texas Press, 2002).

9. See Musimbi R. A. Kanyoro, *Introducing Feminist Cultural Hermeneutics: An African Perspective* (Cleveland: Pilgrim, 2002).

tion that understands itself as a radical democratic[10] political rhetoric of liberation permeates these reflections. Hence, I hope this approach will provide the impetus for further feminist thought about the*logy and church in modernity and postmodernity.

Feminism/Feminist

The word "feminist," especially when associated with the word "critical," still has strong negative associations for many. I prefer an understanding of "feminist" that sounds very simplistic and modern at first glance but on closer inspection reveals itself to be a complex postmodern challenge to the *modern*. According to this definition, feminism is "the radical notion that wo/men are people." That is, wo/men are "free and equal individuals who govern their own lives through the formation of a democratic will."[11]

According to this understanding, feminist the*logy is a radical democratic political the*logy of liberation dedicated to wo/men's social and ecclesial radical democratic emancipatory struggles. In contrast to male-dominated liberation the*logies, it does not simply adopt a Marxist or postcolonial analysis. Unlike academic research on the feminine or gender, it also avoids adopting the dualistic thought frameworks of a functionalist gender analysis. Instead, it shifts its focus to a complex radical democratic social analysis of "kyriarchally" interwoven and mutually multiplicative structures of domination.

Radical democracy is best understood as a congress of equals, or as the self-accountable praxis of equal citizens. Power is not defined by command and obedience, but corresponds to the human ability to join with others and act in concert with them. Radical democracy respects the fundamental dignity and differentiated equality of all people as adult citizens who both take part in communal deliberations and who are equally empowered to make decisions about their own well-being. According to Hannah Arendt, the *polis*, a word from which politics is derived, is "the organization of the people as it arises out of acting and speaking together, and its true space lies between people living together for this purpose, no matter where they happen to be. 'Wherever you go, you will be a *polis*': these famous words . . . expressed the conviction that in acting and speaking a [radical democratic] space is created between the participants."[12]

Such a radical democratic articulation of feminism as a social movement for emancipation, a political ethos, and a scholarly way of seeing based on the

---

10. I modify democracy with "radical" to distinguish it from liberal representative democracy.

11. Jürgen Habermas, "Die neue Intimität zwischen Politik und Kultur," in *Die Zukunft der Aufklärung*, ed. Jörn Rüsen, Eberhard Lämmert, and Peter Glotz (Frankfurt: Suhrkamp, 1988), 65.

12. Hannah Arendt, *The Human Condition* (Chicago: University of Chicago Press, 1958), 198.

conviction "that wo/men[13] are people" alludes to the claim "We, the people." If "people" is understood in the singular, it has very modern valences and for German-speakers "Volk" recalls the racially-laden nationalist concept of "blood and soil." But if "we, the people" is understood as plural, that is, ordinary citizens coming from many different directions, it echoes the postmodern radical democratic equal dignity of the many, of which Hannah Arendt speaks.[14]

In short, under "feminist" I understand a theory and praxis concerned with the elimination of kyriarchal systems and the creation of radical democratic conditions and ethos. This feminist approach takes up the radical democratic claim of modernity, but at the same time it makes clear, in a postmodern sense, that the European Enlightenment from the beginning failed to fulfill this universal claim and promise for all. The theoretical and practical contradiction between kyriarchal and egalitarian society therefore repeatedly produces discursive systems of legitimation that seek to normalize and naturalize kyriarchal domination.

Social and religious movements for emancipation therefore have also repeatedly sought to validate the claim to equality, maturity, and full citizenship for all. Hence, it is necessary to write anew, in feminist postmodern terms, the history of modernity as a history of radical democratic movements for emancipation of people who, because they were assumed not to be fully human, were excluded from democracy, which seeks to engender the "equal dignity of the many."[15] Thus it should be clear that I understand democracy not primarily as a representative form of government, but rather as a social vision and egalitarian ethos that rejects the anthropological framework of gender difference.

Equality and Difference

The tension between modern and postmodern is often treated in feminist discourses as the either-or alternative "equality or difference." In this "either-or" argument the concept of equality is equated with "modernity," because equality is often confused in everyday and in scholarly usage with sameness. Such a

---

13. For the problematic notion of the concept of "woman/women," see Denise Riley, *Am I That Name? Feminism and the Category of Women in History* (Minneapolis: University of Minnesota Press, 1988); Judith Butler, *Gender Trouble: Feminism and the Subversion of Identity* (New York: Routledge, 1990).

14. For Hannah Arendt, see Seyla Benhabib, *The Reluctant Modernism of Hannah Arendt* (Thousand Oaks: Sage, 1996); Susan Bickford, *The Dissonance of Democracy: Listening, Conflict, and Citizenship* (Ithaca: Cornell University Press, 1996); John McGowan, *Hannah Arendt: An Introduction* (Minneapolis: University of Minnesota Press, 1998); Bonnie Honig, ed., *Feminist Interpretations of Hannah Arendt* (University Park: Pennsylvania State University Press, 1995); and especially Christa Schnabl, *Das Moralische im Politischen: Hannah Arendt's Theorie des Handelns im Horizont der theologischen Ethik* (Frankfurt: Peter Lang, 1999).

15. Feminist the*logy as such an intercultural discourse has been formulated especially by Kwok Pui-lan, "Feminist Theology as Intercultural Discourse," in *The Cambridge Companion to Feminist Theology*, ed. Susan Frank Parsons (Cambridge: Cambridge University Press, 2002), 23-39.

modern understanding of equality as sameness, however, leaves no room for differences and diversity.[16]

The classical Aristotelian concept of equality assumes: "equals should be treated as the same, but unequals should be treated differently."[17] Behind this formal definition of equality lurks a broad inequality whose *tertium comparationis* is the *kyrios*, the master or lord. He defines who or what is equal or unequal and should be treated accordingly.[18] Thus political philosophy justified the exclusion of freeborn wo/men and other subordinated persons because they are not full human beings and full citizens.

Such a standardizing concept of equality as sameness tolerates no real difference because it refers equality to a single criterion and simply negates all diversity insofar as it thinks of diversity as subject to elimination. It is a kyriarchal concept that quietly legitimizes unequal treatment.[19] Either you are a white, educated gentleman, in which case you may expect to receive equal treatment, or you are not such a gentleman; then you will be regarded as different from him and accordingly treated unequally. But it must not be overlooked that this hegemonic concept of equality in Aristotle's sense equates difference with inequality. In contrast, emancipation movements insist that equality must always be understood in the sense of a radical democratic ethos according to which equality and difference are not mutually exclusive.

In modernity as in antiquity, the *kyrios* (emperor, lord, master, father, husband), the white, Western, propertied, educated, Christian gentleman, has simply posited himself as representing the nature of humanity.[20] He defines all other people in reference to himself, either as despised, inferior sub-humans or as romantically idealized saviors. His domination (kyriarchy) rests on heterosexism, racial and class prejudices, and colonial exploitation and thus further inscribes difference structurally as inequality. The struggle for equality seeks to overcome these unequalizing differences.

Kyriarchal equality—that is, an equality oriented to gentlemen—together with the theory of the uniformity of the world has propagated Eurocentric colonialism that, under the cloak of equality, either appropriates other peoples and cultures or devalues them. The struggle for emancipation and liberation according

---

16. See the discussion in Avigail Eisenberg, "Diversity and Equality: Three Approaches to Cultural and Sexual Difference," *Journal of Political Philosophy* 11/1 (2003): 41-64.

17. Lisa Schmuckli, *Differenzen und Dissonanzen: Zugänge zu feministischen Erkenntnistheorien in der Postmoderne* (Königstein: Helmer, 1996), 346.

18. Birgit Rommelspacher, *Dominanzkultur: Texte zu Fremdheit und Macht* (Berlin: Orlanda, 1995), 346.

19. See Hedwig Meyer-Wilmes, *Zwischen lila und lavendel: Schritte feministischer Theologie* (Regensburg: Pustet, 1996), 29-44.

20. The deconstruction of the subject in postmodern discourses is appropriate when it applies to this gentleman-subject. See Kwok Pui-lan, "Historical, Dialogical, and Diasporic Imagination in Feminist Studies of Religion," *Jahrbuch der Europäischen Gesellschaft für theologische Forschung von Frauen* 10 (2002): 57-80.

to this postmodern reading of equality always includes both kyriarchy and dehumanization, since the philosophy of the Enlightenment, in the name of reason, associated the ideal of equality with the exclusionary politics of inequality.[21]

Such a postmodern definition of equality as sameness and uniformity, however, does not sufficiently investigate the concept of difference it seeks to rehabilitate. Kyriarchal structures—not equality—produce difference and diversity as inequality, rather than as uniformity. Kyriarchal difference manifests itself as inequality, which is continually reinscribed by structures of oppression and socialization. Racism, colonialism, anti-Judaism, poverty, and heterosexism make most people not only "wholly other," but inferior others, subhumans.[22]

From a critical feminist point of view, I argue, difference always means both: on the one hand structures of oppression and ideologies that measure the lives of wo/men as wo/men by kyriarchal standards, and on the other hand egalitarian social-ekklesial structures, cultural religious visions, and emancipatory heritages, factors that make it possible to understand wo/men as multi-gifted persons with unique dignity and the authority to make decisions. Both meanings—difference as kyriarchally determined inequality and difference as a rich cultural-religious diversity of power, gifts, and possibilities—must be heard simultaneously when we speak about "equality and difference."

In short, in critical-feminist terms difference is best understood as multiplicity and diversity, a diversity that is created not by exclusion and definition as "other," but through reflection on oneself and the perception of one's own personal possibilities and potentials. Oppressed and marginalized groups of people have always derived their understanding of equality from such a self-awareness won in struggles for liberation.

Sexual Difference

The postmodern feminist discourse on equality and difference cannot critically challenge the concept of difference because it has chosen sex-gender and sexual difference as its central analytical category. In particular, Italian and French feminists have developed the theory and praxis of sexual difference in the 1980s. This theory grew out of the alleged failure of the emancipatory politics of equality. Even if wo/men increasingly have rights equal to those of men, it is argued, they do not achieve substantial equality but are only assimilated to the male social and

---

21. According to Rommelspacher, *Dominanzkultur* 19, John Locke and Thomas Hobbes, for example, justify English colonialism by saying that people who behave irrationally are to be treated not as people but rather as animals or machines. If rationality is the criterion of humanity, then according to this logic only "rational" people can expect to be treated humanely and with respect.

22. Daniel Boyarin, *A Radical Jew: Paul and the Politics of Identity* (Berkeley: University of California Press, 1994), 24.

symbolic order.[23] In this assimilation man is and remains the social measure of the world. Equality means adapting wo/men to male standards.

These authors emphasize that attaining substantial equality requires recognizing that the human being is twofold. There are two genders, and neither represents the whole human race. Sexuality and gender difference are ineradicable basic givens of human existence. Female gender is rooted in the gender difference that constitutes it; that is, women who want to be free have to turn to other women in order to determine the foundation of their womanhood. According to Adriana Cavarero, female subjectivity is acquired "in the interaction between women who are similar to each other, and not in confrontation with the male gender."[24] This theory of female difference is thus, as Cornelia Klinger rightly observes, a theory of femaleness, but not a feminist theory, which analyzes the relations of gender as kyriarchal relations and seeks to change them.[25]

In recent years a great number of feminist the*logical publications in the United States have given a positive theological reception to this theory of female difference. This reception of so-called French feminist theory interprets the rhetoric of sexual difference and of the feminine, which is easily misunderstood in a biological-essentialist sense, as the attempt to propose a new female subject within the horizon of sexual difference. But some authors critically observe that, for example, although Luce Irigaray seeks to articulate the differences between "women," she retains racial or cultural differences as the "unspoken" in her work.[26] An approach that thinks of difference as original gender difference, therefore, must be critically reasoned out today in response to so many sociocultural differences.

Like postfeminism, a feminist the*logy of the feminine or motherhood[27] seems insufficiently critical of the effects of its rhetoric in a social and religious context in which the media market femininity and sexuality as Western products. Hence it must be remembered that many today hear the rhetoric of feminine difference in the context of a "new" discourse of femininity, that is, as a discourse of oppression. Although feminist discourses do not understand the theory of sexual difference in the sense of kyriarchal womanhood, the theory of the feminine and motherhood nevertheless has cultural and the*logical resonance precisely

---

23. See Gunhild Buse, *Macht, Moral, Weiblichkeit: Eine feministisch-theologische Auseinandersetzung mit Carol Gilligan und Frigga Haug* (Mainz: Grünewald, 1993).

24. Adriana Cavarero, "Die Perspektive der Geschlechterdifferenz," in *Differenz und Gleichheit: Menschenrechte haben (k)ein Geschlecht*, ed. Ute Gerhard, et al. (Frankfurt: Helmer, 1990), 105.

25. Cornelia Klinger, "Welche Gleichheit und welche Differenz?" in ibid., 116.

26. Penelope Deutscher, *A Politics of Impossible Difference: The Later Work of Luce Irigaray* (Ithaca: Cornell University Press, 2002), 194. See also Ellen T. Armour, *Deconstruction, Feminist Theology, and the Problem of Difference: Subverting the Race/Gender Divide* (Chicago: University of Chicago Press, 1999).

27. See Andrea Günter, *Weibliche Autorität, Freiheit, und Geschlechterdifferenz: Bausteine einer feministischen politischen Theorie* (Königstein: Helmer, 1996), with reference to Irigaray and Luisa Muraro.

because hearers or readers can understand it in terms of traditional and current notions of femininity.[28]

Scholars like Oyerónké Oyéwùmí have, however, shown that the central feminist analytical category of gender/sex as well as the so-called "woman question" is a colonial Euro-American import into African societies whose languages have no grammatical gender and thus are not androcentric. The precolonial, political-social organization of the Yoruba, according to Oyéwùmí, knew no social construction of gender/sex, and social position was determined not by gender, but by seniority.[29] The categories of "woman" and "gender" are accordingly Western ontological categories that are biologically determined and did not exist among the Yoruba before their contact with the West. Feminist theories that presuppose these anthropological, bodily-determined categories as basic analytical categories not only newly inscribe and re-inscribe Western gender relationships. They also serve Euro-American colonization,[30] since both racial and gender theories are social and biological cultural constructs from the West. This approach opens a rich field of work for feminist the*logians that, if it is taken seriously, will fundamentally change Western-dominated Christian the*logy, since language is a central the*logical problem and thus belongs at the heart of the*logical scholarship.

Dehumanizing Kyriarchal Differences

But gender difference is not only Western-defined; it also functions as a Western kyriarchal discourse. The European Enlightenment emphasized, on the one hand, the equality of all human beings *qua* humans over against feudalistic class privileges, but on the other hand it insisted on the gender and racial difference and inferiority of subordinated peoples.[31] As Andrea Maihofer rightly observes, these people are denied precisely the characteristics and abilities

> that designate human beings as human in the sense of having human and civil rights, and upon which their rights are founded. In other words:

---

28. Comparative feminist studies have shown that the official discourse of the three biblical religions—Judaism, Islam, and Christianity—works with the doctrine of female complementarity. This is a modern discourse that has replaced the classical discourse about the inferiority of woman in Catholicism since the Second World War, as can be traced in papal statements.

29. Oyéronké Oyéwùmí, *The Invention of Women. Making an African Sense of Western Gender Discourses* (Minneapolis: University of Minnesota Press, 1997).

30. For the German discussion of colonialism see especially Andreas Foitzik, Rudi Leiprecht, Athanasios Marvakis, und Uwe Seid, eds., *Ein Herrenvolk von Untertanen: Rassismus—Nationalismus—Sexismus* (Duisburg: DISS, 1992).

31. For the close association of racial thinking and fascism, see especially Paul Gilroy, *Against Race: Imagining Political Culture Beyond the Color Line* (Cambridge: Belknap, 2001). For the right-wing conservative tendencies of the "biologizing process" of womanhood in fascism, see Renate Bridenthal, Antina Grossmann, and Marion Kaplan, eds., *When Biology Became Destiny: Women in Weimar and Nazi Germany* (New York: Monthly Review Press, 1984).

the idea of the equality of all human beings with reference to which the emancipation of civil society is demanded, and the discourse about gender difference with which the exclusion of women from civil rights and their relegation to the private sphere was legitimated, are not only historically simultaneous in origin, but are a central moment in *the gender dialectic of the Enlightenment*.[32]

In light of Oyéwùmí's thesis, however, such a critical social theory of gender falls short insofar as it does not consider that actual wo/men are defined not only by gender difference, but always also by race, class, and cultural kyriarchal differences. Like gender difference, so also race, class, and national differences were formulated in and through the discourses of the Enlightenment in order to exclude "second class" people from full humanity and democratic rights and dignity.

Western political philosophy, as Susan Moller Okin showed more than thirty years ago,[33] first formulated this kyriarchal discourse of domination, of inferiority, exclusion, and subordination in the context of the classical democracy of Athens. Ancient philosophers articulated kyriocentric theories to argue why certain groups of people, such as freeborn wo/men or slave wo/men, are unable to participate in democratic self-government and in the exercise of full citizenship because of their deficient or absent rationality. Such explicit justification is always needed, throughout history, when democratic values and institutions are considered as part of a kyriarchally structured society.

According to this theory, philosophical theories of the exclusion of particular groups from democratic self-government and power on the basis of a lack of rationality are sustained by the contradiction between an egalitarian democratic self-concept and the actual kyriarchal socioeconomic social structures of exclusion. According to the theoretical ideal of democracy, all citizens have equal rights and should be able to participate in the power of government and self-determination. But in historical reality, only a few powerful gentlemen or lords have shared in democratic power.

This contradiction between the ethos of the radical equality of the many and the actual sociopolitical conditions of kyriarchy has produced, and continues to produce, the dualistic discourses about "natural" essential differences between humans and G*d, between elite men and wo/men, between free and slave, between Greeks and barbarians, between landowners and farmworkers, between natives and foreigners, between the civilized and the uncivilized world.

---

32. Andrea Maihofer, "Geschlecht als hegemonialer Diskurs: Ansätze zu einer kritischen Theorie des Geschlechts," in *Denkachsen. Zur theoretischen und institutionellen Rede von Geschlecht*, ed. Theresa Wobbe and Gesa Lindemann (Frankfurt: Suhrkamp, 1994), 239-40.

33. Susan Moller Okin, *Women in Western Political Thought* (Princeton: Princeton University Press, 1979).

Modern democracies, as *fraternal*-capitalistic-kyriarchal democracies, are imitations of the classical ideal and also heirs of its ideological contradictions inasmuch as theoretically all members of the state are seen as equal human beings who have the "natural" right to "liberty and happiness." But at the same time the so-called "natural" kyriarchal, sociopolitical, structurally conditioned inequalities are retained. Privileged status based on property and education, not biological maleness, constitutes the citizen and gives him the right to participate in the democratic kyriarchal rule of the few over the many.[34] As Friedericke Hassauer and Peter Roos laconically remark: "They wanted to be citizens . . . in liberty, equality, and fraternity. . . . When their sisters demanded their rights as woman and citizen, *citoyenne*, the great and glorious French Revolution put its daughters under the guillotine. . . . In 1793 Olympe de Gouges was beheaded—she who in 1791 had rewritten the Declaration of Human and Civil Rights for women."[35]

The ideology of the asymmetrical kyriarchal dualism between human and animal, man and woman, barbarian and Greek, or free and slave, articulated in classical philosophy as natural difference, is also inscribed in the discourse of modern Eurocentric philosophy and the*logy. This classic kyriarchal discourse of difference and subordination was conveyed to the West through Christian scripture and the*logy and is constantly re-inscribed through modern scholarship.

The influence that this middle-class discourse of womanhood has on the concept and place of religion, however, is often overlooked. Since the Industrial Revolution and the Enlightenment, religion in Europe and America has been forced out of the public realm and pressed into the private sphere of individual piety, charity, and the maintenance of culture, home, and family. Nevertheless, both the Christian churches and middle-class wo/men had a significant share in the maintenance of the public interest in the antithetically understood "others" and in the formation of social-national identity.[36]

---

34. For France see Joan B. Landes, *Women and the Public Sphere in the French Revolution* (Ithaca: Cornell University Press, 1988), who shows that the French Revolution created a strictly male-determined public sphere that banished wo/men to the private sphere of the home: "Stated baldly, the early modern classical revival—with its political, linguistic, and stylistic overtones— invested public action with a decidedly masculine ethos" (3). Landes then argues further: "Although women failed to achieve political emancipation, the Revolution bequeathed them a moral identity and a political constitution. Gender became a socially relevant category in post-revolutionary life. Indeed, both domesticity—including republican motherhood—and feminism might be viewed as two variant but interrelated outcomes of the transformation of the absolutistic public sphere" (13).

35. Friedericke Hassauer and Peter Roos, "Aufklärung: Futurologie oder Konkurs," in Rüsen et al., eds., *Die Zukunft der Aufklärung* (1988), 40-41.

36. See Joan Jacobs Brumberg, "The Ethnological Mirror: American Women and their Heathen Sisters, 1870–1910," in *Women and the Structure of Society: Selected Research from the Fifth Berkshire Conference on the History of Women*, ed. Barbara J. Harris and JoAnn K. McNamara (Durham: Duke University Press, 1984), 108-28.

Feminist The*logy as a Different Political The*logy of Liberation

Political the*logy and liberation the*logies to date have had difficulty analyzing critically the intersections of sexism, racism, heterosexism, classism, and nationalism in modern sociopolitical and religious-the*logical discourses. Johann Baptist Metz, for example, has argued that the modern processes of secularization increasingly reveal themselves to be "processes of the disempowerment and dissolution of the human being as previously known and entrusted to us."[37] But in saying this he ignores the critical voices that have shown that this human being *"as we know him"* was identified in Christian the*logy and Enlightenment political philosophy with the white European gentleman. Metz continues to oppose the death of G*d and the death of the subject announced by Nietzsche and the Postmodern with the alternative "the Enlightenment within the horizon of the memory of G*d," in order to resist the "disappearance of the human" and to save the human "desire for maturity" and "political capability."

But this argument disregards the critical feminist and postcolonial challenges to the biblical idea of G*d, is silent about the "injustices that cry out to heaven" that were inflicted in the name of the biblical G*d, and forgets that the the*logical definition of the Others—wo/men, homosexuals, heretics, "savages," Gentiles, Jews, to name just a few—was grounded in biblical the*logy. It always has qualified the people thus excluded as inferior, subordinate, and dependent and deprived them of freedom and denied them justice. If political the*logy hopes to recover the humanity and dignity of human beings that are threatened by postmodern globalization, it must acknowledge a critical feminist the*logy of liberation and recognize the evil caused or enabled by the church and the biblical tradition of G*d as a structural sin and must self-critically articulate its own complicity in it.

While Metz does not recognize the challenges of feminist and postcolonial the*logy to the Enlightenment religious discourse about "the human," Andrea Günter, who was one of the first to stimulate discussion of postmodern thought in German-speaking feminist the*logy, has energetically questioned the proposal for a critical feminist political the*logy of liberation:

> Behind the thus generalized victim- and liberation-model stands an understanding of freedom, happiness, and the life of women which assumes that a woman must not only first become something, namely free, but that the world itself must become utterly different. This conveys the idea that a woman—like the world itself—is nothing as she is now, but must first become utterly different before she can acquire value and meaning and

---

37. Johann Baptist Metz, "Wider die zweite Unmündigkeit: Zum Verhältnis von Aufklärung und Christentum," in Rüsen et al., eds., *Die Zukunft der Aufklärung* (1988), 81.

achieve "female freedom"—a judgment that is contrary to most women's self-esteem and sense of their lives.[38]

Here several levels seem to be confused. A critical feminist the*logy of liberation has always worked with the notion of structural sin, precisely because it seeks to strengthen wo/men and other subordinated people so that they do not regard situations of injustice such as, for example, rape as personal guilt. Speaking of structural sin does not mean that a woman and the world "as it is" is "nothing." Rather, because a concrete woman is socially "as she is," namely a second- or third-class citizen, she must insist on the transformation of the world and herself if she wants to achieve full personhood and citizenship.

In order not to regard situations of oppression as "given" and internalize them as lack of self-esteem, oppressed people—men as well as wo/men—need a critical liberationist analysis that does not see "injustices that cry out to heaven" the*logically as the will of G*d but can name them as structural sin. This does not mean that wo/men and other oppressed people should be seen merely as victims. Both wo/men and men are always also agents as well as perpetrators. As the history of slavery and colonizing missions teaches us, wo/men can very well rule over other wo/men or become the exploited victims of other wo/men, since wo/men as much as men are always bound up in kyriarchal structures of domination and either collaborate with them or seek to change them. The postmodern objection that feminist liberation the*logy further inscribes the binary oppositions of modernity overlooks the complexity of the category of kyriarchy.

Modern science and the*logy have articulated not only the "man of reason," but also the racist-colonialist-defined ideology of the "White Lady," to the extent that they have stylized white, educated woman as the model of womanhood and the vehicle of culture and religion. Thus it is clear that emancipatory discourses rely upon the ruling discourses in kyriarchal societies, churches, and scholarly institutions in which they work; they are inextricably entangled with and determined by their kyriarchal discourses. Hand in hand with the ruling ideologies of gender differences, the*logical discourses further emphasize that gender and race are "natural" categories because they allow gender and racial differences to appear as "real" and "ordinary." This is achieved by attributing deep symbolic meaning for our lives to the existing kyriarchal differences instead of seeking to "denaturalize" and demystify such differences as sociopolitical and socioreligious constructs.

Rather than universalizing the characteristics of the white privileged woman either as an object of research or as a subject of scholarship, a critical-political-feminist the*logy seeks to create a discursive forum, where wo/men can recognize

---

38. Andrea Günter, ed., *Feministische Theologie und postmodernes Denken: Zur theologischen Relevanz der Geschlechterdifferenz* (Stuttgart: Kohlhammer, 1996), 57.

themselves as politico-religious subjects of action without being forced to conceal kyriarchal structurally-caused divisions and prejudices among wo/men. Through dialogue, controversy, and reflection the*logical discourses can transform simplified kyriarchal formations of identity into creative diversity and develop corresponding political strategies for a multivocal and multilayered feminist the*logy.

To give a political-the*logical name to such a critical alternative site to the discourses of kyriarchy, I have introduced the concept of the *ekklēsia* of wo/men. *Ekklēsia* is qualified by the genitive "of wo/men," which points to the non-citizens of modernity. The intention here is to bring to public awareness the fact that neither church nor democracy is what they pretend to be: *ekklēsia*, that is, the radical democratic assembly of responsible full citizens. Historically and politically the concept of *ekklēsia* of wo/men is an oxymoron, that is, a combination of mutually contradictory concepts intended to articulate a feminist-political "other."

I have argued that such a theoretical frame is able to replace the modern kyriarchal construct of woman as the other of man—further inscribed by theories of womanhood and motherhood—with the radical-democratic construct of the *ekklēsia*, which is both unfulfilled vision and historical reality. This concept draws no narrow boundaries of identity, but instead joins the social and the ecclesial spheres, individual groups and global movement. *Ekklēsia* of wo/men constitutes itself wherever responsible people gather both to articulate, discuss, and celebrate their problems, visions, and goals and together decide on strategies and ways to political and religious self-determination. *Ekklēsia* of wo/men emphasizes that wo/men are such responsible full citizens. It is already reality but still being realized.

The eschatological tension between kyriarchy and *ekklēsia* not only orients *ekklēsia* to the transformation of the kyriarchal church and society. It also sustains awareness that the *ekklēsia* is not a community of the liberated, but participates both in kyriarchal oppression and in the reality of a liberated world toward which it is moving. Democratic principles such as maturity, liberty, and justice are to be understood in this approach not as frozen principles, but as practices that create meaning.

A political-feminist the*logy seeks to understand the *ekklēsia* of wo/men as a theoretical site where we can imagine political-cultural-religious transformation and engage on behalf of a radical democratic pluralism. It is critically aware that its social liberation analysis and vision bear a Western stamp. Nevertheless, it is not only relevant for European and American people but appears to be more and more necessary worldwide in the wake of capitalist globalization.

Feminist and other emancipation-oriented movements and the*logies must engage in the struggles against global control and capitalistic commodification of knowledge and information in order to keep the vision of radical equality alive for those deprived of their rights and of power, whose radical democratic dreams are undermined daily.[39] In the last centuries radical democratic movements throughout the world have struggled for the dream of liberty, justice, and equality of all people.[40] Today unscrupulous economic exploitation, militarist might, and nationalist interests have destroyed many of these movements or are in the process of doing so.

Economists point out that only the best-qualified 15 to 20 percent of the world's population profit from the global capitalist economy, while two-thirds of the population are being increasingly forced into the status of working poor, unemployed, and welfare recipients.[41] The economic decline and loss of education in the so-called middle class has created a geopolitical situation in which the dividing line no longer runs between the so-called third and first worlds but extends right across the entire world, separating the propertied and those who have nothing who live in the same city, state, or country. In other words, my neighbor who works in an international computer firm has more in common with the corresponding employees in Europe, Latin America, or Japan than with the woman two streets over who lives on welfare. In view of both worldwide exploitation and global communication, we are faced today with the alternative: either the "global village" that is being created will be a radical democratic confederation, an *ekklēsia* of wo/men that considers itself obligated to the economic well-being and political rights of all citizens without exception, or this global situation will be subject to a strongly controlled, "velvet-pawed" dictatorship that concentrates all economic and cultural resources in the hands of a few and degrades the majority of the world's peoples to a permanent impoverished and dehumanized under-class.[42]

---

39. As an outstanding case study and critical analysis of the interweaving of religion with this worldwide exploitation, see especially the works of the journalist Penny Lernoux, *Cry of the People: United States Involvement in the Rise of Fascism, Torture, and Murder and the Persecution of the Catholic Church in Latin America* (Garden City: Doubleday, 1982); *In Banks We Trust* (Garden City: Doubleday Anchor, 1986); and her last book before her premature death, *People of God: The Struggle for World Catholicism* (New York: Viking, 1989).

40. See Seyla Benhabib, *The Claims of Culture: Equality and Diversity in the Global Era* (Princeton: Princeton University Press, 2002). See also Jill M. Bystydzienski and Joti Sekhon, eds., *Democratization and Women's Grassroots Movements* (Bloomington: Indiana University Press, 1999), 9. This book analyzes the variety of ways in which wo/men from sixteen different countries struggle "for more control over their daily lives while simultaneously creating and extending opportunities for greater participation" (18). See also Susan Zaeske, *Signatures of Citizenship: Petitioning, Antislavery, and Women's Political Identity* (Chapel Hill: University of North Carolina Press, 2003) for the nineteenth century.

41. See Robert B. Reich, *The Work of Nations: Capitalism in the Twenty-First Century* (New York: Knopf, 1991).

42. Joan Smith, "The Creation of the World We Know: The World-Economy and the Re-Creation of Gendered Identities," in *Identity Politics and Women: Cultural Reassertions and Feminism in International Perspective*, ed. Valentine M. Moghadam; Boulder: Westview, 1994), 27-41.

This global conflict compels feminist economics and the*logy to emphasize the necessity for a worldwide systemic analysis of culture and religion.[43] In view of postmodern relativist and often nihilistic theories, feminist the*logy and religious studies must articulate their critical religious visions of liberation anew and in such a way that they contribute to the formation of subjects who know themselves obligated to a radical democratic praxis.[44]

Otherwise, religion in general and Christian the*logy in particular will remain a dangerous weapon in the hands of the powerful, who misuse them for conservative and oppressive ends. In the United States, for example, religion is deployed to further a "bunker mentality" or to brand disadvantaged "lower classes" and "single welfare mothers" as scapegoats.[45] Around the globe conservative political forces lay claim to religion largely as cover for the interests of those who are economically better off, though their security has decreased since the 1980s because of the continuing decline of their economic and educational potential.

Rightwing fundamentalist movements—whether the so-called "electronic churches" in the United States, or Islamist groups,[46] Jewish ultra-right movements,[47] Christian fundamentalist movements in Latin America, or the religious movement of Hindu nationalism—everywhere in the world reveal a common profile:[48] They skillfully employ modern media and technologies and generally present absolutist nationalistic and religious claims. While on the one hand they positively regard modern technology, science, industrialism, and nationalism, on the other hand they reject many of the political and ethical values of modern democracies, including basic personal rights, pluralism, freedom of speech, the right to housing, health care, and work, equal pay for equal work, social market mechanisms, a democratic ethos, a division of power, and political responsibility, and especially equal rights for wo/men.

The politico-religious Right claims to determine and define the true nature of biblical religions against liberation the*logies of all colors. Their financially well-endowed "think tanks" are supported by reactionary political and financial

---

43. See especially the declaration of the Division for the Advancement of Women on "International Standards of Equality and Religious Freedom. Implications on the Status of Women," in ibid., 425-38.

44. Courtney W. Howland, ed., *Religious Fundamentalisms and the Human Rights of Women* (New York: St. Martin's, 1999).

45. See Rebecca F. Klatch, "Women of the New Right in the United States: Family, Feminism, and Politics," in Moghadam, *Identity Politics and Women*, 367-88.

46. Most of the essays in Moghadam, *Identity Politics and Women*, refer to wo/men and Islam in different parts of the world.

47. See Madeleine Tress, "Halakha, Zionism, and Gender: The Case of Gush Emunim," in ibid., 307-28, and Debra Renée Kaufman, "Paradoxical Politics: Gender Politics Among Newly Orthodox Jewish Women in the United States," in ibid., 349-66.

48. Sucheta Mazumdar, "Moving Away from a Secular Vision?: Women, Nation, and the Cultural Construction of Hindu India," in ibid., 243-73, and Radha Kumar, "Identity Politics and the Contemporary Indian Feminist Movement," in ibid., 274-92.

institutions that defend kyriarchal capitalism. The association of religious, anti-democratic arguments with the debate over "true womanhood" and the "role of woman" is neither accidental nor only the*logical in its significance.[49]

For several decades, right-wing religious-fundamentalist movements through-out the world have represented emancipated wo/men as the embodiment of Western decadence or modern atheistic secularism, while they regard male power as the expression of divine power.[50] Whether it will be possible to change exclusive, kyriocentric forms of religion[51] and whether religion can make a contribution to the worldwide struggle for a radical democratic world order will depend largely upon whether critical-political-feminist the*logies can transform church and the*logy such that they can articulate a new spiritual vision of radical equality, justice, and well-being in this global situation of exploitation. The struggles for radical democracy and the acknowledgment of the religious-the*logical author-ity of wo/men are closely bound up with one another. The power of the gospel for wholeness and well-being throughout the world, I argue, depends on the the*logical articulation of such a radical democratic, critical-emancipatory vision and its implementation through political religious and the*logical praxis.

---

49. For documentation and analysis see the three-part, prize-winning PBS series, "God and Politics," in which Bill Moyers investigates the relationship between state and church and their influence on United States foreign policy.

50. See Valentine M. Moghadam, "Introduction: Women and Identity Politics in Theoretical and Comparative Perspective," in Moghadam, *Identity Politics and Women*, 3-26; Hanna Papanek, "The Ideal Woman and the Ideal State: Control and Autonomy in the Construction of Identity," in ibid., 42-75; and Ira Yuval-Davis, "Identity Politics and Women's Ethnicity," in ibid., 408-24.

51. Diana L. Eck, *Encountering God: A Spiritual Journey from Bozeman to Banaras* (Boston: Beacon, 2003), 176, writes: "A new wave of exclusivism is cresting around the world today. Expressed in social and political life, exclusivism becomes ethnic or religious chauvinism, described in South Asia as communalism. . . . As we have observed, identity-based politics is on the rise because it is found to be a successful way of arousing political energy" (176).

3

Method in Wo/men's Studies in Religion

A Critical Feminist Hermeneutic and Rhetoric

To approach the topic of women's studies and feminist hermeneutics, I must first explicate my own perspective and location, since feminist theory together with malestream[1] hermeneutics has insisted that scholarship is not done from a disembodied value-neutral position or a "god's eye view" but that it is always perspectival and sociopolitically situated. My own work therefore has sought to articulate feminist the*logy and feminist studies in religion not just as hermeneutical—but rather as rhetorical-critical studies.[2]

Feminist interpretation is best understood as a practice of rhetorical inquiry that engages in the formation of a critical historical and religious consciousness. Whereas hermeneutical theory seeks to understand and appreciate the meaning of texts, rhetorical interpretation and its the*-ethical interrogation of texts and symbolic worlds attends to the kinds of persuasive effects that religious discourses produce and how they produce them.

While wo/men always have participated in religion and interpreted Scriptures[3] and traditions, feminist hermeneutics as the theoretical exploration

---

1. I use this expression not in a pejorative but in a descriptive sense. Until very recently mainstream scholarship has been malestream.

2. This chapter has appeared as "Method in Wo/men's Studies in Religion: A Critical Feminist Hermeneutics," in *Methodology in Religious Studies: The Interface with Women's* Studies, Arvind Sharma, ed. (Albany: SUNY Press, 2002), 207-41.

3. See the discussions in Kwok Pui-lan and Elisabeth Schüssler Fiorenza, *Wo/men's Sacred Scriptures* (Maryknoll: Orbis, 1998).

of the cultural and political presuppositions of religious inquiry and feminist interpretation in the interest of wo/men is of very recent vintage. Only in the context of the wo/men's movement of the last century, and especially in the past twenty-five years or so, have feminists in religion begun to explore the possibilities and implications of scholarship that takes the silencing of wo/men by institutionalized religions as its point of departure. In the last decade numerous books and articles on wo/men's, gender, and feminist studies in religion have appeared. They have not only won a wide general readership but also made inroads, albeit very slowly, into the academy. This growing body of feminist research and publications seeks to address and redress the centuries of wo/men's silencing and exclusion from religious leadership and the*logical studies.

Feminist studies in religion must therefore be understood as critical research that explores the history of wo/men's subordination and exclusion. Hence, the starting point and interests of feminist hermeneutics are different from those of malestream hermeneutics, which is concerned with understanding, appreciating, and validating cultural and religious traditions. Feminist Studies are therefore closer to critical theory, rhetoric and ideology critique than to a universalizing ontological hermeneutics. Nevertheless, a critical hermeneutics is important for feminist inquiry. Thus, it is necessary to critically explore and assess the contributions that a critical hermeneutics understood as a rhetoric of emancipation makes to feminist studies in religion. Yet before I can engage this question, it is necessary to address the hermeneutical impediment that the word "feminism/feminist" constitutes for popular and scholarly audiences.

A Critical Theoretical Perspective and Methodological Framework

Since for many feminism is associated with ideological prejudice and unscientific bias, it is necessary to explain why and how I use the term. I begin with the insight that being a wo/man is not sufficient for generating feminist knowledge. Rather feminist inquiry is a critical theory[4] and intellectual practice that requires a process of conscientization[5] and engagement in struggles for transformation. The title wo/men's studies is ambiguous and can be understood either in an objectifying scientific sense as study *about* wo/men[6] or in feminist terms as study *by* wo/men. In contrast, feminist studies explicitly stress wo/men's agency and authority as intellectual religious subjects. They seek not just to understand but

---

4. See Marsha Aileen Hewitt, *Critical Theory of Religion: A Feminist Analysis* (Minneapolis: Fortress Press, 1995).

5. For the context of this expression see Maria Pilar Aquino, "Latin American Feminist The*logy," *JFSR* 14 (1998): 89-108. The practice presupposes a systemic political analysis and hence it is not identical with the individualistic notion of "consciousness-raising."

6. See, for example, Jean Holm with John Bowker, eds., *Wo/men in Religion* (New York: Pinter, 1994), which discusses the status and role of wo/men in diverse religions.

to change and transform wo/men's situation of religious-the*logical silencing, marginalization, and oppression. Strictly speaking, feminist studies move beyond hermeneutics. Therefore, it is necessary to braid together the theoretical approaches of hermeneutics, rhetoric and ideology critique for fashioning a method of critical inquiry that is oriented toward justice, emancipation, and liberation.

Feminist "conscientization" makes one realize that cultural common sense, dominant perspectives, scientific theories, and historical knowledge are not only androcentric but that they are kyriocentric, that is, elite male or master-centered. Malestream language and science do not give an objective, value-neutral account of reality. Rather, by making marginalization and stereotypes appear as "natural" or "common sense," they interpret, construct and legitimize reality from the elite western male perspective and in the interest of relations of exclusion and domination.

The "root-experience" of feminism realizes that cultural "common sense," dominant perspectives, scientific theories, and historical knowledge are andro-centric—that is, male biased—and therefore not objective accounts of reality but ideological mystification of domination and subordination. Generally feminists have used patriarchy as a key concept for analyzing such relations of oppression. Whereas prior to feminism patriarchy was understood in anthropological and social studies as the power of the father over his kinship group, in the 1970s feminists developed theories of patriarchy as a social system which maintains "men's social, ideological, sexual, and political dominance"[7] over wo/men.

Since black and so-called two-thirds-world feminists have consistently criti-cized such a universalizing dualistic analytic of patriarchy since the late seventies, I have redefined patriarchy in the classical Aristotelian sense as subordination and exploitation of wo/men who are differently located on the patriarchal pyramid of intermeshed structural oppressions. However, no theory or praxis of emancipa-tion and liberation is adequate that does not explicitly consider the multiplica-tive interlocking structures—sexism, racism, colonialism, class-exploitation and ageism—of wo/men's oppression.

Feminism as I understand it is not concerned only with gender inequities and marginalization. Kyriarchy perpetrates not only dehumanizing sexism and gender stereotypes but also other forms of wo/men's oppression, such as racism, poverty, religious exclusion, and colonialism. Feminist studies therefore have the goal to alter fundamentally the nature of our knowledge of the world by exposing its deformations and limitations in and through androcentrism, racism, classism and cultural imperialism as well as by reconstructing more comprehensive and adequate accounts of the world.[8]

---

7. Caroline Ramazanoglu, *Feminism and the Contradictions of Oppression*, 33.
8. See Rosemary Hennesy, *Feminism and the Politics of Discourse* (New York: Routledge, 1993).

Feminist movements have always emerged from the participation of wo/men in emancipatory struggles such as the struggles for full democratic citizenship, religious freedom, abolition of slavery, civil rights, national and cultural independence as well as those of the ecological, labor, peace or gay movements. In these struggles for religious, civil and human rights, feminists have learned that words such as "human" or "worker" or "civil society" are gender typed and often do not refer to nor include the rights and interests of wo/men. Therefore it becomes necessary to focus specifically on the struggle for wo/men's rights and self-determination in society and church.

As such a theory and practice of justice, feminist studies in religion can be appreciated only if seen in their entirety and particular historical-social location. Their rhetorical aims, theoretical arguments, and the*logical passion must be understood as both empowered and limited by the sociopolitical and academic-religious contexts in which they operate. Consequently, I have introduced and developed a critical feminist hermeneutics of liberation that aims to transform malestream hermeneutical and the*logical discourses. In order to elaborate the theoretical framework of such a critical feminist hermeneutics, it is necessary to delineate the key methodological components that are braided together in this theoretical articulation.

Since "voice," positionality and heterogeneity are key categories in feminist studies, feminist theory and the*logy always have insisted that scholarship cannot be done from a disembodied value-neutral position. Research is always perspectival and sociopolitically situated. Since they share this critique of positivist science with malestream hermeneutics, feminist religious studies and the*logies have found hermeneutical method and theory helpful. However, although hermeneutics appreciates tradition, it does not sufficiently consider the centuries of wo/men's silencing and exclusion and the resulting systematically distorted communication.

Although I have introduced and to a great part shaped the field of feminist biblical hermeneutics,[9] my own work has sought to articulate not only feminist biblical studies but also feminist the*logy and studies in religion not simply as hermeneutical but as critical rhetorical studies.[10] By rhetoric and rhetoricality I mean a new form of cultural practice and critical investigation that is no longer

---

9. See the panel discussion at the 1982 AAR/SBL Annual meeting on my article "A Feminist Biblical Hermeneutics and Liberation The*logy," in *The Challenge of Liberation The*logy: A First World Response*, ed. L. Dale Richesin and Brian Mehan (New York: Orbis, 1981), 91-112, which was prepared for a conference at Chicago Divinity School in 1979 where I introduced the term "feminist hermeneutics." See also the contributions in Letty M. Russell, ed., *Feminist Interpretation of the Bible* (Philadelphia: Westminster, 1985), especially her introduction.

10. For the significance of this change see Francis Schüssler Fiorenza, "From Interpretation to Rhetoric: The Feminist Challenge to Systematic Theology," in *Walk in the Ways of Wisdom: Essays in Honor of Elisabeth Schüssler Fiorenza*, ed. Shelly Matthews, Cynthia Briggs Kittredge, and Melanie Johnson-DeBaufre (Harrisburg: Trinity International, 2003), 17-45.

circumscribed by the scientistic notions of objectivism, subjectivism, liberalism and nationalism of the Enlightenment and of Romanticism that have relegated classical rhetoric to the dustbins of history.

> Rhetoricality, by contrast, is bound to no specific set of institutions. . . . For this reason it allows for no explanatory meta-discourse that is not already rhetorical. Rhetoric is no longer the title of a doctrine and a practice, nor a form of cultural memory; it becomes instead something like the condition of our existence. . . . Rhetoricality names the new conditions of discourse in the modern world and, thus, the fundamental category of every inquiry that seeks to describe the nature of discursive action and exchange.[11]

In a rhetorical research paradigm method is understood differently. Whereas methods are understood in the scientific positivist paradigm as rules and regulations, they are seen in a critical-rhetorical paradigm of study as modes of inquiry, as questions to be asked and perspectives to be clarified.

Feminist studies in religion cannot simply assume that scholars will produce knowledge that changes rather than just describes and analyzes kyriarchal relations of domination. They must submit their methods to a critical process of rhetorical analysis and reconfiguration, of "braiding" or "blending together" various methods if they should serve liberatory goals. Such a braiding or hybridization of methods must be accomplished within a critical feminist framework.

In short, by *method* I do not mean primarily technical procedures and rules but rather modes of critical reflection and analysis. Even though I have consistently elaborated a critical feminist biblical hermeneutics, I have also argued nevertheless that feminist interpretation must be developed not just in terms of hermeneutics, but rather in terms of critical theory and feminist the*logies of liberation. As a theory and practice of justice critical feminist studies cannot be limited to hermeneutical studies, which seek to understand, appreciate and appropriate the texts and traditions of malestream culture and religion. Rather they must draw on and braid together several methodological approaches in order to reconfigure them as a critical feminist rhetoric of liberation.

What do I mean by *critical*? Since "critique" and "critical" are often understood in a negative, deconstructive, and cynical sense, I use the term in its original sense of "crisis," which is derived from the Greek words *krinein/krisis* meaning judging and judgment. A critical method is interested in weighing, evaluating and judging, in crisis situations and adjudications. A critical method thus has the opposite goals and functions from those that a positivist scientist method espouses. Moreover, in contrast to hegemonic hermeneutics it focuses not only

---

11. John Bender and David E. Wellbery, "Rhetoricality: On the Modernist Return of Rhetoric," in *The Ends of Rhetoric: History, Theory, Practice,* ed. John Bender and David E. Wellbery (Stanford: Stanford University Press, 1990), 25-26.

on the rhetoricality of all inquiry and the rhetoricity of texts but also on the power relations in which they are embedded.[12]

Whereas the literary formalist and historical positivist paradigms of interpretation were still reigning in religious studies two decades ago, today epistemological, ideology critical and hermeneutical discussions that are critical of the positivist scientific paradigm of religious studies determine academic discourses. Their theoretical and practical force has destabilized the foundations of the field of religious studies.

Feminist hermeneutics has played a great part in this transformation of academic scholarship in religion. Nevertheless, even a cursory glance at the literature can show that the hermeneutical contributions of critical feminist scholarship are rarely recognized and much less acknowledged by the Euro-American malestream academy and religious institutions. Even feminist scholars still feel compelled to "prove" the legitimacy and validity of their arguments by showing how these "fit" into the hermeneutical frameworks and epistemological theories of the "great men" in the field.[13]

Hermeneutics[14]

The notion of hermeneutics derives from the Greek word *hermēneuein* and means "to interpret, exegete, explain, or translate." It owes its name to Hermes, the messenger of the Gods, who has the task to mediate the announcements, declarations and messages of the Gods to mere mortals. His proclamation, however, is not a mere communication and mediation but always also an explication of divine commands in such a way that he translates them into human language so that they can be comprehended and obeyed.

---

12. See my book *Rhetoric and Ethic*.

13. See, for example, Erin White, "Figuring and Refiguring the Female Self: Toward a Feminist Hermeneutics," in *Claiming Our Rites: Studies in Religion by Australian Women Scholars*, ed. Morny Joy and Penelope Magee (Wollstonecraft: Australian Association for the Study of Religion, 1994), 135-55. After claiming that "feminist scholarship lacks extended discussion of hermeneutical questions," she goes on to claim that Phyllis Trible's and my own work "focus on the text" and in my case "on the communities of wo/men and men who produced the text" but that we do not focus "on the relation between text and (female) self-identity" (136). In her elaboration of my alleged position she does not refer to my books *Bread Not Stone*, *But She Said*, nor *Vision of a Just World*, nor to any of my other hermeneutical-epistemological essays. Instead she (mis)reads *In Memory of Her* in a positivist historical vein and claims that I do "not sufficiently recognize the place of both text and present context in the construction of any community of the past" (138). She concedes that her critique might seem "niggardly" [sic] and then goes on to show how much better off we would be if we had read Ricoeur, although a reading of *Bread Not Stone* and my discussion of Sandra Schneiders' proposal could have shown that I have considered this approach but found it wanting.

14. For this section see especially also Francis Schüssler Fiorenza, "History and Hermeneutics," in *Modern Christian Thought*, vol. 2, ed. James Livingston and Francis Schüssler Fiorenza (Upper Saddle River: Prentice Hall, 1999), chap. 11. See also the collection of essays edited by Kurt Mueller-Vollmer, *The Hermeneutics Reader* (New York: Continuum, 1988).

While hermeneutics can be understood with Derrida as a matter of the free play of signs[15] and with Rorty[16] as merely keeping the lines of communication open, according to Gadamer[17] hermeneutics has the task of translating meaning from one "world" into another.[18] Like Hermes, the messenger of the Gods, hermeneutics not only communicates knowledge but also instructs, directs, and enjoins. Hermeneutics thus has affinities to manticism and prophecy. It conveys revelation and interprets signs and oracles. It is a matter of practical understanding, which involves the Aristotelian virtue of *phronesis*—practical judgment and adjudication—which is not secured by an a priori method but only in the process of understanding.

As a discipline, philosophical hermeneutics is rooted in biblical interpretation. It is best understood as a theory and practice of interpretation that explores the conditions and possibilities of understanding not just of texts but of other practices[19] as well. As such hermeneutics is not so much a disciplined scientific method or technique but rather an epistemological perspective and approach. It "represents not so much a highly honed, well-established theory of understanding or a long-standing, well-defined tradition of philosophy as it does a family of concerns and critical perspectives."[20]

Since Schleiermacher, Dilthey, and Gadamer,[21] hermeneutics has maintained over against scientific positivism that understanding takes place as a process of engagement in the hermeneutical circle or spiral, which is characterized by the part-whole relation. It stresses that understanding is not possible without preunderstandings or prejudices and therefore that understanding is always contextually dependent. Hermeneutics does not ground intelligibility in the "pregiven, essentially changeless human subject, but in the public sphere of evolving, linguistically mediated practice."[22] Thus hermeneutics seeks to remain open for change and difference.

Hermeneutics insists on the linguisticality of all knowledge, on its contextuality and its immersion in tradition. It stresses that human understanding can

---

15. Jacques Derrida, "The Ends of Man," *Philosophy and Phenomenological Research* 30 (1969), 31-57.

16. Richard Rorty, *Philosophy and the Mirror of Nature* (Princeton: Princeton University Press, 1979), 315.

17. See Hans Georg Gadamer, *Truth and Method* (Berkeley: University of California Press, 1976).

18. See Richard Bernstein, "What Is the Difference that Makes a Difference? Gadamer, Habermas, and Rorty," in *Hermeneutics and Modern Philosophy*, ed. Brice R. Wachterhauser (Albany: SUNY Press, 1986), 343-76.

19. Paul Ricoeur's theory of interpretation has argued that action may be regarded as a text. If an action like a text is a meaningful entity, then the "paradigm of reading" can also be applied to socioreligious practices. See Paul Ricoeur, *Hermeneutics and the Human Sciences*, ed. and trans. John B. Thompson (Cambridge: Cambridge University Press, 1981), 197-221.

20. See Brice R. Wachterhauser, *Hermeneutics and Modern Philosophy*, 5.

21. See Paul Ricoeur, *Hermeneutics and the Human Sciences*, 43-62.

22. Wachterhauser, *Hermeneutics and Modern Philosophy*, 8.

never take place without words and outside of time. Its key concepts are *empathy, historicity, linguisticality, tradition, preunderstanding, fusion of horizons,* and *the classic* with its notion of *effective history.* However, all seven theoretical emphases of hermeneutics are problematic from a critical feminist perspective because they do not sufficiently take into account relations of domination and power.

Empathy

Empathy invites one to cultivate emotional identification, sympathy, and appreciation in the process of understanding. Wilhelm Dilthey[23] has argued that "through an act of "empathy" [of "sich einfühlen"] one could achieve objective validity. In such an act of empathy the historian of religion can extricate herself from her own immersion in history and contextual determination and transpose herself into the minds and lives of those whom she studies.

Rita Gross for instance has emphasized the centrality of empathy in the study of religion. She argues that the hermeneutical approach of empathic understanding involves two steps: first, bracketing one's own worldview, values and visions as much as possible and second, imaginatively entering into the world of the text or religious practice that is being studied. She concedes that a feminist hermeneutics cannot relinquish critical evaluation, but nevertheless insists on empathy as a central method in the feminist study of religion. "Although empathy involves appreciatively entering into the spirit of that which is being studied, one could not agree with all the positions that one understands empathically because many are mutually exclusive."[24]

I would argue instead that feminists cannot adopt such an empathic hermeneutical method, not because positions and theories are mutually exclusive, but because kyriarchal religious texts, traditions and practices destroy wo/men's well-being. Gross quotes as a compliment the statement of her student that she teaches all those religions as if they were true, but this highlights the practical implications of such an empathic hermeneutics. For instance, teaching kyriarchal religious vilifications of wo/men "as if they were true" intensifies kyriarchal identifications and socialization rather than interrupts and changes them.[25]

Historicity

Historicity (*Geschichtlichkeit*) and contextuality are central to hermeneutic method. Historicity signifies our participation in and belonging to history and

---

23. Wilhelm Dilthey, *Selected Writings,* ed. and trans. H. P. Rickman (Cambridge: Cambridge University Press, 1976).

24. Rita M. Gross, *Feminism and Religion: An Introduction* (Boston: Beacon, 1996), 11-12.

25. For the role such an empathic hermeneutic plays in the rehabilitation of the holocaust and National Socialism see Michael Brumlik, "Geisteswissenschaftlicher Revisionismus—auch eine Verharmlosung des Nationalsozialismus," in *Rechtsextremismus: Ideologie und Gewalt,* ed. Richard Faber, Hajo Funke, and Gerhard Schoenberner (Berlin: Hentrich, 1995).

makes us through and through historical beings. It colors our rational capacity to know and make sense out of the world. By shaping our pre-understandings and prior assumptions it makes it impossible for scholars of religion to free our-selves from the impact of our own historical context in order to represent other religions or the past "as they actually are." Scholars can produce more or less true accounts but we can never free ourselves from the influences of our historical context and location.

Moreover, historicity means that we can never be reduced to an essential ahistorical core or to a universal "human nature" that is the same in all historical circumstances. Rather who we are must be understood as a function of the his-torical circumstances, languages and communities in which we live. "According to the hermeneutical perspective, human beings are neither given an immutable essence by God or nature, nor do we make ourselves (at least not as isolated indi-viduals), but we are rather the particular mode of historical existence we in part find ourselves in and in part shape in co-operation with others."[26]

Yet while hermeneutics stresses that "human beings *are* their history," femi-nist theory specifies that wo/men are determined by the historical power rela-tions of domination in which we live. Historicity and contextuality always also mean domination. Utilizing the hermeneutical emphasis on historicity and the liberationist critique of contextuality and social location, feminists have criti-cally destabilized the foundational concept of "woman." In her book *Am I That Name?*[27] Denise Riley distinguishes three overlapping and blurred levels of inde-terminacy that are characteristic of "woman": the individual, the historical and the political level.

Wo/men are not a unitary group. They are not just determined by their gender and sex but also by their race, class, able-bodiedness and ethnicity. My practice of writing the word with a slash indicates that I do not understand "wo/men" in essentialist or naturalized terms. In this way I seek to lift into consciousness that "wo/man or wo/men" is an ambiguous concept. This way of writing highlights that there are many historical and structural differences *between* wo/men and *within* wo/men ourselves, which cannot be reduced to gender difference. Moreover, in light of a systemic analysis the term *wo/men* can be seen as being inclusive of all non-persons, to use an expression of Gustavo Gutiérrez. It is not female nature or feminine essence that defines the concept of wo/man but historical-political contextuality.[28]

---

26. Wachterhauser, *Hermeneutics and Modern Philosophy*, 7.

27. See Denise Riley, *Am I That Name? Feminism and the Category of "Women" in History* (Minneapolis: University of Minnesota Press, 1988).

28. Anne-Louise Eriksson, *The Meaning of Gender in Theology*, does not understand these hermeneutical-epistemological dimensions of my work (Stockholm: Almqvist, 1995), 135-50. See also Elina Vuola, *Limits of Liberation: Praxis as Method in Latin American Liberation Theology and Feminist Theology* (Helsinki: Suomalainen Tiedekatemia, 1997), who summarizes Eriksson: "It seems that the problems in Ruether's and Fiorenza's theology are derived from the scarcity of

Linguisticality

Hermeneutics insists further that all knowledge and understanding is determined by and mediated through language. Language transports meaning from one context to another. The notion of linguisticality underscores that all understanding is historically and culturally mediated. By learning a language or the discourse of specialized fields of study we come to understand our world and ourselves. Although recognizing the totalizing linguisticality of our being in the world is crucial for feminist work, it also raises difficult problems for feminist theory, knowledge and understanding.

Feminist analyses have underscored that grammatically masculine, so-called generic language is a major cultural force in maintaining wo/men's second-class status in culture and religion. If according to Wittgenstein the limits of our language are the limits of our world,[29] then grammatically masculine language that constructs the universe of wo/men and men in kyriocentric terms engenders a world in which wo/men are marginal or not present at all. Hence, it does not suffice to understand the kyriocentric religious-cultural language, tradition, or classic. It is necessary to change them.

A critical feminist hermeneutics, therefore, insists that we must analyze language as an instrument of power and ideology rather than as simply descriptive and communicative. Language is always rhetorical. Hence hermeneutical theory must be "braided" with rhetorics, for rhetoric not only inscribes but also makes explicit the relation of language and power in a particular moment.[30] "If all language is rhetorical, if even objectivity is the product of a certain strategy, then discourses are no longer to be measured in terms of their adequacy to an objective standard (which Nietzsche's perspectivism exposes as a myth) but rather to be analyzed in terms of their strategic placement within a clash of competing forces themselves constituted in and through the very rhetorical dissimulations they employ."[31]

Tradition

Tradition is a foundational term in hermeneutics and religious studies. Gadamer stresses that we always stand within a tradition and likens this to our standing

---

this sort of reflections. It is the lack of explicit theorizing of epistemological issues—with the help of non-theological feminist theory—that makes their theology vulnerable and open for different readings." Not only is the work of Ruether and my own theoretically lumped together here, but also its consistent engagement with feminist theory is totally overlooked. One wonders whether such failure of research is tolerated in dissertations because the dissertation advisors and publishers lack theoretical competence in feminist studies or whether it is politically motivated.

29. On religious language and hermeneutics see Dan R. Stiver, *The Philosophy of Religious Language: Sign, Symbol, and Story* (Cambridge: Blackwell, 1996), 37-111.

30. See Cheryl Glenn, *Rhetoric Retold: Regendering the Tradition from Antiquity through the Renaissance* (Carbondale: Southern Illinois University Press, 1997) and Loraine Code, *Rhetorical Spaces: Essays on Gendered Locations* (New York: Routledge, 1995).

31. Bender and Wellbery, *The Ends of Rhetoric*, 27.

within a river of life. Hermeneutics is the attempt to understand the stream of tradition of which we are a part. However, Gadamer understands tradition affirmatively "as belonging" rather than critically as a place of distortion and domination. Belonging to a tradition means sharing language and/or understanding. Still, hermeneutics does not sufficiently problematize that traditions are rhetoricized, valorized and shaped by those in power.

The emphasis of hermeneutics on tradition and its authority clearly stands in tension with feminist pre-understandings and goals because in most societies and religions, law and custom have excluded wo/men from the authoritative traditions and classic texts of their culture or religion.

Preunderstanding

The well known hermeneutical circle insists that all understanding is conditioned by our preunderstanding. If we are part of a language and world that is not of our own making we can never leave it behind even if we adopt a "disinterested" theoretical attitude. Presupposition-less understanding is impossible. "The languages we speak, the practices we unconsciously appropriate, the institutions we live out our lives in, the theoretical debates we inherit, and so forth, all form a loosely packed amalgam of meaningful relations that we can never entirely objectify and that we always presuppose in our thematic understanding of anything whatever."[32]

In short, our very ability to understand becomes defined by our preunderstandings, which we cannot simply cast off as we would a coat or a hat. Presuppositions are not roadblocks that prohibit a true grasp of reality; rather, they are a set of inherited, linguistically mediated preunderstandings that make it possible for us to understand the world. Utilizing this insight a feminist hermeneutics insists that critical scholarship requires the critical articulation of one's kyriocentric preunderstandings. Yet, it does not suffice to understand the kyriocentric world of the text, whether it is behind or before it. Feminist studies in religion seeks to enable wo/men to recognize this world for what it is, a world of subordination and oppression. At this point it becomes evident that a critical feminist hermeneutics must move beyond hermeneutics to the critique of ideology that can lift into consciousness the distortions and rhetorical constructedness of this world.

Fusion of Horizons

Gadamer understands the hermeneutical event as a fusion of horizons (*Horizontverschmelzung*). The well-known "hermeneutical circle" means that understanding can only take place if we situate a phenomenon in a larger context, that is, the parts of some larger reality can only be grasped in terms of the whole. In this "to and fro" of the hermeneutical circle or spiral, we can fuse or broaden our horizon with that which we seek to understand.

---

32. Wachterhauser, "History and Language in Understanding," 21.

All interpretation involves a fusion of horizons between that of the text and that of the reader, between past and present, between the classic and its contemporary interpreter. Such a fusion of horizons presupposes a conception of the actual course of history linking the past with the present situation and its horizon of the future [that] form the comprehensive horizon within which the interpreter's limited horizon of the present and the historical horizon of the text fuse together. For only in that way are the past and the present preserved in their historical uniqueness and difference in contrast to one another within the comprehensive horizon.[33]

The image of the fusion of horizons seeks to articulate effective hermeneutic communication. The appropriation of a tradition through understanding can be likened to translation. The horizon of the present is not formed without the past. Such an interlacing of horizons belongs to the very conditions of hermeneutic work. No horizon is closed because we can place ourselves in another point of view and comprehend another culture.

However, it has been pointed out that Gadamer does not mean to say that past and present are separate horizons, although the image suggests a melting or flowing into each other of two distinct horizons. "When we understand the past, with its many differences, we are expanding our horizon, not stepping out of our horizon into the other horizon."[34]

Yet to understand the fusion of horizons either as expanding our horizon with that of the other's horizon or as submission of one's own to that of the other means to construe understanding in kyriarchal terms either as appropriation or as submission. Instead, it is necessary, as Susan Shapiro has argued,[35] to articulate hermeneutics as rhetoric. If horizon means "the field to which the perceptual object belongs," or is the "inactual, nonthematic halo that surrounds and decisively affects the structure of the thematic object,"[36] then hermeneutics must become a critical inquiry into the rhetoricity of the structures of domination and goals of emancipation.

The Classic

Finally, the notion of the *classic* and its history of effects underscores the authority of the great works of the tradition and pays attention to the effects of the classic and its reception history. Over against the modern hermeneutical emphasis on regarding all texts including sacred texts in the same critical manner, David Tracy

---

33. Wolfhart Pannenberg, "Hermeneutics and Universal History," in Wachterhauser, *Hermeneutics and the Human Sciences*, 135.

34. David Couzens Hoy, "Is Hermeneutic Ethnocentric?" in *The Interpretive Turn: Philosophy, Science, Culture*, ed. David R. Hiley, James F. Bowman, and Richard Shusterman (Ithaca: Cornell University Press, 1991), 165.

35. Susan Shapiro, "Rhetoric as Ideology Critique: The Gadamer-Habermas Debate Reinvented," *Journal of the American Academy of Religion* 62/1: 123-50.

36. Ibid., 424.

has argued that the classic text exerts a previous claim upon us. We expect such a text, especially a sacred text, to be significant, to speak to us, to be meaningful, and to have a certain authority which is based on tradition. We always read in front of the cultural or religious "influential" classic or canonical text. Cultural classics and canonical scriptures in turn always already inform our readings. Insofar as they are cultural or religious "classics," they have "performative authority" that is of continuing significance and influence in shaping people's thought and life. They function as persuasive rhetorical texts that continue to influence western cultures and biblical religions. Because of their persuasiveness we must critically scrutinize how much they re-inscribe structures of domination and silencing.

Tracy insists that "the interpreter must risk being caught up in, even being played by, the questions and answers"[37] which the classic raises for us today. However, such advice is dangerous for those whose subordination and silencing the classics such as Scripture have promoted and legitimated. Feminist and ideological criticism have pointed out that a culture's or religion's classics are selected and valorized by those in power.

The claim of hermeneutics that one must accept and enter the classics' world of vision cannot be sustained by a critical feminist hermeneutics. Rather, the rhetorical structures of domination in this claim must be critically scrutinized as distorted communication. One must investigate the genealogy of the kyriocentric classic in order to evaluate its persuasive impact and power. Since the debates of the "culture wars" have amply documented that relations of power condition the formulation, function and effective history of the classic, works considered as classics require especially critical rhetorical investigation.

Hermeneutic as Ideology Critique

With Jürgen Habermas, a representative of the Frankfurt School's critical theory, a critical feminist hermeneutics insists over against the hermeneutical program of Gadamer that the question of power is integral to understanding, linguisticality, tradition, and the classic. Habermas distinguishes "three basic forms of our scientific interest in knowing about the world: the empirical-analytical, the hermeneutical-historical, and the critical-emancipatory. We seek to know in order to control social and natural realities (the empirical-analytic interest), to qualitatively understand and interpret such realities (the hermeneutical-historical interest), and to transform our individual and collective consciousness of reality in order to maximize the human potential for freedom and equality (the critical-emancipatory interest)."[38]

---

37. David Tracy, *The Analogical Imagination: Christian Theology and the Culture of Pluralism* (New York: Crossroad, 1981), 154.

38. Raymond A. Morrow with David D. Baron, *Critical Theory and Methodology* (Thousand Oaks: Sage, 1994), 146.

Whereas hermeneutics is concerned with the surplus of meaning, critical theory focuses on the lack and distortion of meaning through contextualization and relations of domination. Feminist analysis and critical theory both stress the distortion of language and tradition. For instance, the endurance of the classic is not so much due to its outstanding representation of meaning but rather to the persistence of kyriarchal power constellations that legitimate it and in turn are legitimated by it. Cultural and religious linguistic practices and traditions are constituted within unequal power relationships. A feminist critical theory thus insists on and enables the concrete analysis of structures of power and domination. It engages in hermeneutics for the sake of ideology critique.

With the feminist theorist Michèlle Barrett I understand ideology as referring to a process of mystification or misrepresentation. Ideology is distorted communication rather than false consciousness. "The retrievable core of meaning of the term ideology is precisely this: discursive and significatory mechanisms that may occlude, legitimate, naturalise, or universalise in a variety of different ways but can all be said to mystify."[39]

A fundamental assumption of critical theory holds that every form of social order entails some forms of domination and that critical emancipatory interests fuel the struggles to change these relations of domination and subordination. Such power relations engender forms of distorted communication that result in self-deception on the parts of agents with respect to their interests, needs and perceptions of social and religious reality. The*logically speaking they are structural sin. "The notion of ideology must be situated with a theory of language that emphasizes the ways in which meaning is infused with forms of power. . . . To study ideology is not to analyze a particular type of discourse but rather to explore . . . the modes whereby meaningful expressions serve to sustain relation of domination."[40]

John B. Thompson has pointed to three major modes or strategies that are involved in how ideology operates: legitimization, dissimulation, and reification (literally, "making into a thing").[41] All three modes can be identified in the discourses of wo/men's silencing and censure. The first strategy is an appeal for legitimacy on traditional grounds, whereas the second conceals relations of domination in ways that are themselves often structurally excluded from thought. Or as Habermas puts it, ideology "impede[s] making the foundations of society [and, I would add, of religion] the object of thought and reflection."[42]

---

39. Michèlle Barrett, *The Politics of Truth: From Marx to Foucault* (Stanford: Stanford University Press, 1991), 177.

40. Raymond A. Morrow with David D. Baron, *Critical Theory and Methodology*, 130-49.

41. John B. Thompson, *Studies in the Theory of Ideology* (Cambridge: Polity, 1984), 254.

42. Jürgen Habermas, "Ideology," in *Modern Interpretations of Marx*, ed. Tom Bottomore (Oxford: Blackwell, 1981), 166.

The third form of ideological operation is reification or naturalization which represents a transitory, culturally, historically and socially engendered state of affairs as though it were permanent, natural, outside of time or directly revealed by G*d. This ideological strategy comes to the fore in the questionable the*logical arguments for wo/men's special nature. Ideology moreover contributes to the distorted self-understanding of oppressed people who have internalized belief in the legitimacy of their own subordination and innate inferiority. Religious texts and traditions that represent kyriocentric texts and kyriarchal structures of domination as revealed truth call for ideology critique.

In short, relying on a critical theory of language and the insights of liberation movements, I have sought to develop such an ideology critique as a critical feminist *metic* of liberation and transformation. Such a critical hermeneutical theory attempts to articulate interpretation both as a complex process of reading and reconstruction and as a cultural-religious praxis of resistance and transformation. It moves from the traditional understanding of "hermeneutic" to a form of interpretation that can best be described as metic.

Understanding Hermeneutic as Metic

Since feminist studies in religion are primarily interested in the critical-emancipatory interests of knowledge production, "hermeneutics" as it is traditionally understood seems to be a misnomer for the method used to pursue such emancipatory interests. It is not the myth of Hermes but that of Metis and Athena that articulates the task of a critical feminist rhetoric. Athena, the patron Goddess of the classic Athenian city-state, was not only the patron of the arts, technological and scientific knowledge, but also a war goddess. According to Hesiod, she came fully-grown and armored from the head of her father Zeus. However, she only appears to be motherless. Her real mother is the Goddess Metis, the "most wise woman among Gods and humans."[43]

According to the myth, Zeus, the father of the Gods, was in competition with Metis. He duped her when she was pregnant with Athena because he feared that Metis would bear a child who would surpass him in wisdom and power. Hence he changed Metis into a fly. But this was not enough! Zeus swallowed the fly Metis whole in order to have her always with him and to benefit from her wise counsel. This mythical story of Metis and Zeus reveals not only the father of the Gods' fear that the child of Wisdom would surpass him in knowledge but it also lays open the conditions under which wo/men in kyriarchal cultures and religions are able to exercise wisdom and to produce knowledge.

---

43. See my article "Der 'Athenakomplex' in der theologischen Frauenforschung," in *Für Gerechtigkeit straiten: Theologie im Alltag einer bedrohten Welt*, ed. Dorothee Sölle (Gütersloh: Kaiser, 1994), 103-11.

Read with a hermeneutics of suspicion, the myth of Metis and Athena shows that kyriarchal systems of knowledge and power objectify wo/men and swallow them up in order to co-opt their wisdom and knowledge for their own interests of domination. Wo/men's or gender studies remains therefore an ambiguous notion since it has wo/men or gender as objects of its research, rather than structures of domination. Feminist studies in contrast seeks to empower wo/men by recognizing and changing such knowledges and structures of marginalization and oppression.

Since the goal of feminist hermeneutics is not simply to interpret and communicate divine revelations and religious insights, but to undo kyriarchal mystification and dehumanization, it must derive its inspiration from Metis and not from Hermes, the trickster god. A feminist critical hermeneutic—perhaps best described as *metic*—critically investigates how much malestream religious myths, texts, traditions and practices marginalize, make invisible, or distort experience, tradition, language, knowledge and wisdom such that they eliminate wo/men from cultural and religious consciousness and records. Positively, it seeks to produce knowledge not as divinely or naturally given, which is hidden and must be unearthed, but as practical wisdom—*sophia*, not just *phronesis*.

I have proposed, therefore, a complex method for the critical process of a feminist interpretation for liberation.[44] Such a critical feminist hermeneutic-rhetorical method of interpretation does not subscribe to one single reading strategy or method but employs a variety of theoretical insights and methods for articulating its own practices of interpretation. I have developed the "dance of interpretation" with the following seven hermeneutical strategies of interpretation to constitute such a critical rhetorical model. They are a hermeneutics of *experience*, of an *analytics of domination*, of *suspicion*, of critical *evaluation*, of *imagination*, of *memory* and reconstruction, reaching its goal in a hermeneutics of *transformation*.

This model seeks to recast interpretation not in positivist but in rhetorical terms. It recognizes that religious texts are rhetorical texts, produced in and by particular historical debates and struggles. This model of a critical feminist interpretation for liberation argues for the integrity and indivisibility of the interpretive process as well as the primacy of the contemporary starting point of interpretation. This complex model of reading, which engages in a hermeneutical process of deconstruction and reconstruction, of critique and retrieval, applies both to the level of text and to that of interpretation. It seeks to overcome the hermeneutical splits between sense and meaning, between explanation and understanding, between critique and consent, between distanciation and empathy, between reading "behind" and "in front of" the text,[45] between the pres-

---

44. See especially *But She Said*, 51-76 and 195-218, for the elaboration of this process with reference to a particular text.

45. For such a hermeneutical reading, see Sandra Schneiders, *The Revelatory Text: Interpreting the New Testament as Sacred Scripture* (New York: HarperSanFrancisco, 1991).

ent and the past, between interpretation and application,[46] between realism and imagination.

Such a critical method and process of feminist interpretation for liberation requires feminist conscientization and systemic analysis. Its interpretive process or "hermeneutical dance" does not commence with placing malestream texts and traditions at the center of its attention. Rather it begins with a *hermeneutics of experience*.[47]

A critical feminist rhetoric of liberation focuses in particular on the struggles of wo/men at the bottom of the kyriarchal pyramid of domination and exploitation, because their situation lays open the fulcrum of oppression and dehumanization threatening every wo/man. The victories in the struggles of multiply oppressed wo/men reveal at the same time the liberatory presence of G*d in our midst. In short, a feminist critical interpretation for liberation does not simply begin with experience. Rather it begins with a reflection of the experience of wo/men on the bottom of society who struggle for survival and well-being.

The starting point of feminist liberation the*logies of all colors is the experience and voices of the oppressed and marginalized, of those wo/men traditionally excluded from articulating the*logy and shaping religious life. Long before postmodern feminist theories, feminist liberation the*logies have not only recognized the perspectival and contextual nature of knowledge and interpretation but also asserted that knowledge and the*logy are—knowingly or not—always engaged for or against the oppressed. Intellectual neutrality is impossible in an exploitative and oppressive historical world. Yet as the Brazilian educator Paolo Freire pointed out a long time ago, the oppressed have also internalized oppression and are divided in and among themselves. "The oppressed, having internalized the image of the oppressor and adopted his [sic] guidelines, are fearful of freedom. Freedom would require them to eject this image and replace it with autonomy and responsibility. Freedom . . . must be pursued constantly and responsibly."[48]

Since both the oppressed and their oppressors are "manifestations of dehumanization,"[49] the methodological starting point of all liberation studies must be systemically analyzed and reflected experience, rather than simply "common sense" experience. Since wo/men also have internalized and are shaped by kyriarchal "common sense" mindset and values, the hermeneutical starting point of feminist interpretation must be the experience of wo/men that has been

---

46. Klaus Berger, *Hermeneutik des Neuen Testaments* (Gütersloh: Gütersloher, 1988), insists on the distinction in order to safeguard the distanciating power of exegetical-historical interpretation and the freedom of selectivity in the application of texts in contemporary situations.

47. For a critical discussion of the category of experience in feminist thought see Joan W. Scott, "Experience," in *Feminists Theorize the Political*, ed. Judith Butler and Joan W. Scott (New York: Routledge, 1992), 22-40.

48. Paolo Freire, *Pedagogy of the Oppressed* (New York: Seabury, 1973), 31.

49. Ibid., 33.

critically explored through the process of "conscientization" as to its location in the systems of oppression and struggles for liberation.

To that end, one must develop a feminist analytics of domination that insists on a systemic analysis that can both disentangle the ideological (religious-the*logical) ways that sacred texts and traditions inculcate and legitimate the kyriarchal order but also explain their potential for fostering justice and liberation.[50] Feminist readings that do not prioritize wo/men's struggles against multiplicative oppression but privilege the religious text itself and malestream doctrinal, the*logical, spiritual, or theoretical frameworks cannot be liberative.

After having applied a critical systemic analysis of kyriarchal structures of domination and dehumanization, a critical feminist hermeneutics continues the interpretive process with a *hermeneutics of suspicion*. A hermeneutics of suspicion scrutinizes both the presuppositions and interests of interpreters, as well as the androcentric strategies of the text itself. I concur that a hermeneutics of suspicion does not employ "a hermeneutics of discovery assuming that there is some order in the world . . . that can be discovered. . . . Truth is something discovered by employing a hermeneutics of suspicion, wherein one is suspicious of the various disguises one can use to cover up and distort reality."[51]

Kyriocentric language does not cover up but constructs reality in a certain way and then mystifies its own constructions by "naturalizing" them as revelation. Kyriocentric texts, literary classics and visual art, works of science, anthropology, sociology or the*logy do not cover up reality "as it is." Rather they are ideological constructs that produce as given reality the invisibility and marginality of wo/men. A hermeneutics of suspicion must be understood as a denaturalizing and demystifying practice, rather than as working away at the layers upon

---

50. Although Anthony C. Thiselton, *New Horizons in Hermeneutics: The Theory and Practice of Transforming Biblical Reading* (London: HarperCollins, 1992), 449, claims in his discussion of my work that "what is at stake is hermeneutical theory," he does not bother to discuss *Bread Not Stone* but rather focuses on a particular exegetical topic regarding wo/men's witness to the resurrection discussed in *In Memory of Her.* In so doing he seeks to show that I did not take all possible interpretations into account. Yet such a criticism overlooks the limits set by my choice of genre for this work, mistaking a work of historical reconstruction for one of hermeneutical critical theory. The interests driving his misreading come to the fore in his emotionally laden comparison of my own work with that of Susanne Heine. Although Heine's work has appeared later and is dependent on my own work, albeit without acknowledging it, she finds Thiselton's favor because she attacks the work of other feminists. Thiselton's own interests come to the fore also in his repeated question as to how much a given tradition can undergo transformation before it ceases to be *this tradition* as well as in the question of whether the transformation of which I speak comes "into being by imposing one's community values upon another in a hermeneutic of conflict, or by progress toward a universal commitment to a transcendental critique of justice and of the cross that speaks from beyond given context-bound communities in a hermeneutic of openness?" Obviously, Thiselton is not able to understand either commitment to wo/men as a universal stance nor feminist struggle as a commitment to a "transcendental critique of justice" or to the "cross" as the symbolic expression of such struggles.

51. Bible and the Culture Collective, *The Postmodern Bible* (New Haven: Yale University Press, 1995), 249.

layers of cultural sediment which hide or repress a "deeper truth." A critical feminist interpretation insists on a hermeneutics of suspicion in order to disentangle the ideological functions of kyriocentric text and commentary. It does not do so because it assumes a kyriarchal conspiracy of the classics and their contemporary interpreters, but because wo/men never know whether we are addressed by grammatically masculine generic texts.

A *hermeneutics of ethical and the*logical evaluation* assesses the rhetoric of texts and traditions. It seeks to adjudicate the oppressive or liberatory tendencies inscribed in religious texts as well as their function in contemporary struggles for liberation. It does not, however, reify texts and traditions either as oppressive or as emancipatory. Rather it seeks to adjudicate repeatedly how they function in particular situations. The well-being of every wo/man must be established and reasoned out as its standard of evaluation in terms of a systemic analysis of kyriarchal domination. For the*logical reasons it insists that Christians must cease preaching kyriarchal texts as the "word of G*d," since by doing so they proclaim G*d as legitimating kyriarchal oppression.

A *hermeneutics of creative imagination and ritualization* in turn seeks to generate utopian visions and to "dream" a world of justice and well-being. It seeks to retell scriptural stories, reshape religious vision, and celebrate those who have brought about change. To that end it utilizes not only historical, literary, and ideology critical methods that focus on the rhetoric of religious texts and their historical contexts. It also employs methods of storytelling, role-play, bibliodrama, pictorial arts, dance and ritual for creating a "different" religious imagination.

Yet our imagination and utopian visions are always informed and determined by our present sociopolitical location. Hence, we also need to scrutinize them with a hermeneutics of suspicion. When seeking for future vision, we can only extrapolate from present experience that is always already determined by the past. Thus, we need to analyze the present in order to articulate the vision and imagination for a new humanity and religious community. Only if we want to work for a different future can our imagination transcend past and present limitations. As Toni Morrison so forcefully states in her novel, *Beloved*: "She did not tell them to clean up their lives or to go and sin no more. She did not tell them they were the blessed of the earth, its inheriting meek or its glory bound pure. She told them that the only grace they could have was the grace they could imagine. That if they could not see it, they would not have it."[52]

Such a hermeneutics of imagination is always also a hermeneutics of desire. Alicia Suskin Ostriker characterizes such a hermeneutics of desire as "you see what you want to see."

---

52. Toni Morrison, *Beloved* (New York: Knopf, 1987), 88.

I am engaged both theoretically and practically in the question of what will happen when the spiritual imagination of women, women who may call themselves Jews or Christians, pagans or atheists, witches or worshippers of the great Goddess, is released into language and into history. . . . I feel desperately fractured much of the time, as anyone in a pathological culture must. But I strive for healing. And so I must confront what is toxic—but I must do more than that.[53]

A *hermeneutics of remembrance and reconstitution* works not only to increase the distance between ourselves and the time of the text but also seeks for an increase in historical imagination. It displaces the androcentric dynamic of the text in its literary contexts by re-contextualizing the text in a sociopolitical model of reconstruction that can make the subordinated and marginalized "others" visible. It attempts to recover wo/men's religious history and the memory of their victimization, struggle, and accomplishments as wo/men's heritage. It seeks not only for historical retrieval but also for a religious reconstitution of the world. With postmodern thinkers it is fully conscious of the rhetoricity of its own reconstructions but nevertheless insists that such work of historical remembrance is necessary in support of wo/men's struggles for survival and transformation. If it is a sign of the total oppression of a people not to have a written history, then feminists cannot afford to eschew such historical, reconstructive work.

The shared spiritual visions of traditional religions can evoke powerful emotions and responses and thereby create a sense of community necessary to sustain the struggles and visions for an alternative society and world. Hence, such a critical feminist interpretative process or "hermeneutical dance" climaxes in a *hermeneutics of transformation* that aims to change relations of domination that are legitimated and inspired by kyriarchal religion.

Feminist religious interpretation and inquiry has to explore avenues for changing and transforming relations of domination inscribed in texts, traditions and everyday life. It must stand accountable to those wo/men who struggle at the bottom of the kyriarchal pyramid of discriminations and dominations. It needs to articulate religious studies as a site of social, political and religious transformation.

Such a critical process of interpretation for liberation is not restricted to Christian religious texts but has been applied successfully to traditions and Scriptures of other religions. It has been used in graduate education, in parish discussions, in college classes, and in work with illiterate Andean wo/men. This critical rhetorical model of feminist hermeneutics conceives of religious studies as well as of the*logy as sites of struggle and conscientization. It challenges other approaches in Religious Studies to become more comprehensive and

---

53. Alicia Suskin Ostriker, *Feminist Revision and the Bible* (Cambridge: Blackwell, 1993).

sophisticated by problematizing their sociopolitical locations and functions in the global struggle for a more just and inclusive religion and world.

Reconceptualizing the Authority of Scripture and Tradition

Such a critical process of interpretation requires a reconception of the authority of scriptures and traditions. Understanding this authority as challenging possibility rather than as norm redefines Scriptures as formative root models rather than as normative archetypes. Instead of reducing the symbolic richness of scriptural and other religious expressions to abstract principle, timeless norm, de-contextualized essence or ontologically immutable type which should be repeated and translated from generation to generation, a critical feminist hermeneutics of liberation seeks to reclaim religion and the sacred as an open-ended paradigm that makes transformation possible.[54]

To be sure, the experiences that religious traditions and practices have generated are not always liberating. They often are oppressive not simply because of unfaithful or false interpretations and bad readings. Religious texts and traditions do re-inscribe relations of oppression if they were formulated in the first place for maintaining kyriarchal sociopolitical structures and religious identity formations. Therefore a critical interpretation for liberation must clearly identify and mark both the religious texts and traditions that promote kyriarchal structures and their contexts and ideological functions in ever changing situations.

Religious identity that is grounded in Scripture and tradition as its formative prototypes must be deconstructed and reconstructed in terms of a global praxis for the liberation of all those dehumanized by kyriarchal societies and religions. As a root metaphor (the tension between *is* and *is not*) malestream traditions and scriptures inform but do not provide the the*logical lenses for a critical feminist reading of particular texts in the interest of liberation.

As I have argued above, unlike a hermeneutic-aesthetic inquiry that strives for textual understanding, appreciation, application, and consent, a critical feminist rhetorical inquiry pays careful attention to the power structures and interests that shape language, text and understanding. In contrast to hermeneutics, a critical feminist *metic* is not just concerned with exploring the conditions and possibilities of understanding and appreciating kyriocentric texts and traditions but also with critically assessing and dismantling their persuasive powers in the interest of wo/men's liberation. To that end one must construct a feminist theoretical framework of interpretation that can articulate a critical rhetoric of inquiry, an epistemological move which is often overlooked. Such a critical rhetoric of inquiry calls for redefining the notion of truth in the *metic*-emancipatory terms of wisdom.

---

54. See my book *In Memory of Her* for the development of the notion of Scripture as paradigm and prototype.

Examining ancient Greek legal, philosophical, and literary texts on torture, Page duBois has argued that classical Greek philosophy developed the concept of truth as something hidden to be excavated or extracted by the torture of slaves. "This logic demands a closed circle, an other, an outside, and creates such an other. And in the case of the Greek city, the democracy itself used torture to establish this boundary, to mark the line between slave and free, and to locate truth outside."[55]

In contrast, the myth of Metis makes clear that central kyriarchal power deforms and swallows up wisdom and truth. Truth is not located outside but within kyriarchal relations of domination. Western philosophy understands truth as something that is unknown, buried, secreted in the earth, in the body, in the wo/man, in the slave, in the totally "other": something that must be extricated through torture or sexual violence. In a similar fashion, revelation has been understood in traditional the*logy as an uncovering of a hidden mystery which is located in the unknown and in the beyond. It is directly known only to a select few and can be extracted only through arduous labor. For instance, the "canon within the canon" approach seeks to uncover, to distill or to extract a universal truth or authoritative norm from the multilayered meanings of sacred texts and the often-contradictory writings collected in them.

According to duBois, this kyriarchal understanding of "truth" is articulated in reaction to the "logic of democracy" as the notion of equal power among members of a society which required the radical distribution of wealth and the elimination of social and political hierarchies. For some ancient thinkers, even slavery itself was eventually called into question. This "logic of democracy" is not represented by Zeus or Hermes but by Metis. It was Zeus, the Father of the gods, who violated "this logic of equality" by dedivinizing and dehumanizing Metis and by not acknowledging her different power.

Such a recontextualization of religious hermeneutics in the paradigm of radical democracy produces a different notion of truth. It does not understand truth or the sacred as a metaphysical given buried in the "other" but seeks to comprehend it in and through the interactive deliberation of a multiple, polyvalent assembly of voices. Truth is a not a process of discovering the hidden or lost sacred, but rather of public deliberation and creation for establishing radical democratic power relations. The truth of religion, understood according to the logic of democracy, is produced in struggle and debate between equals as an alternative discourse to torture and inquisition. In this radical democratic paradigm the truth or the sacred is best understood as an "absent presence," as a moment in an interpretive political process, a progressive extension of rights and equality to all residents of our expanding world community. Such a conception of "truth" comes close to the biblical notion of "doing the truth" that will set us free.

---

55. Page duBois, *Torture and Truth: The New Ancient World* (New York: Routledge, 1991).

A critical feminist hermeneutics of liberation, therefore, attempts to recover the biblical notion of "discerning the spirits" as a deliberative rhetorical practice. As religious subjects, feminists, I argue, must claim their spiritual authority to assess both the oppressive as well as the liberating function and imagination of particular religious texts and traditions in particular historical situations. We need to do so because of the kyriarchal functions of authoritative religious claims that demand obedience and acceptance. Critical feminist discourses can deconstruct the all-encompassing kyriarchal rhetoric and politics of subordination and thereby generate new possibilities for the communicative construction of religious identities and emancipatory practices.

Reclaiming wo/men's authority for shaping and determining religions, feminist scholars ask new questions in order to re-conceptualize the act of religious interpretation as a moment in the global praxis for liberation. Hence, a critical feminist hermeneutics cannot simply take over malestream hermeneutical theory or interpretive methods. Rather it must position itself within the epistemological paradigm shift engendered by critical theories and liberation the*logies.

To that end it also seeks to interrogate religious texts, traditions, and institutional practices for religious visions that foster equality, justice and the hermeneutics of desire that envisions and practices *ekklēsia* as a feminist public counterspace[56] to that of kyriarchal domination. Yet, feminist hermeneutics will only be able to identify its radical democratic religious roots when it questions the kyriarchal discourses of exclusion inscribed in religious Scriptures and traditions. A critical hermeneutical integration of liberty, equality, and radical democracy with radical egalitarian religious visions, I argue, can engender critical religious studies and discourses of possibility for a different understanding of human well-being. The task of feminist studies in religion is to articulate and envision a Spirit Center for a radical democratic citizenry of global dimensions.

In short, such a shift from a modern western malestream to a critical liberation the*logical frame of reference engenders a fourfold change in hermeneutical-rhetorical inquiry: a change in interpretive goals, a change in epistemology, a change in consciousness, and a change in central the*logical questions.

As I have elaborated above, the task of feminist interpretation is *not just to understand* religious texts and traditions *but to change* western idealist hermeneutical frameworks, individualist practices and sociopolitical relations. For so doing, feminist liberation studies shift attention to the politics of religious studies and its sociopolitical contexts. They claim the hermeneutical privilege of the oppressed and marginalized for reading and evaluating religious texts and traditions. For instance, whereas Schleiermacher, the "father of hermeneutics,"

---

56. For the notion of a feminist "counter-public" (I would prefer "alternative") sphere see Rita Felski, *Beyond Feminist Aesthetics: Feminist Literature and Social Change* (Cambridge: Harvard University Press, 1989), 164-75.

addressed the "cultured critics of religion," Gustavo Gutiérrez argues that liberation the*logians take up the questions of the "non-persons."[57]

Such an articulation of religious studies in view of the wo/men living at the bottom of the kyriarchal pyramid of domination is not confessional and doctrinal but ecumenical and interreligious. It seeks to enable and defend sentient life that is threatened or destroyed by hunger, destitution, sexual violence, torture and dehumanization. Liberationist studies seek to give dignity and value to the life of the non-person as the presence and image of G*d in our midst. Therefore, they do not restrict salvation to the soul but aim to promote the well-being and radical equality of all.

As long as kyriarchal religion hinders wo/men struggling for emancipation, promotes patriarchal kyriarchy, and distorts wo/men's self-understandings and perception of the world, feminist interpretation must pay attention not only to kyriocentric texts and traditions but also to the frameworks or "lenses" of wo/men readers. Recognizing the kyriocentric dynamics of religious texts and traditions, a critical feminist rhetoric of liberation, I have argued throughout, must abandon the quest for a liberating canonical text, unitary essence or revealed pre-given truth; instead, it must shift its focus to the process of interpretation in which wo/men as religious-the*logical subjects grapple with oppressive and liberating meanings of particular religious texts and traditions and their function in wo/men's lives and struggles.

Since feminist critical reflection is motivated by the hunger and thirst for justice, it seeks to reclaim those religious visions, memories, and unrealized possibilities that can sustain resistance to oppressive structures and inspire energy and hope for their transformation. It struggles to transform kyriarchal religions because the "productive imagination"[58] of religion has not only sanctioned kyriocentric ideologies, but also articulated visions and utopias for a more just world. The task of feminist studies in religion is both the deconstruction of kyriarchal religions and the re-articulation of their emancipatory values and visions in the global struggles for wo/men's dignity, justice, and the well-being of all creation.

---

57. See also Sharon Welch, *Communities of Resistance and Solidarity* (Maryknoll: Orbis), 7: "the referent of the phrase 'liberating God' is not primarily God but liberation."

58. Paul Ricoeur, *Hermeneutics and the Human Sciences*, 38-39.

PART II

Feminist The*logy and Feminist Struggles

4

Domination Divides Us, Feminist Differences Make Us Strong

The Ethics and Politics of Liberation

Postmodern feminist theories have pointed out that the ways we situate our texts and choose our rhetorical strategies raise questions about power that need to be made clear again and again.[1] In her poem, "Heroines,"[2] the American poet Adrienne Rich drew attention to the place of feminist theory and the*logy defined by the divided heritage of the nineteenth-century white wo/men's movement. She pointed out that this heritage is still important today, but speaks to us "in the shattered language of a partial vision." Therefore she asks the nineteenth-century white suffragists: How can we fail to love your "clarity and fury . . . give you all your due, take courage from your courage, honor your exact legacy as it is, recognizing as well that it is not enough?"

1. First published as "Patriarchale Herrschaft spaltet/Feministische Verschiedenheit macht stark: Ethik und Politik der Befreiung," in *Frauenkirchen: Vernetzung und Reflexion im europäischen Kontext*, ed. Angela Berlis, Julie Hopkins, Hedwig Meyer-Wilmes, and Karoline Vander Stichele (Kampen: Kok Pharos, 1995), 5-29. I am indebted to Professors Lieve Troch and Hedwig Meyer-Wilmes. They not only encouraged me to work on this theme but also insisted that I engage theoretically with the general discussion of feminist theory. The often-technical language of my essay is required by this engagement with theory. At the same time I want to extend my great thanks for the interest and enthusiasm with which the wo/men's movement in the churches of the Netherlands has supported and enriched my work. I also want to thank Linda Maloney for her translation of this chapter.
2. Adrienne Rich, *A Wild Patience Has Taken Me This Far: Poems 1978–1981* (New York: Norton, 1981), 33-36.

Like our white feminist predecessors of the nineteenth century, so also most of us who are able to participate in feminist conferences are, in the words of Gayatry Chakravorty Spivak, "infinitely privileged" wo/men.[3] Since even feminists remain entangled in the web of kyriarchal super- and subordination, feminist discourses must make theoretically visible the institutional structures and academic or ecclesiastical kyriarchal locations from which we speak.

The place from which I begin my critical intervention is North American feminist the*logy.[4] In order to mark this location, I have prefaced my theoretical reflections with a reference to the poem "Heroines," by Adrienne Rich. I will close my reflections with an extract from an address given by the African-American intellectual Anna Julia Cooper in 1893 at a world congress of wo/men in Chicago. By marking my text in this way, I attempt to locate my discussion of a feminist ethics and politics of liberation explicitly within the historical discourses of the North American wo/men's movement and its heritage. In doing so I want to invite readers to judge for themselves whether and to what extent my theoretical reflections may contribute to feminist conversations in other geopolitical situations.

Although I speak out of the context of the United States wo/men's movement in the*logy and church, I speak not as a "native" but as a "resident alien," a foreigner living there. The label "resident alien" situates me as someone who is both "inside and outside": On the basis of my long residency and my professional position in the United States I "belong." But at the same time I remain a foreigner because of my German accent, my experience, and my history. When I visit Germany I am regarded as a "native" on the basis of citizenship, culture, and language. At the same time I am seen as "a foreigner" who as a "representative" of American feminist the*logy does not "belong." For similar reasons, though these are rooted in quite different experiences, Patricia Hill Collins has argued that black citizens, especially womanist intellectuals, always have to assume a "double" insider/outsider position.[5]

I therefore suggest that the metaphor of the "resident alien" is an appropriate image for a feminist movement and politics of liberation in the context of

---

3. Gayatra Chakravorty Spivak, *The Post-Colonial Critic: Interviews, Strategies, Dialogues*, ed. Sarah Harasym (New York: Routledge, 1990), 42.

4. Here, I refer also to "womanist" and "mujerista" the*logy. African American feminists have adopted the concept of "womanist" from Alice Walker. See also Katie G. Cannon, *Black Womanist Ethics* (Atlanta: Scholars, 1998) and the round table discussion, "Christian Ethics and Theology in a Womanist Perspective," *Journal of Feminist Studies in Religion* 5/2 (1989): 83-112. As far as I know, the expression "mujerista" was first used by Ada María Isasi-Díaz, see "The Bible and Mujerista Theology," in *Lift Every Voice: Constructing Christian Theologies from the Underside*, ed. Susan Brooks Thistlethwaite and Mary Potter Engel (New York: Harper and Row, 1990), 261-69. Maria Pilar Aquino and others speak of "Latina Feminist Theology."

5. Patricia Hill Collins, "Learning from the Outsider Within: The Sociological Significance of Black Feminist Thought," *Social Problems* 33 (1986): 14-32.

Western societies and churches. If the "White Lady"[6] has served as the agent of civilization and simultaneously as feminine "glue" holding Western-kyriarchal domination together, then white wo/men, who are relatively recent "immigrants" in the*logical scholarship and church offices, must be on our guard not to assume alibi functions for Western kyriarchal civilization. We must refuse to produce or disseminate knowledge that legitimates intellectual or religious structures that degrade, subordinate, or restrict wo/men. In order to practice such disloyalty toward kyriarchal authority, feminist theory and the*logy need to hold to to their "foreign" character by understanding themselves as "second-order reflection" that is simultaneously responsible to the initiative for liberation.

Academic research on wo/men and especially on gender often seeks to overcome its position as "resident alien" by accommodating itself to the academic system. Of course it is necessary for academic feminists to formulate their discourse in accordance with the scholarly standards of the university. But such a survival strategy must be seen for what it is: a collaboration with andro-kyriocentric-academic discourses that pass over the existence of wo/men with silence or marginalize wo/men as "the others." Similarly, ordained wo/men are often forced to accept certain ecclesiastical discourses in order to exercise their office. But such a decision to collaborate in the dominant discourse must always be ethically justified and legitimated as a strategic-tactical undermining of kyriarchal systems of knowledge and governance. Otherwise, feminist-the*logical discourse as well as women's and gender studies run the risk of simply reproducing the knowledge about "woman" that objectifies, marginalizes, and silences wo/men.

If we understand ourselves at one and the same time as "resident aliens" and as "insiders and outsiders," instead of settling as "others" in the margins of feminist sex-gender discourses, we need to articulate an ethos and ethics of kyriarchal critique, common political initiatives, and multicultural visions of liberation. Such an ethos both expresses and constitutes who we are. It requires a permanent critique of our own projects and their possible ideological entanglement, cooptation, and limitation by the kyriarchal-institutional structures within which we have to think and act.

Articulating feminist strategies of liberation situated in the tension between center and margin does *not* mean favoring fixed positions of opposition. Rather, it demands a situation-appropriate weighing and careful selection of theoretical and practical strategies that can do justice to the constantly changing feminist struggles against kyriarchal systemic oppression. Such a concentration on the theory and praxis of struggle for transforming situations of domination constitutes both an actual and a normative principle of a feminist ethics of liberation.

---

6. Hazel V. Carby, "On the Threshold of Woman's Era: Lynching, Empire, and Sexuality," in *Race, Writing, and Difference*, ed. Henry Louis Gates Jr. (Chicago: University of Chicago Press, 1986), 301-28.

In the nineteenth century, a slave named Isabella experienced her own liberation as part of the emancipation movement and was transformed by it. She marked her experiences of liberation in religious terms by choosing a new name: Sojourner Truth.[7] Although the mutual interaction between a provisional, temporary stay (sojourn) and truth can be understood, interpreted, and interrelated in different ways, the dynamic tension between sojourn and truth articulates, in my opinion, an enduring vision for an ethics of transformation. If, in the words of Nelle Morton, "the journey is home,"[8] it is important to create feminist intellectual and religious spaces as "refueling stations" for solidarity, empowerment, and friendship in the feminist struggles for liberation.

Patriarchy as Sex-Gender Dualism

Feminist discourses have from the beginning sought to create free spaces for wo/men not at the margins, but in the center of academy and church. Therefore feminist theory has analyzed and criticized androcentric dualisms and asymmetrical, binary constructions of gender difference. Nevertheless, feminist discourses have not entirely avoided repeating dualistic classifications and representing them as exclusive alternatives: either reformist or radical, socialist or liberal, private or public, oriented to equal rights or womanhood, psychoanalytical or sociopolitical, essentialist or constructivist, European or American, white or black, wo/men of the so-called First or Third Worlds.

The religious ethicist Carol Robb has persuasively argued that the differences in theoretical approaches of feminist ethics are caused by different analyses of wo/men's oppression and its roots.[9] Rather than rehearse here the different, now well-known, and much-belabored typologies of feminist-theoretical approaches, I would like to turn to the concepts of patriarchy and kyriarchy.

Whereas some feminist theoreticians reject the concept of patriarchy[10] as an unhistorical, universalistic, and totalistic notion, others use it as a key theoretical concept to name the origins and continuation of sexual, social, political, and ideological domination of men over wo/men. Hence in feminist theory the concept of patriarchy is no longer restricted to the power of the head of household, the father, over the extended family, as is largely still the case in the social sciences.

---

7. See Bert James Loewenberg and Ruth Bogin, eds., *Black Women in Nineteenth-Century American Life* (University Park: Pennsylvania State University Press, 1976), 234, 242.

8. Nelle Morton, *The Journey Is Home* (Boston: Beacon, 1985).

9. Carol S. Robb, "A Framework for Feminist Ethics," in *Women's Consciousness, Women's Conscience: A Reader in Feminist Ethics*, ed. Barbara Hilkert Andolsen, Christine E. Gudorf, and Mary D. Pellauer (Minneapolis: Winston, 1985), 211-34.

10. For discussion and definition of the concepts, see Maggie Humm, *The Dictionary of Feminist Theory* (Columbus: Ohio State University Press, 1990), 159-61 and Gerda Lerner, *The Creation of Patriarchy* (New York: Oxford University Press, 1986), 231-43. Unlike Lerner, I am not interested in the origins of kyriarchal dominance but in developing it as a heuristic historical category.

Rather, the concept is used to name the social structures of domination and the androcentric ideologies that have permitted men to subordinate women over the course of history and to rule over them.

As discussed previously, if the concept of patriarchy is understood in the sense of male-female gender dominance, then gender difference becomes the primary form of domination and oppression. The difference between male and female becomes the fundamental and essential difference between human beings. Such an essentialist idea of gender difference can take a constructivist turn when it is assumed that binary gender dualism is not biologically determined or divinely ordained, but socially constructed. Such ideological construction of gender difference supports kyriarchal domination and may appear to be natural and common sense, not only to men but also to wo/men. Although the majority of feminists represents a form of constructivist-social gender analysis, some tend to assume biological determinism or philosophical essentialism concerning the feminine or to assert both.[11]

Although feminists in general agree that the dominant sociocultural sex-gender system must be demystified, they disagree on how a positive standpoint in the struggle for liberation can be defined after the concepts of the "maternal-feminine" have become problematic. Hence, feminist theory must seek an alternative theoretical site because only a critical-theoretical standpoint that differs from the dominant system of gender can demystify and unmask the sociocultural and religious ideologies of domination. However, in my opinion the possibility of finding such a theoretical site depends on the existence of a social movement that struggles for the removal of patriarchal conditions of domination. Vice versa, the theoretical articulation of such a feminist site empowers the feminist movement as a social movement for liberation.

The theoreticians of the "new," "wholly different" maternal-feminine seek to name such a feminine site not only on the epistemological but also on the social level, by seeking to extract the concept of the feminine from the dominant gender system, to assign it to a new theoretical place, and to evaluate it. The Italian feminist Adriana Cavarero formulates such a female theoretical standpoint:

> By essential and original difference I mean that the "being-in-difference" that is called into existence is for women not a matter of discussion, since for everyone born female it is always already so and not otherwise. It is rooted in their being not as something superfluous or additional, but as what she necessarily is: female/feminine.[12]

---

11. For the problem complex and discussion of the essentialist/constructivist opposition, see Diana Fuss, *Essentially Speaking: Feminism, Nature, and Difference* (New York: Routledge, 1989).

12. Adriana Cavarero, "L'elaborazione filosofica della differenza asessuale," in *La Ricerca delle Donne: Studi Femministi in Italia*, ed. Maria Christina Marcuzzo and Anna Rossi-Dura (Turin: Rosenberg and Sellier, 1987), 180. See also her essay, "Die Perspektive der Geschlechterdifferenz,"

It is true that feminist scholars attempt to emphasize that the theory of the maternal-feminine undermines the assumed objectivity of logo- and phallocentric principles, representations, and knowledge, destabilizing existing forms of writing and knowing in ways previously unthinkable. Nevertheless, the American reception of so-called French feminist theory and its emphasis on the feminine as metaphor and construct has tended to re-inscribe and solidify the cultural feminine. This danger exists especially in the popular reception of the feminine by religious feminists: fluidity, softness, plurality, ocean, nature, peacefulness, nourishing, body, life, Mother-Goddess are understood as the opposites of solidity, hardness, rigidity, aggressively, reason, control, death, Father-God. As a result, the theory of the maternal-feminine is in danger of reproducing in the form of deconstructive language the traditional cultural-religious attributions of femininity and motherhood, ascriptions all too familiar to Catholic feminists from papal pronouncements.

In the 1980s, feminist theory, so the story is told, moved beyond the liberal critique of the sexism of knowledge and the structural critique of patriarchal theories to a critique of phallocentrism, which represents both sexes in terms that are only appropriate to the male/masculine. Autonomous feminism has supposedly moved away from a theory that focuses its analysis on sexism and woman to a critical examination of theory as hiding its masculine character. An open acknowledgment of the "masculinity of knowledges" is needed, so the argument goes, in order to open up a space within the "universal" for woman as woman, a site where female difference can be articulated. "In exploring the language of femininity and autonomy, feminist theory has introduced the possibility of a dialogue between knowledges now accepted as masculine and the 'alien' or 'other' voice of women."[13]

And yet such a periodizing depiction of the rediscovery of the feminine is silent about—indeed, represses—the fact that the emergence of many different feminist voices around the world and the associated deconstruction of a unified, essentialist understanding of "woman" represents the most important breakthrough for feminist theory in the 1980s. Hence, it is very disturbing that white feminist theory and the*logy in the United States is so fascinated by the European-American articulation of sexual difference and the valorization of the feminine at the very moment when major important theoretical works from feminists in the two-thirds world are appearing, works that not only call into question the primacy of gender oppression but also theorize it differently.[14]

---

in *Differenz und Gleichheit: Menschenrechte haben (k)ein Geschlecht*, ed. Ute Gerhard et al. (Frankfurt: Helmer, 1990), 95-111.

13. Elizabeth A. Grosz, "The In(ter)vention of Feminist Knowledges," in *Crossing Boundaries: Feminisms and the Critique of Knowledge*, ed. Barbara Caine, Elizabeth A. Grosz, and Marie de Lepervanche (Sydney: Allen and Unwin, 1988), 97, 103.

14. See bell hooks, *Feminist Theory: From Margin to Center* (Cambridge: South End, 1984); *Talking Back: Thinking Feminist/Thinking Black* (Boston: South End, 1989); and *Yearning: Race, Gender, and Cultural Politics* (Boston: South End, 1990). See also Paula Giddings, *When and*

Patriarchy and Kyriarchy

In order to approach a new definition of the center of feminist discourse, I argue, feminist the*logy and theory must abandon the privileging of a binary gender dualism as its theoretical framework in which "sexual difference" determines "the horizon" of our thought (Irigaray). To do so, I have attempted to reconceptualize and theorize the concept of patriarchy, as the primary analytical category of feminist theory, by replacing it with *kyriarchy* so that it can articulate the intersecting relations of the various mutually conflicting forms of wo/men's oppression. Instead of postulating a dualistic structure of male-female domination, we must understand it theoretically as a pyramidal political-cultural system of domination and subordination.[15]

European and American feminist theories and the*logies that absolutize and universalize the Western discourse of sexual difference conceal not only the complex intersection of kyriarchal structures of domination that shape the individual experiences of wo/men and the relationships between wo/men. They also cover up the participation of white privileged wo/men and Christian religion in kyriarchal oppression, to the extent that both have served as civilizing channels for kyriarchal knowledge and cultural values.

In short, it is both the interlacing of the exclusion of privileged Western women from democratic rights and citizenship with the exclusion of all other "nonpersons" (Gustavo Gutiérrez) and the ideological legitimation of gender, race, class, and cultural differences as natural or G*d-given that must be explored in a feminist theoretical analytic. This is overlooked when some feminists construct a contrast between the feminism of the 1960s and 1970s, which allegedly struggled only against sexism and for equal rights for wo/men, and that of the 1980s, which supposedly was the first to fight for the autonomy and self-determination of all wo/men.[16] That kind of dualistic periodization of feminist intellectual history in the last thirty years misunderstands two crucial points.

Where I Enter: The Impact of Black Women on Race and Sex in America (New York: William Morrow, 1984); Cheryl A. Wall, ed., *Changing Our Own Words: Essays on Criticism, Theory, and Writing by Black Women* (New Brunswick: Rutgers University Press, 1989); Henry Louis Gates Jr., ed., *Reading Black, Reading Feminist* (New York: Meridian, 1990); Patricia Hill Collins, *Black Feminist Thought: Knowledge, Consciousness, and the Politics of Empowerment* (Boston: Unwin Hyman, 1991); and Joanne M. Braxton and Andrea Nicola McLaughlin, eds., *Wild Women in the Whirlwind: Afro-American Culture and the Contemporary Literary Renaissance* (New Brunswick: Rutgers University Press, 1990).

15. Sylvia Walby, *Patriarchy at Work: Patriarchal and Capitalist Relations in Employment* (Minneapolis: University of Minnesota Press, 1986), 5-69. The author understands patriarchy as a complex system of interrelated social structures. The various groups of patriarchal relationships shift over time and bring about different constellations at different times and in different cultures.

16. Elizabeth Gross, "Conclusion: What Is Feminist Theory?" in *Feminist Challenges: Social and Political Theory*, ed. Elizabeth Gross and Carol Pateman (Sydney: Allen and Unwin, 1986), 195.

First, emancipatory movements, including the movement for the liberation of wo/men, fight not for equal rights so that wo/men may become like privileged men but for the rights, responsibilities, and privileges of equal citizenship that legitimately belong to them but are denied to them in democratic-capitalist kyriarchy. Emancipatory movements are discursive communities founded on democratic rights and values, calling exclusions into question and establishing claims to authority and dignity for people without rights. In the last decades the feminist wo/men's liberation movement in society and religion has been one of the most vital examples of such an emancipatory countermovement. It has constituted itself as an open forum for the analysis of kyriarchal oppression and the articulation of wo/men's interests and hopes. However, to the extent that feminist movements have presented themselves as a unified oppositional front and articulated a universalizing critique of sexism from the standpoint of "woman," they have always been in danger of constituting a feminist counter-public as the hegemonic territory of privileged white Western women.

Second, oppositional discourses like feminist theory and the*logy are not independent of the dominant discourses of the kyriarchal societies, churches, and institutions in which they live. On the contrary, they are inevitably entangled in their kyriarchal discourses to the extent that they are conditioned by them. The revived feminist theory and the*logy of the feminine is thus closely interlinked with the kyriarchal ideology of domination that "naturalizes" and reifies biological gender differences, as if gender definitions were the same in all situations and locations for all wo/men.

Hand in hand with the kyriarchal ideologies of gender difference, oppositional discourses of the feminine inculcate the idea that gender and race are "natural" categories, since they make gender and racial differences appear as "real" and "ordinary." This is achieved by attributing deep symbolic significance for our lives to "biological differences" instead of trying to "denaturalize" and demystify such differences as sociopolitical and religious constructs. Instead of universalizing the characteristics of the white privileged lady as natural and essential gender difference, a critical feminist the*logy of liberation must seek to create a discursive forum in which wo/men can establish themselves as subjects of political action without being forced to repress kyriarchally and structurally conditioned divisions and prejudices among wo/men. Through dialogue, argument, and reflection, the*logical discourse can help transform generalized kyriarchal identity formations into creative difference, and develop corresponding political strategies for a multivocal and multilayered feminist movement.

Third, instead of regarding kyriarchy as an all-embracing totality that feminists can escape only through the leap into the "beyond" or the flight into a conjectured liberated community, we must, I argue, articulate an "other," alternative theoretical location in the heart of democratic kyriarchy, from where we can name so-called anthropological differences as sociopolitical-religious structures of domination.

The *Ekklēsia* of Wo/men

As I argued in previous chapters, I have introduced the image of the *ekklēsia* of wo/men in order to name such a critical-alternative site in political-the*logical terms. John McGowan's study points to the possibility of such an alternative site when he speaks of the "troubled and perhaps even necessarily antithetical" relationship of democracy to capitalism and emphasizes that only the appeal to the political and ethical principles already inherent in a society can secure pluralism and difference.[17] Democratic principles such as liberty and equal rights are to be regarded within kyriarchal-democratic societies and religions not as rigid formal norms, but as meaningful action concepts.

If feminist theory and the*logy were to understand democratic society or church as a "social whole" that is subdivided into quasi-autonomous areas and has democracy as its social norm, it could conceive a political location from which it could view difference in a theoretically positive way. We would then be able to understand the *ekklēsia* of wo/men as a theoretical site from which political-cultural transformation can be articulated and action can be taken on behalf of a democratic pluralism.

Locating feminist theorizing and the*logizing within the praxis and vision of the *ekklēsia* of wo/men, one can grasp so-called natural sexual difference, similarly to racial, ethnological, and class-determined differences, as a sociopolitical, religio-cultural-ideological construct for legitimating kyriarchal democracy that has excluded wo/men from full citizenship. Wo/men live in societies that are not simply pluralistic. Rather, societies are divided into classes, subdivided into social groups with unequal status, unequal power, and unequal access to resources.

These axes of inequality have developed along the kyriarchal lines of class, gender, race, ethnic identity, and age.[18] Therefore feminist theory must be on guard against further re-inscribing these kyriarchal status differences and divisions between wo/men as positive feminist difference and plurality. Instead, a critical-feminist the*logy and praxis of liberation needs to "denaturalize" and relativize kyriarchal status determiners such as race, gender, class, or heterosexuality. It can only do this if it understands that sexual difference is welded to a multitude of other biological, social, cultural, and religious differences among wo/men themselves and between wo/men.

Thus it is possible to understand the *ekklēsia* of wo/men as a theoretical site where the meaning of wo/men as sociopolitical category and as collectivity can be thought both practically and theoretically. Starting from such a theoretical place, feminist the*logy can "denaturalize" and politicize social-cultural assumptions

---

17. John McGowan, *Postmodernism and Its Critics* (Ithaca: Cornell University Press, 1991), 14-15, 220-80.

18. Nancy Fraser, *Unruly Practices: Power, Discourse, and Gender in Contemporary Social Theory* (Minneapolis: University of Minnesota Press, 1989) 165.

about gender, sexuality, or femininity. Such a sociopolitical deconstruction of the concepts of woman and the feminine need neither repress nor dispute gender differences that have become part of history. Rather, it must avoid inserting these axes of inequality into an essentialist, dualistic thought-framework and thereby assigning them ontological-symbolic significance as well as universalizing their historically-culturally determined meanings.[19]

The *ekklēsia* of wo/men may also not be defined with reference to what is common to all wo/men as "women." Feminist-political analyses have demonstrated that feminist proposals for constructions of a just political order remain within the boundaries drawn by Plato and Aristotle. Plato's idea of a politically created common life that will bring together a heterogeneous population in a hierarchically organized meritocracy is reflected in the liberal feminist rhetoric of negatively determined freedom, formal legal equality, and political participation. Aristotle's confusion of equality with sameness as the precondition for political membership in a *polis is* echoed in the critique and dream of exclusive feminist separatism.[20]

The *ekklēsia* of wo/men, understood as a feminist-imaginary congress, must therefore avoid the exclusivist alternatives of classical philosophy: either formal equality, which does not examine the kyriarchal divisions of wo/men by race, class, sexuality, religion, or ethnocentrism but instead re-inscribes them, or a feminist equality that creates feminist spaces by passing over the theoretical and practical differences between wo/men.

In short, the *ekklēsia* of wo/men cannot constitute itself in the sense of formal equality that does not touch on the continuing kyriarchal divisions; it also may not understand itself in terms of equality as sameness, presuming homogeneity among wo/men. Instead, its praxis and theory needs to create a feminist public space in which equality and full citizenship for wo/men can be pursued. It can only do this by naming kyriarchal divisions theoretically, courageously confronting them, and practically struggling against them, but not by presenting itself as a liberated community. Instead it is challenged to plumb the theoretical and practical differences between wo/men as democratic-discursive opportunities for praxis.

In her book *The Bonds of Love*,[21] Jessica Benjamin seeks to clarify why, despite our conscious commitment to equality and freedom, we accept and live rela-

---

19. Rita Felski, *Beyond Feminist Aesthetics: Feminist Literature and Social Change* (Cambridge: Harvard University Press, 1989), 170. Precisely this critique of an oppositional, genderized identity confirms its prominent existence not as something ontologically given but as an actually existing discursive form that has brought in its wake a wave of different and contradictory political and cultural activities.

20. Mary E. Hawkesworth, *Beyond Oppression: Feminist Theory and Political Strategy* (New York: Continuum, 1990), 156.

21. Jessica Benjamin, *The Bonds of Love: Psychoanalysis, Feminism, and the Problem of Domination* (New York: Pantheon, 1988).

tionships of domination and subordination. After demonstrating the complex interweaving of familial-gender and sociopolitical domination that produces such a psychological process of complicity, she offers intersubjective theory in the place of the construction of a female counter-concept as a framework for feminist-psychological interpretation.

> The intersubjective view maintains that the individual grows in and through the relationship to other subjects. Most important, this perspective observes that the other whom the self meets is also a self, a subject in his or her own right. . . . Thus intersubjective theory, even when describing the self alone, sees its aloneness as a particular point in the spectrum of relationships rather than as the original, "natural state" of the individual. . . . I am not suggesting that gender can or should be eliminated, but that along with a conviction of gender identity, individuals ideally should integrate and express both male and female aspects of selfhood (as culturally defined). . . . Thus a person could alternatively experience herself as "I, a woman; I, a genderless subject; I—like-a-man [or: like a woman]." A person who can maintain this flexibility can accept all parts of herself, and of the other.[22]

According to Benjamin, this intersubjective frame is best symbolized in the metaphor of an "open-bounded space." In my opinion this concept can be applied not only to individuals, but points to a location where the feminist difference of the *ekklēsia* of wo/men can be imagined as an open rhetorical forum, a space that is rooted in the struggle of wo/men against multiple forms of oppression. The *ekklēsia* of wo/men, not defined as sisterhood or womanhood, but as an "open-bounded" space, can give voice to feminist community and historical continuity without denying the existing differences in experience and power between wo/men and those between men and wo/men. Instead of a uniform discursive oppositional entity, the *ekklēsia* of wo/men is best conceived as a coalition of overlapping feminist communities and quasi-independent realms that have a common interest in changing kyriarchal domination. As a feminist open space, the *ekklēsia* or parliament/congress of wo/men is not to be seen as a unified monolithic block, but as a heterogeneous, multi-voiced forum of competing discourses, all of which have the goal of transforming kyriarchal structures of oppression.

An Ethics and Politics of Solidarity in the *Ekklēsia* of Wo/men

The *ekklēsia* of wo/men is located at the intersection of a number of public feminist discourses and a site of disputed sociopolitical contradictions, feminist alternatives, and still unrealized possibilities. Hence, it requires a rhetorical—not a

---

22. Ibid., 19-20, 113.

scientific—positivistic conceptualization of feminist theory and the*logy.[23] To constitute *ekklēsia* as a discursive, public, and democratic forum that can conceptualize "woman" as a political-historical category, feminist the*logical discourses must simultaneously employ different rhetorical strategies and at the same time move back and forth among them instead of regarding such strategies as rigid, contradictory positions that are mutually exclusive. I suggest as such important feminist the*logical strategies the following: the rhetoric of liberation, the rhetoric of differences and not merely difference, the rhetoric of solidarity, and the rhetoric of vision.

Feminist theoretical discourses can best be understood in the sense of classical deliberative rhetoric. Such a rhetoric seeks to persuade democratic assemblies and weigh arguments in order to reach decisions for the good of the *ekklēsia*. Feminist the*logy and strategy must, for example, mediate between arguments for the eternal feminine or exclusive sisterhood and arguments for the historical-political particularity of wo/men that at the same time keep in mind class, race, gender, ethnic identity, and sexual preference. Such a reasoning together in the *ekklēsia* of wo/men, in the context of diverse struggles and political coalitions, can recognize different discursive feminist voices expressed in a multitude of intellectual visions and competing interest groups.

When different feminist publics formulate their analyses, presuppositions, and strategies in different ways, it is necessary to discuss and adjudicate such competing feminist definitions of reality and alternative constructions of symbolic worlds. Competing feminist analyses of kyriarchal reality and diverging articulations of feminist goals and utopias are not simply true or false. They should not be understood as doctrinaire positions, but must be judged as strategic proposals for action. As a form of such rhetorical interventions, feminist the*logy needs public discussion and evaluation if it is not to degenerate into dogmatic sectarianism. If there is no single feminist strategy and no single correct position, but only a multitude of feminist strategies and discourses, feminist the*logy and praxis must be embodied in and through responsible debates and pragmatic solutions.

The *ekklēsia* of wo/men can make available such multilingual feminist discourses in which individual wo/men can bring their own histories into dialogue with the histories of contemporary, historical, or biblical wo/men. Such discourses must make visible and audible the wo/men who until now, even in feminist discourses, have not been sufficiently present. Only when they insist on the theoretical and practical audibility of wo/men of color, lesbians, old, poor, differently abled, or foreign wo/men can feminist theory and the*logy make it clear that wo/men have no unified female nature, but represent a historically-developed cultural and religious multiplicity, not only as groups but also as

---

23. See my book, *But She Said: Feminist Practices of Biblical Interpretation* (Boston: Beacon, 1992).

individuals. Thus, for example, many American wo/men have not only African, but also European, Native American, and Asian ancestry. Finally, the feminist discourse of the *ekklēsia* of wo/men must see to it that it does not represent a particular group of wo/men—such as lesbians—as a monolithic and undifferentiated entity free of contradictory interests, values, and conflicts.[24]

In short, such a conceptualization of the *ekklēsia* of wo/men as a democratic-feminist forum for practical deliberation and responsible choice need not repress the debates over different theoretical approaches and strategies, but can evoke and cultivate such debates. Instead of sweeping theoretical-practical differences under the table as something divisive in the wo/men's liberation movement, we must foster a culture of debate that can show how feminist positions and arguments are intertwined with dominant discourses or are connected to conflicting needs of subgroups within the wo/men's movements. By constantly arousing friendly criticism, discussion, and confrontation, the *ekklēsia* of wo/men can seek better strategies and more persuasive visions in order to prevent systemic-kyriarchal divisions and create a better feminist reality. By clarifying and judging disputed concepts and presuppositions, feminist discourses of liberation can advance a long process of ethical reflection and practical solidarity in different, often competing feminist groups.

The development of an ethics and politics of solidarity is important for the dialogical and strategic praxis of the *ekklēsia* of wo/men because its various subgroups differ not only in terms of race, class, culture, or religion but also in terms of diverse institutional positions, professional education, and confessional convictions.[25] Hence, they can appeal to a broad spectrum of theoretical approaches. Since such a feminist-rhetorical praxis engenders different theoretical and strategic strategies, such differences must not degenerate into a crippling pluralism that can put forward even the most reactionary policies as feminist. An ethic of solidarity must clearly name especially those kyriarchal contexts of domination that are inscribed in its own discourses and strategies. It must formulate feminist criteria of judgment and evaluation that favor the theories and strategies of those feminists who speak out of the daily experience of the self-multiplying kyriarchal structures of oppression.

If there is not just one single correct feminist position but a multitude of feminist discursive possibilities for action, a feminist ethics and politics of solidarity cannot consist of uncritical agreement. Rather, it must be realized in responsible debate and practical judgment. In its dialogical evaluations of ethical-political possibilities for action it should prove equal to the test by not only deciding what

---

24. Elizabeth Frances White, "Africa on My Mind: Gender, Counter Discourse, and African-American Nationalism," *JWH* 2/1 (1990): 87.

25. Rita Felski, *Beyond Feminist Aesthetics*, 171.

the best course of action may be but also what is best in a particular situation and for a particular group of wo/men.

A feminist ethics and politics of solidarity therefore presupposes that wo/men must have full authority of democratic action and self-determination as a *conditio sine qua non*. Wo/men have the right and the power to interpret their own reality and determine their own goals. But no group of wo/men may claim to speak for all wo/men. The interests of feminists who are in conflict with one another must be expressed in public discussion and evaluated so that strategies of solidarity between wo/men can be forged. The *ekklēsia* of wo/men needs at the same time to examine critically its own discursive practices in order to assure the self-determination of individual wo/men and feminist subgroups. What voices may speak? What voices are never raised or never heard? Who may speak, what stories are still to be told, and what suggestions are still to be made? Acknowledging mutually contradictory interests as valid can mean for white Western feminists that they need to surrender power. In short, the *ekklēsia* of wo/men seeks to create models for how people can work together in complex situations and power relationships without mutual exploitation.

Positively, a feminist ethics and politics of solidarity seeks to develop a multifaceted consciousness of liberation that seeks to get to the roots of the multiplicative intersections of kyriarchal hegemony both in dominant society and in liberation movements themselves in order to call these intersections into question. It insists that wo/men, who suffer under multiple structures of oppression, are not only victims, but also have developed strategies for daily resistance. At the same time it challenges the glorification of the victimized "other" and the romanticizing of wo/men of color or poor wo/men—a romanticizing that is so typical of Western privileged wo/men.

As a radical democratic *ekklēsia*, feminists of different cultural backgrounds can work together as individuals without always having to speak as representatives of their race, class, culture, or religion. An ethics and politics of solidarity therefore seeks to advance respect and "befriending" between wo/men, but does not base this on the "natural" solidarity of womanhood or the feminist friendship of sisterhood. If ultimately it is not gender and biology, but historical experience and struggles against kyriarchal domination that are constitutive for the discovery of feminist identity in the *ekklēsia* of wo/men, an ethics and politics of solidarity needs to pay attention to how we tell our stories and how we write the history of wo/men.

I began this chapter with a reference to Adrienne Rich's poem "Heroines," but even that poem by a famous American feminist tells the story of feminist struggles for transformation as the history of white privileged wo/men. The original inhabitants of America, the African slaves, and the white immigrants from the European lower classes appear only as victims. Even in feminist reconstructions of history the wo/men who have struggled for equal rights as wo/men and also as Africans, immigrants, poor, or natives are largely absent.

Into this historical silence must be spoken the visions and struggles of marginalized or silenced wo/men, if the feminism of white, privileged wo/men is to move beyond its dualistic "gender imprisonment" and complicity. I want therefore to conclude with a speech by the African American feminist Anna Julia Cooper, who expresses such an inclusive vision that leads us into the open-bounded space of the *ekklēsia* of wo/men.

> Now, I think if I could crystallize the sentiment of my constituency, and deliver it as a message to this congress of women, it would be something like this: Let woman's claim be as broad in the concrete as in the abstract. We take our stand on the solidarity of humanity, the oneness of life, and the unnaturalness and injustice of all special favoritisms, whether of sex, race, country, or condition. If one link of the chain be broken, the chain is broken. . . . We want, then, as toilers for the universal triumph of justice and human rights, to go to our homes from this Congress, demanding an entrance not through a gateway for ourselves, our race, our sex, or our sect, but [through] a grand highway for humanity. The colored woman feels that woman's cause is one and universal; and that not till the image of God, whether in parian or ebony, is sacred and inviolable; not till race, color, sex, and condition are seen as the accidents, and not the substance of life; not till the universal title of humanity to life, liberty, and the pursuit of happiness is conceded to be inalienable to all; not till then is woman's lesson taught and woman's cause won—not the white woman's, nor the black woman's, nor the red woman's, but the cause of every man and of every woman who has writhed silently under a mighty wrong. Woman's wrongs are thus indissolubly linked with all undefended woe, and the acquirement of her "rights" will mean the final triumph of all right over might, the supremacy of the moral forces of reason, and justice, and love in the government of the nations of earth.[26]

---

26. Anna Julia Cooper, "The Intellectual Progress of the Colored Women in the United States since the Emancipation Proclamation," address to the World Congress of Representative Women (1893) in *The Voice of Anna Julia Cooper*, ed. Charles Lemert and Esme Bhan (Oxford: Rowman and Littlefield, 1998), 204-5.

5

Ties That Bind

Violence against Wo/men[1]

Domestic violence[2] is at the heart of patri-kyriarchal relations of oppression. Violence against wo/men and their children remains all-pervasive. It is not limited to one specific class, geographical area, or type of persons. Rather it cuts across social differences and status lines: white and black, rich and poor, Asian and European, Hispanic and Anglo-Saxon, urban and rural, religious and secular, professional and illiterate, heterosexual and lesbian, able-bodied and differently abled, young and old wo/men face daily violence in North America and across the world because they are wo/men. In a poem published almost forty years ago, the African American writer Ntozake Shange summed up this life-threatening danger in which wo/men of all classes, races, religions, and cultures find themselves caught up daily:

> Every three minutes a woman is beaten,
> every five minutes a woman is raped
> every ten minutes a little girl is molested.
> Every day women's bodies are found
> in alleys and bedrooms/at the top of the stairs . . .[3]

---

1. This is the published version of a talk given at the Intercontinental Women's Dialogue on Violence against Women of the Ecumenical Association of Third World Theologians in June 1995. It was published in *Voices from the Third World* 18/1 (1995), 122–67.

2. Ann Jones, *Next Time She Will Be Dead* (Boston: Beacon, 1993) problematizes the expression "domestic violence" as insinuating "domesticated violence." However, I would argue that the concept of domestic violence underscores that the patri-kyriarchal household—the paradigm of society, religion, and state—produces, sustains, and legitimates violence against wo/men.

3. "With no immediate cause" in Ntozake Shange, *Nappy Edges* (New York: St. Martin's, 1972).

In the intervening years feminist work has documented and analyzed the multifarious forms of violent attacks against wo/men just because they are wo/men.[4] Such violence can take many forms and the list of abuse is endless: sexual and domestic abuse,[5] child pornography, sexual harassment in schools and jobs, lesbian bashing, right-wing neo-Nazi terror against wo/men,[6] eating disorders, psychiatric hospitalization, battered wo/men and children, incest, homelessness, poverty, intellectual colonization, spiritual exploitation, refusal of wo/men's equal rights, HIV, impoverishment of widows and older wo/men, sexual abuse of the mentally ill, mistreatment of illegal aliens and imprisoned and disabled persons, emotional violence in all forms, cosmetic surgery, strip search and prison rape, sex clinics, forced sterilization, welfare harassment, surrogacy, incarceration of pregnant wo/men with substance abuse, witch burning, stranger rape, rape in marriage, acquaintance rape, food deprivation, serial murder, sadomasochism, soft and hard pornography, sexual objectification, psychiatric dehumanization, femicide.

Despite the legislative Violence against Women Act and government offices to implement the law, wo/men still experience the same violence as twenty years ago when this essay first was written. For instance, in her February 2011 report, Susan B. Carbon, director of the governmental Office of Violence against Women, states:

> February marks the 2nd Annual Teen Dating Violence Awareness and Prevention Month as dedicated by the U.S. Senate. Each year, approximately one in four teens reports being the victim of teen dating violence, ranging from physical abuse, to stalking, to emotional abuse to sexual violence. Women age 16 to 24 experience the highest rates of rape and sexual assault, and people age 18 and 19 experience the highest rates of stalking. One in five high school girls has been physically or sexually abused, not by a stranger but by a dating partner. This prevalence of teen dating violence is alarming and simply unacceptable.[7]

---

4. See J. Hammer and M. Maynard, eds., *Women, Violence, and Social Control* (London: Macmillan, 1987); Kate Young, Carol Wolkowitz, and Roslyn McGullagh, *Of Marriage and the Market: Victim's Subordination in International Perspective* (London: CSE, 1981); Roxana Carillo, *Battered Dreams: Violence against Victims as an Obstacle to Development* (New York: United Nations Development Fund for Victims, 1992); Margaret Schuler, ed., *Freedom from Violence, Strategies from around the World* (New York: United Nations Development Fund for Victims, 1992); Jessie Tellis Nayak, "Institutional Violence against Victims in Different Cultures," *In God's Image* 8 (September, 1989) 4-14.

5. Yvonne Yayori, ed., "Prostitution in Asia," *In God's Image* 9 (June, 1990); Elizabeth Bounds, "Sexuality and Economic Reality: A First and Third World Comparison," *In God's Image* 9 (December, 1990): 12-18; Mary Ann Millhone, "Prostitution in Bangkok and Chicago: A Theological Reflection on Victim's Reality," *In God's Image* 9 (December, 1990): 19-26.

6. Charlotte Bunch, *Gender Violence: A Development and Human Rights Issue* (New Brunswick: Center for Women's Global Leadership, 1991).

7. www.ovw.usdoj.gov/messages.htm.

Such violence is not always forced upon wo/men but also can be self-inflicted in the interest of feminine self-esteem, love, and marriage. For instance, in the United States more than millions of wo/men have "freely elected" breast implants. The number of wo/men who have "chosen" cosmetic surgery has increased. When wo/men tell me that they are not feminist or are post-feminist because they do not experience any discrimination but are equal and even privileged, I point to this endless list of abuse. Femicide,[8] the murder of wo/men, is the deadly outcome of domestic violence. Most wo/men in the United States are murdered in their homes by men with whom they have shared daily life. Nine out of ten wo/men murdered are killed by men known to them; four out of five are murdered at home.[9]

The media almost always report domestic violence and femicide from the perspective of the batterer. They sensationalize such incidents but do not bring to public consciousness that statistically a woman is more likely to be raped, battered, or killed at night in her own house than on the most crime-infested streets. At least one-third and probably one-half of all femicide victims are murdered by their husbands and lovers who almost never have any criminal record or a known psychiatric history. Nevertheless, the public perception still prevails that such murders are rare and are committed by hardened criminals or psychiatric cases.

Headlines such as "woman shot by jealous lover" or "woman stabbed by cuckolded husband" make femicide not only anecdotal but also "deserved." If the batterer says: "I hit her and then she deliberately defied me until I had to hit her again," it is reported that he was provoked into losing his self-control. If he says that he battered or killed his wife or girl friend because he loved her so much, the media report it as an understandable "crime of passion." Although the man wages an assault, the woman is portrayed as retaliating by deliberately trying to provoke his jealousy or anger. In many cases the battered woman is held responsible for the problem: her uppity demeanor, her sloppy dressing, her withholding sex or other marital services, her nagging and accusations, her low self-esteem, her indirect expression of needs, her love for her children, her whining, or worst of all her sexual promiscuity—all these and more are construed as "provocative" and hence as a valid excuse for battering or murder.

However, such practices of overt physical and sexual violence are not isolated incidents or perverse behavior but must be explored as structural normative practices. Whether psychological and journalistic discourses, democratic courtroom hearings, or religious morality and biblical laws, they often do not hold

---

8. Jill Radford and Diana E.H. Russel, *Femicide, the Politics of Woman Killing* (New York: Twayne, 1992).

9. *Women's Action Coalition Stats: The Facts about Women* (New York: New, 1993), 56.

perpetrators to be responsible for practices of victimization but presume that the wo/men, either those who are victimized by acts of crime or those close to the victimizer, are to blame. Worse, wo/men victims of battery, rape, or incest often have internalized such guilt themselves.

The increased violence against wo/men and the backlash against the limited feminist gains which have been made in the past decades is spearheaded by very vocal and well financed political New Right organizations which are often championed by conservative wo/men. In the United States the Moral Majority of the Reagan era has been replaced by the Christian Coalition which was funded by Pat Robinson after his unsuccessful bid for the presidency in 1988. This coalition has overcome centuries of religious divisions and has unified old religious enemies by bringing together not only conservative evangelicals and Roman Catholics, but also orthodox Jews and Greek Orthodox Christians. By being pro-family and pro-censorship while at the same time insisting on their own religious freedom, the religious right seeks to restore America to its greatness as a Christian nation and society that maintains biblical values. Today the Christian Coalition and now the Tea Party claims to control the Republican Party. All across the country the Christian Coalition has taken over local school boards and set out to enforce traditional family values in public education.

The common ground of the political right is not just the defense of the "traditional family" but also that of traditional biblical religion that excludes wo/men from its leadership ranks and relegates us to second-class citizenship while at the same time extolling or special natural gifts of nurture and self-sacrifice. Wo/men themselves are often among the most fervent spokespersons of the Christian right. They utilize the methods of protest developed by emancipatory movements in the 1970s for asserting fetal rights, prayer and creationism in public schools, or workfare for wo/men on welfare, and for fighting against sex education, gay and lesbian rights, any marriage other than the union between a man and a woman, abortion, teenage mothers, sex education, birth-control, and illegitimacy as destroying the American family.

While the religious right overtly advocates "traditional family values," its real interest is to uphold the patri-kyriarchal form of the middle class nuclear heterosexual family. In the name of love, this family ethos legitimates the chastizing and battering of wo/men and children in the home, the silence about incest and child abuse, the attack on shared parenting, child care programs, and reproductive rights, and the rejection of affirmative action programs that would guarantee economic justice for wo/men. In short, since feminist movements around the world[10] have challenged patri-kyriarchal regimes that sustain physical, sexual,

---

10. For documentation, see Robin Morgan, ed., *Sisterhood Is Global: The International Women's Movement Anthology* (Garden City: Anchor, 1984).

cultural, and religious violence against wo/men, they have become primary targets for the political and religious right.

Just as the religious right, so also feminists have identified the central role of the traditional family in social organization. But whereas political conservatives and liberals view the family as the basis of social cohesion and societal order that transmits accepted values, shapes national identities, and engenders basic loyalties, feminists have seen it as reproducing patriarchal social relations and hence as the primary site for the production and continuation of such violence not only in the private but also in the public realm. Although wo/men's political and economic roles have changed, the ethos of the patri-kyriarchal heterosexual family has, throughout modernity, declared wo/men's place to be the home, to be supported by and subordinated to their husbands, and to maintain the well-being of the family by socializing children to their proper adult roles, caring for the sick and aged, and overseeing the household.

Systemic Analysis

Verbal, emotional, economic, political, physical, or sexual violence against wo/men must not be reduced either to abstract statistic or to episodic evidence and isolated incidence. Rather, such violence must be understood in systemic terms and placed on a continuum of elite male power and control over wo/men and children that encompasses not only incidents of physical violence but also dehumanizing impoverishment. Most analyses of domestic violence and femicide point out that such violence against wo/men and children is motivated by proprietary control and jealousy which are deeply ingrained in western cultural, political, and religious traditions and self-understandings.

Both proprietary control and love-sick jealousy are engendered by patri-kyriarchal understandings of family. However, I argue that they belong to two different historical formations of the family[11] that operate simultaneously in sustaining relations of domination and the ethos of submission and interiority. This ethos and regime of the traditional family is maintained not only by the power and control of male heads of households but also sustained by the cultural and religious construction of docile feminine bodies and subservient feminine selves. This simultaneity of patri-kyriarchal rule is overlooked when it is argued that in pre-industrial society patriarchal rule was exercised in the private sphere by the male head of the household who controlled the labor, property, and lives of all members of the household, whereas with the arrival of industrial capitalism patriarchal authority shifted from the male head of household to the market place and the state.

---

11. My classification is different however from the division into private and public family forms. See Sylvia Walby, *Theorizing Patriarchy* (Cambridge: Blackwell, 1990).

As familial patriarchy gave way to social or public patriarchy, the state assumed regulatory functions previously confined to the family including greater regulation of marriage, inheritance, child custody, and employment. . . . The transition signalled by an attack on public aid (outdoor relief) and the rise of institutional care (indoor relief) made public aid very harsh and punitive. The Marxist explanation of these "reforms" suggests that state regulated deterrence became necessary to discipline the newly industrialized labor force. The feminist analysis adds that social welfare changes also operated to enforce new ideas about family life. Punitive relief programmes assured that wo/men chose any quality of family life over public aid.[12]

However, such a socialist feminist analysis conceptualizes patriarchal social relations within a dual systems theory of productive and reproductive labor that seeks to integrate the radical feminist social analysis of patriarchy as fundamental gender domination with a Marxist analysis of capitalist class and property relations. The weakness of such a conceptualization is its inability to adequately theorize racial and colonial oppression as essential to sustaining patriarchal relations. In my own work I have therefore sought to articulate a different systemic analysis and to theorize "patriarchy" differently, by exploring the classical notion of patriarchal kyriarchy that has developed in interaction with notions of democratic equality.

Classical philosophy defines freeborn wo/men and children as well as slaves and indentured laborers, both wo/men and men, not as independent citizens but as dependent on and subordinate to the male head of household. Such a conceptualization of patri-kyriarchy allows one to understand not only sexism but also racism, property-class relationships, and all forms of exploitation or denigration as basic structures of every wo/man's oppression. Yet such a mapping of patri-kyriarchy as an overarching system of elite male domination must not be misconstrued as an universal ahistorical "master paradigm" but must be seen as constantly being adapted to new situations. For instance, unlike modern political theory, Greek political thought was not interested in articulating a universal political order. Rather it understood itself as a concrete reflection of the particular sociopolitical situation in the Athenian city-state which was undertaken for the sake of the common good.

The Roman imperial form of patri-kyriarchal rule resembles the monarchical pyramid of the patriarchal household while also incorporating elements of democratic practices. The model of Roman kyriarchy was legitimated by Neo-Aristotelian philosophy which found its way into Christian Scriptures in the form of the patri-kyriarchal pattern of submission or the so called Household-Code texts. The First Epistle of Peter, for instance, admonishes

---

12. Mimi Abramovitz, *Regulating the Lives of Women: Social Welfare Policy from Colonial Times to the Present* (Boston: South End, 1988), 33.

Christians who are servants to be submissive even to brutal masters (2:18-25) and instructs freeborn wives to subordinate themselves to their husbands, even to those who are not Christians (3:1-6). Simultaneously it entreats Christians also to be subject and give honor to the emperor as supreme as well as to his governors (2:13-17). The post-Constantinian ancient church most closely resembles this Roman imperial pyramid in Christian terms.

However, it must not be overlooked that these patri-kyriarchal arguments were introduced over against a Christian communal understanding of *ekklēsia* as a discipleship community of equals. Because of the historical impact of the patri-kyriarchal ethos, I have argued, Christian the*logy and practice has never developed a notion of family and church that would embody such a discipleship community of equals.[13] Hence the much-touted Christian family is not Christian at all but continues the classical form of the Greco-Roman patri-kyriarchal familia.

Feminist political theorists[14] have shown that in response to the emergence of democratic notions, both classical and modern political philosophy has articulated a theory of kyriarchal democracy in order to justify why certain groups of people are incapable of participating in democratic government. Classical philosophy argues that whole groups of people, such as freeborn wo/men or slave wo/men and men, were unfit to rule or to govern, on grounds of their deficient natural powers of reasoning. Such an explicit ideological justification of patri-kyriarchal relations is necessary at a point in history when it becomes obvious that those who are excluded from the political life of the *polis* (the city state)— such as freeborn wo/men, educated slaves, wealthy metics (alien residents), and mercenaries—are actually indispensable to it.

Philosophical rationalizations of the exclusion of these people from government thus are engendered by the contradiction between the democratic vision of the *polis* and its actual patriarchal socioeconomic and political practices. In short, this contradiction between the logic of democracy and its tension with historical sociopolitical patriarchal practices has produced the kyriocentric (master-centred)[15] theory of "natural differences" between elite men and wo/men,

---

13. For a fuller argument, see my book *Bread Not Stone: The Challenges of Feminist Biblical Interpretation* (Boston: Beacon, 1984) and Clarice J. Martin, *"The Haustafeln in African American Biblical Interpretation:* 'Free Slaves' and 'Subordinate Women,'" in *Stony the Road We Trod: African American Biblical Interpretation*, ed. Cain Hope Felder (Minneapolis: Fortress, 1991), 206-31.

14. Susan Moller Okin, *Women in Western Political Thought* (Princeton: University Press, 1979); Page duBois, *Centaurs and Amazons and the Pre-History of the Great Chain of Being* (Ann Arbor: University of Michigan Press, 1982); Du Bois, *Torture and Truth*; M. E. Hawkesworth, *Beyond Oppression: Feminist/Theory and Political Strategy* (New York: Continuum, 1990); E. C. Keuls, *The Reign of the Phallus: Sexual Politics in Ancient Athens* (New York: Harper and Row, 1985); and A. Rouselle, *Porneia: On Desire and the Body in Antiquity* (New York: Basil Blackwell, 1988).

15. By *kyriocentric* I mean to indicate that Western cultural ideological frames of reference are not just androcentric. The Western view of the world is identical with the perspective of elite, Western, educated, propertied, Euro-American men who have articulated and benefitted from the

between freeborn and slaves, between property owners and farmers or artisans, between Athenian born citizens and other residents, between Greeks and Barbarians, between the civilized and the uncivilized world.

As the work of Elizabeth Spelman has underscored, the articulation of "natural" gender difference applies in classical philosophy solely to freeborn elite men and wo/men. Strictly speaking, slave wo/men and alien resident wo/men are not *woman*. They are "gendered" not with respect to slave-men or alien resident men, but with respect to their masters. They are subordinated to and therefore "different in nature" in relation not only to elite men but also in relation to elite wo/men. As a result, the patri-kyriarchal pyramid of dominance and subordination engenders not only male-female and male-male but also female-female "natural differences."[16] This different location of wo/men in the classical patri-kyriarchal system, which with the abolition of overt status stratifications in modern democracy seems constantly shifting, still comes to the fore in the different valuations of family and kinship among feminists. Whereas for elite (freeborn) wo/men the family has often been a site of oppression, for slave wo/men, indentured servants, or immigrant wo/men who were not allowed to have their own families, the family has been a site of struggle and resource of resistance.

A similar contradiction between democratic vision and sociopolitical kyriarchal reality becomes evident again with the emergence of modern democratic politics in the West which has articulated itself as *fraternal* capitalist kyriarchy.[17] Since modern capitalist democracy is modeled after the classical ideal of kyriarchal democracy, it continues the contradiction between patri-kyriarchal practices and democratic self-understandings which are inscribed in the discourses of democracy in antiquity. At first, modern democracy excluded propertied and all other free wo/men, as well as immigrant, poor, and slave men and wo/men from democratic rights and full citizenship. "Property" and elite male status by birth and education, not simply biological-cultural masculinity, entitled one to participate in the government of the few over the many.

Susan Moller Okin has argued convincingly that substantive inequalities between the sexes continue to exist because conservative and liberal politics have tacitly assumed that "the individual" or "the citizen" is the male head of the traditional household. Hence contemporary theories of justice assume but do not discuss that this "individual" is the subject of their theories of justice. They not only presuppose the division of the human in two sexes but also assume that the social relations of the gender structured family are just. Consequently

---

exploitation of "unpersons." See my article, "The Politics of Otherness: Biblical Interpretation as a Critical Praxis for Liberation," in *The Future of Liberation Theology: Essays in Honor of Gustavo Gutiérrez,* ed. M. H. Ellis and O. Maduro (Maryknoll: Orbis, 1989), 311-25.

16. Elizabeth V. Spelman, *Inessential Woman: Problems of Exclusion in Feminist Thought* (Boston: Beacon, 1988), 19.

17. See Christine Faure, *Democracy without Women* (Bloomington: Indiana University Press, 1991).

they are not able to recognize the family as a political institution of primary importance for a democratic society. "To a large extent, contemporary theories of justice, like those of the past, are about men and wives at home."[18] Whereas the political-religious right seeks to restore today classical patri-kyriarchal family structures, liberal policies seek to reform the traditional family in such a way that wo/men are better able to manage their work responsibilities without having to give up their household and family responsibilities at home. Yet such liberal policies have served wo/men poorly and hence are threatening to many middle class wo/men.

Moller Okin further argues that a genderless democratic family would be more unprejudiced than the patri-kyriarchal family because it would result in greater justice for wo/men understood as free moral agents and citizens, it would be more conducive to equal opportunity both for wo/men and children of both sexes, and it would be more conducive to the rearing of citizens of a just society. A just family, she concludes, would not only increase justice for wo/men and children but also result in just social institutions and a genderless society that is truly democratic.[19] A just family as the primary institution of society, however, would not only need to be conceptualized as genderless but also as free from structures of race, class, and colonialist exploitation if it should benefit all wo/men and children.

Most importantly, the argument for a just society and family would need to reconceptualize masculinity in terms of equality and responsibility and thereby undo men's need for control and socialization to violence. Whereas in classical kyriarchal democracy elite men exercised the power over life and death of freeborn wo/men, children, slaves, and servants of their households, in modern kyriarchal democracy every man is believed to be entitled to exercise physical control and legal power over the wo/men and children belonging to "his" family, race, class, or nation. Personal and national power is expressed through control and violence against wo/men who signify all who are weak and subordinate. Hence, violence against wo/men is not just generated by heterosexist patriarchal but also by colonialist kyriarchal power.[20] Only if feminist discourses focus on the struggles of wo/men at the bottom of the kyriarchal "new world order," I have consistently argued, will we be able to explore and comprehend the full complexity of domestic violence. Violence against wo/men constitutes the heart of kyriarchal oppression. It is sustained by multiplicative structures of control, exploitation, and dehumanization: the oppressive powers of hetero-sexism are

---

18. Susan Moller Okin, *Justice, Gender, and the Family* (New York: Basic, 1989), 13.
19. See her closing chapter, 170-86.
20. For such a distinction, see my books *Discipleship of Equals: A Feminist Ekklēsia-logy of Liberation* (New York: Crossroad, 1993) and *But She Said: Feminist Practices of Interpretation* (Boston: Beacon, 1992).

multiplied by racism, poverty, cultural imperialism, war, militarist colonialism, homophobia, and religious fundamentalism.

The Kyriarchal Love Ethic and Its Disciplining Practices

Since in modernity wo/men are no longer forced to marry, one could argue that they are free to choose their husbands and to determine the number of their children. Why then do wo/men continue to choose marriage and family after they have achieved citizenship in their own right and are on the way of gaining economic independence and sexual and reproductive freedom? That even educated and privileged wo/men remain in violent and abusive relationships shows that it is not just important to change political and domestic institutions in order to achieve a just family and society. It also is crucial to fashion a cultural-religious ethos that is truly just and democratic.

Feminist studies have pointed out over and over again that wo/men continue to put themselves in harm's way because culture and religion tell them they are nothing without a man or without children. Wo/men's self-worth and self-esteem is defined by their being attached to a man and or by becoming a mother. Yet rather than speaking of wo/men's perduring "false consciousness" that keeps them in such violent social situations, it is important to trace the cultural and religious disciplining practices that play a decisive role in securing wo/men's continuing collaboration in and their acquiescence to domestic and sexual violence.

Feminist analyses also have amply documented how the disciplining practices of culture and religion enact and re-enact received gender norms. The Western kyriarchal family ethos and its educational practices continue to socialize girls and wo/men into self-effacing love and feminine submissive service. This kyriarchal ethos produces the cultural-religious understanding that a woman is nothing without a man and that she has to do everything possible to attain or to keep "wedded status." Such cultural socializing practices are on the one hand the genderization of people and on the other hand the production of the "feminine" body.[21]

Sandra Lee Bartky has pointed out that three disciplining sociocultural practices produce the docile subjected and made-up body as the ideal body of "femininity."[22] However, I suggest that a fourth type of sociocultural and religious discursive practice motivates all three of them. My contention is

---

21. See, for example, Andrea Dworkin, *Woman Hating* (New York: Dutton, 1974); Mary Daly, *Gyn/Ecology: The Metaethics of Radical Feminism* (Boston: Beacon, 1978); and Naomi Wolf, *The Beauty Myth* (New York: William Morrow, 1991).
22. Sandra Lee Bartky, "Foucault, Femininity, and the Modernization of Patriarchal Power," in *Feminism and Foucault: Reflections on Resistance*, ed. Irene Diamond and Lee Quinbee (Boston: Northeastern University Press, 1988), 61-86.

that the first three practices serve to reinforce a fourth one in sustaining and legitimating domestic and sexual violence. A systemic analysis of patriarchal or fraternal kyriarchy can lay open that just like race, class, or colonialism, gender is not about bipolar difference or complementarity but about the inequality of power. As Catherine MacKinnon has pointed out, such kyriarchal gender relations appear to be natural and consensual because they are sustained and perpetrated in and through the eroticization and sexualization of relations of dominance and submission.

Such a four-pronged strategy of bodily discipline in the interest of a kyriarchal family ethic is not "forced" upon wo/men. Rather it is perceived to be "freely chosen" for the sake of beauty and love. Yet the *overt aim* of beauty and love is far removed and indeed contrary to the *covert aim* of such disciplining practices, which seek to produce the feminine body as a "subjected," docile, sexualized body, on which an inferior status has been inscribed.

The *first* assemblage of disciplining practices seeks to produce *the ideal feminine body* as a body of a certain size and general configuration. Its regimes are obsessive dieting in order to produce the slender boyish body as well as forms of exercise that shape the "ideal" feminine body form.[23] However, only one in forty thousand wo/men meets the requirements of a model's size and shape, who today weighs 23 percent less than the average woman. Hence, fourth-grade girls are already dieting, half of of high school girls are unhappy with their body by age thirteen and the majority by age eighteen. Such a negative body image leads to erosion of the self-affirmation and self-confidence of girls as well as to the tendency of wo/men to renounce and devalue their own perceptions, beliefs, thoughts and feelings.[24] Even highly accomplished professional wo/men exhibit such negative self-appraisal and self-worth: they tend to feel "illegitimate, apologetic, undeserving, anxious, tenuous, out-of-place, misread, phony, uncomfortable, incompetent, dishonest, guilty."[25]

The *second* type of disciplining practices seeks to *control wo/men's self-understanding and movement*. It seeks to fashion wo/men as passive containers and selfless signifiers of kyriarchal values and to produce the "docile" female body by enforcing a specific repertoire of gestures, postures, and mannerisms as well as by constricting wo/men's spatiality and movement. Wo/men are taught that when sitting, walking and speaking they must constrict their gestures and should not "let themselves go" in public so as not to give the impression of being a "loose woman." Such a restriction of movement in the

---

23. See Michelle Mary Lelwica, *Starving for Salvation: The Spiritual Dimension of Eating Problems among American Girls and Women* (New York: Oxford University Press, 1999).

24. Lori Stern, "Disavowing the Self in Female Adolescents," in *Women, Girls, and Psychotherapy: Reframing Resistance* (New York: Harrington Park, 1992), 105-18.

25. Peggy McIntosh, "Feeling Like a Fraud," *Work in Progress* 18 (Wellesley: Stone Center Working Paper Series, 1984), 1.

name of "graceful" behavior is reinforced through clothing, for example, high heeled shoes—which are again in fashion—and certain forms of etiquette, such as not to spread one's legs when sitting.

Through their clothing, movements, gestures, and smiles, wo/men must communicate that they are "nice," unthreatening, and subservient, in short that they are "feminine." Their body language must be deferential, timid, and subservient. Wo/men who are "loud," "uppity," or "nagging" bring punishment and violence on themselves. They do not deserve protection and respect. By stressing subordination, refinement and helplessness such bodily feminine inscriptions aim to produce the character of the "White Lady." Furthermore, by construing countries, cities and churches as "feminine," such discourses also create a distinct cultural, national, and religious identity in "feminine" terms. Such a feminine symbolization socializes men into becoming warriors in order to protect the "feminine" body of their own people and to ravish that of the enemy country.

The *third* type of practices is directed toward the *display of the feminine body as an ornamental surface.* Wo/men's faces and bodies must be made up and made over according to normative standards of beauty. No wonder that cosmetics are a multi-billion-dollar industry worldwide. These normative standards of beauty are Eurocentric and racially biased. The blond, blue-eyed, white Barbie doll communicates such a racist standard of "femininity." Hair must be straightened or curled, facial and bodily hair must be excised. Early on wo/men have to become skilled in numerous techniques of hair care and skin care; they learn to practice the narrowly circumscribed "art" of cosmetics, and even to suffer corrective surgery so that the "properly" made up woman can appear in public. Conformity to the prevalent standards of "feminine" dress and make-up is a prerequisite for well-paying jobs and social mobility.

Such inscriptions of the body seek to produce the submissive feminine by inculcating the desirability of the hegemonic feminine, the "White Lady." Again and again womanist scholars have pointed out that beauty standards are not just sexist but also racist. The American ideal of beauty glamorizes elite, young white wo/men's features and bodies. The self-esteem of African-American wo/men is undermined by colorism or pigmentocracy which highly prizes light skin and "good hair," that is, not "kinky hair."[26] Moreover, this racist "politics of beauty" compensates the low self-esteem of white wo/men who do not measure up to the ideal standard of beauty with the ideology that they are "better" by the mere fact of being white. Wo/men of color in turn are stereotyped as "dirty, ugly,

---

26. For these terms, see Katie G. Cannon, "Womanist Perspectival Discourse and Canon Formation," *Journal of Feminist Studies in Religion* 9 (1993): 29-31. See also Kathy Russel, Midge Wilson, and Ronald Hall, eds., *The Color Complex* (New York: Harcourt, Brace, Jovanovich, 1992) and Chandra Taylor Smith, "Wonderfully Made: Preaching Physical Self-Affirmation," in Annie Lally Milhaven, ed., *Sermons Seldom Heard: Women Proclaim Their Lives* (New York: Crossroad, 1991), 243-51.

stupid, lazy, uppity, devious, and promiscuous" in colonialist racist discourses. Such colonialist-racist stereotypes of femininity also serve in courts for labelling white wo/men victims of violence such as rape or wife-beating as uppity, nagging, overbearing, or promiscuous.[27]

A *fourth* assemblage of disciplining practices presupposes and works in conjunction with the first three. It is directed toward producing *kyriarchal heterosexual gender relations not only as natural sex but also as personal desire, pleasure, and love.* It not only articulates the gender of wo/men as the sexualized ideal of cultural-religious submission by inflecting the first three types of disciplinary practices in terms of its overarching goal. It also organizes the social relations between the sexes so that for men domination and for wo/men submission become sexualized. Eroticized submission defines femininity whereas eroticized dominance constitutes masculinity.

Not only gender but also sexuality and desire are socially constructed. While I do not agree with Catherine MacKinnon that the sex-gender system is the primary source of oppression I agree with her that it eroticizes and sexualizes relations of dominance not only between men and wo/men but also between elite and subordinated men.

> Sexuality, in feminist light, is not a discrete sphere of interactions, feelings, sensations or behaviors in which pre-existing social divisions may or may not be played out. It is a pervasive dimension of social life, one that permeates the whole, a dimension along which gender occurs and through which gender is socially constituted; it is a dimension along which other social divisions, like race and class, partly play themselves out. . . . So many distinct features of wo/men's status as second class—the restriction and constraint and contortion, the servility and the display, the self-mutilation and requisite presentation of self as a beautiful thing, the enforced passivity, the humiliation—are made into the context of sex for wo/men. Being a thing for sexual use is fundamental to it.[28]

In short, in order to earn the love of a man and to fulfil their supposedly natural drive to motherhood, wo/men must make themselves not only objects and prey for the sexual consumption of men but also define their identity in terms of romantic love understood as the emotional fulfilment of men's erotic desires and sexual needs. To question these disciplining practices of "femininity" threatens wo/men not only with loss of jobs, family and livelihood but also with loss of self-identity, status and disciplining power over other wo/men. This heterosexist kyriarchal regime is not only sanctioned by loss of patriarchal "patronage," and

---

27. See Martha Mamozai, *Herren-Menschen: Frauen im deutschen Kolonialismus* (Reinbeck: Rowohlt, 1982), 160, and May Opitz, Katharina Oguntoye, and Dagmar Schultz, eds., *Showing Our Colors: Afro-German Women Speak Out* (Amherst: University of Massachusetts Press, 1992).

28. Catherine A. MacKinnon, *Toward a Feminist Theory of the State* (Cambridge: Harvard University Press, 1989), 130.

maintained through wo/men's self-surveillance and collusion in the disciplining of other wo/men, but also perpetrated in and through the construction of religious meaning and spirituality.

The Religious Politics of Meaning

The religious right seeks to recreate the kyriarchal Eurocentric society and world that existed before the changes brought about by the civil rights, the wo/men's liberation, and the gay and lesbian rights movements. By co-opting the politics of meaning engendered by civil rights and liberationist discourses, the religious right casts itself as an oppressed and silenced minority fighting for their cultural and political rights that are believed to be threatened by left-wing "political correctness."[29] Christian American style religious fundamentalism admonishes wo/men to display their "femininity" and to utilize make-up, cosmetic surgery, diets, and fashion for seducing their husbands and maintaining their marriages. They insist on the headship of men in the Christian family as either natural or as G*d-given, teach sexual abstinence in place of reproductive rights—and all this in defense of the "Christian" family.

Still, not only the religious right but also liberal churches and the*logies reproduce the sociocultural discourses of femininity and subordination. As long as Christian faith and self-identity remain intertwined with the sociocultural regime of subordination and its politics of meaning, it cannot but re-inscribe physical and ideological violence against wo/men and the weak. Religious discourses re-inscribe the inferior object status of wo/men and reinforce rather than interrupt the victimization of wo/men and children if they do not question but reproduce the sociocultural inscriptions of "femininity." True, Christian the*logy overtly condemns oppressive forms of exploitation and victimization such as incest, sexual abuse, femicide, or rape. Nevertheless, Christian proclamation of the kyriarchal politics of submission and its attendant virtues of self-sacrifice, docility, subservience, obedience, suffering, unconditional forgiveness, male authority and unquestioning surrender to G*d's will *covertly* advocates in the name of G*d patriarchal practices of victimization as Christian spirituality. In so doing, both types of religious regimes—the conservative and the liberal— the*logically re-inscribe the sociocultural and kyriarchal constructs of femininity and subordination in order to maintain heterosexist kyriarchal structures of submission.

Liberal and liberationist the*logies will not be able to overcome their own violence-producing sociocultural and religious discourses of subordination, economic exploitation and political objectification as long as they do not

---

29. See the analysis of Heather Rhoads, "Racist, Sexist, Anti-Gay: How the Religious Right Helped Defeat Iowa's ERA," *On the Issues* (Fall 1993): 38-42.

publicly condemn the institutionalized structures of heterosexist kyriarchal "Christian" family and church that jeopardize the survival of wo/men who struggle at the bottom of the sociocultural and economic-political pyramid of domination. As long as such structural change does not take place, Christian the*logies will continue to collude in practices of physical and spiritual violence against wo/men.

Feminist the*logical work on violence against wo/men and child abuse[30] has pointed to four key traditional the*logical discourses that are major roadblocks in the way of abused wo/men and children who seek to change their violent situations.

First, as I have argued in the first section of this paper, the Western *socio-politics of subordination* has its roots in Greek philosophy and Roman law and is mediated through Jewish, Islamic and Christian Scriptures. Especially, the so-called Household Code texts trajectory inscribed in the Christian Testament has mediated these kyriarchal discourses of subordination, which demand submission and obedience not only from freeborn wo/men, wives and children, but also from servants, slaves and barbarians—both wo/men and men. This scriptural ethos of the patriarchal politics of subordination is compounded if it is used to provide the interpretive framework for reading originally anti-kyriarchal biblical texts that prohibit divorce as upholding patriarchal marriage relationships.

It also has disastrous effects when it provides the contextual framework of meaning for the Christian the*logical liturgical language about G*d and G*d's relation to the world. A Christian symbolic universe that proclaims an Almighty Father G*d whose will and command is revealed in the patri-kyriarchal texts of Scripture legitimates and religiously re-inscribes not only misogyny, but also racism, status inferiority, homophobia and xenophobia.[31]

Not only do Scriptural inscriptions reproduce this patri-kyriarchal politics of meaning; teachings on headship also maintain patriarchal family relations and church structures. The christological doctrine of male headship and patriarchal authority both legitimate the exclusion of wo/men from ordained ministries and make it impossible for Christian children and wo/men to resist sexual abuse by marital and ecclesial "heads of household," by natural and spiritual "fathers." How can battered wo/men or abused children turn to and trust "priestly authority" for help, if it is the same kind of authority that maims and kills them daily?

---

30. See Regula Strobel, "Der Beihilfe beschuldigt: Christliche Theologie auf der Anklagebank," *Feministisch theologische Zeitschrift* 9 (1993): 3-6, for a review of the discussion.

31. For historical documentation and theo-ethical evaluation of the politics and the*logy of submission, see my books *Bread Not Stone: The Challenge of Feminist Biblical Interpretation* (Boston: Beacon, 1984), 65-92, and *In Memory of Her: A Feminist Historical Reconstruction of Christian Origins* (New York: Crossroad, 1983), 243-314.

Second, already Paul's second letter to Corinth refers to *the image of marriage between Christ and the church and associates it with the deception of Eve* (2 Cor 11:2-3). The pseudo-Pauline Pastoral Epistles explicitly link the kyriarchal the*logy of submission with the teaching on woman's sinfulness. They prescribe the silence of wo/men and prohibit wo/men's authority over men by claiming that not Adam but the woman was deceived and became a transgressor (1 Tim 2:11-15). Hence, the cultural pattern of making the victims of rape, incest, or battering feel guilty and responsible for their victimization has its religious roots in the scriptural teaching that sin came into the world through Eve and that wo/men gain salvation primarily through bearing children when they continue in "faith and love and holiness with modesty." This religious re-inscription of the cultural politics of "femininity" and patri-kyriarchal submission has been amplified by the*logians throughout the centuries. Such the*logical discourses of victimization have either stressed wo/men's sinfulness and culpability or their failure to measure up to the feminine ideal of "faith, love, and holiness with modesty." In either case, the victimized and not the victimizers are held responsible.

Third, both Christian Scriptural texts and traditional christological discourses[32] *the*logize kyriarchal suffering and victimization.* For instance, the Epistle to the Hebrews admonishes Christians to resist sin to the point of shedding their blood. It points to the example of Jesus "who for the joy that was set before him endured the cross, despising the shame." Because they are "sons" they have to expect suffering as disciplining chastisements from G*d. Just as they respect their earthly fathers for having punished them at their pleasure, so they should subject themselves to "the Father of spirit and life" who "disciplines us for or good, that we may share his holiness" (Heb 12:1-11). The First Epistle of Peter, which also stands in the Pauline tradition, explicitly enjoins servants/slaves to practice the kyriarchal politics of submission by pointing to the example of Christ. Servants/slaves are admonished to subordinate themselves not only to kind and gentle but also to unjust and overbearing masters. There is no credit in enduring beatings patiently if one has done wrong. But if one does right and suffers unjustly, one finds G*d's approval. "For to this you have been called because Christ also suffered for you, leaving you an example, that you should follow in his steps . . . for he trusted him who judges justly" (1 Pet 2:18-23).

Such admonitions are not isolated aberrations but go to the heart of Christian faith: trust in G*d, the father, and belief in redemption through the suffering and death of Christ. Feminist the*logy has underscored the pernicious impact of such the*logical and christological discourses which stress that G*d sacrificed his son for our sins. If one extols the silent and freely chosen suffering of Christ who was "obedient to death" (Phil 2:8) as an example to be imitated

---

32. For a critical discussion of christological discourses, see my book *Jesus: Miriam's Child, Sophia's Prophet* (New York: Continuum, 1994).

by all those victimized by patriarchal oppression, especially by those suffering from domestic and sexual abuse, one not only legitimates but also facilitates violence against wo/men and children. The work of Rita Nakashima Brock has shown that christological discourses which are articulated within the paradigm of kyriarchal submission "reflect views of divine power that sanction child abuse on a cosmic scale."[33]

Moreover, Christine Gudorf[34] has pointed out that contrary to René Girard's[35] thesis, the sacrifice of surrogate victims does not contain and interrupt the cycle of violence. Rather, by re-channelling violence, it serves to protect those in power from the violent protest of those whom they oppress. By ritualizing the suffering and death of Jesus and by calling the powerless in society and church to imitate his perfect obedience and self-sacrifice, Christian ministry and the*logy do not interrupt but continue to foster the cycle of violence engendered by kyriarchal social and ecclesiastical structures as well as by cultural and political disciplining practices. A the*logy that is silent about the sociopolitical causes of Jesus' execution, and stylizes him as the paradigmatic sacrificial victim whose death was either willed by G*d or was necessary to propitiate G*d, continues the kyriarchal cycle of violence and victimization rather than empowering believers for resisting and transforming it.

Fourth, when preached to wo/men and subordinated men, *central Christian values such as love and forgiveness* help to sustain relations of domination and to promote acceptance of domestic and sexual violence. Thus Scriptural texts and Christian ethics often continue the cycle of violence by preventing resistance to it. For instance, rape victims who believe obedience to G*d's will requires that they preserve their virginity and sexual purity at any cost not only endanger their lives but also suffer from loss of self-esteem. Hence, rape survivors feel not only that they are "used goods" but also that they are responsible for their own rape. Battered wives, in turn, who believe that divorce is against G*d's will, cannot but remain in violent marriage relationships "for better and for worse."

Children who are taught to trust and obey adults as the representatives of G*d, particularly parents and priests, are especially prone to become victimized. Because of such Christian teachings incest victims do not have the spiritual means to resist the traumatic sexualization, stigmatization, betrayal, and powerlessness that lead to damaged self-image and loss of self-esteem. If such victims are taught that it is essential for a Christian to suffer, to forgive unconditionally,

---

33. Rita Nakashima Brock, "And a Little Child Will Lead Us: Christology and Child Abuse," in *Christianity, Patriarchy, and Abuse: A Feminist Critique,* ed. Joanne Carlson Brown and Carol R. Bohn (New York: Pilgrim, 1989), 43. See also her book *Journeys by Heart: A Christology of Erotic Power* (New York: Crossroad, 1988).

34. Christine E. Gudorf, *Victimization: Examining Christian Complicity* (Philadelphia: Trinity International, 1992), 14-15.

35. See René Girard, *Job: Victim of His People* (Palo Alto: Stanford University Press, 1977) and *Violence and the Sacred* (Palo Alto: Stanford University Press, 1977).

to remain sexually inexperienced and pure, to believe that their sinful nature is in need of redemption, and to be obedient to authority figures,[36] it becomes virtually impossible for them, particularly for little girls, either to remember and to speak about sexual abuse by a beloved father, priest, relative or teacher or to recover their damaged self-image and self-worth.

Although their original intention might have been quite different, scriptural texts such as "blessed are the peacemakers" and "those who suffer for righteousness' sake"; "but I say to you that everybody who is angry with his brother is liable to judgment"; "it is better that you lose one of your members than that your whole body goes to hell"; "love your enemies, and pray for those who persecute you"; or "do not resist evil" (Matt 5–6) construct a sacred canopy that compels victims to accept their sufferings without resistance. Injunctions of Jesus, such as to forgive the one "who sins against you not seven times but seventy times seven" (Matt 18:21-22), or Paul's praise of love as "patient and kind," not jealous or boastful, not insisting on its own way, not irritable and resentful, bearing all things, believing all things, hoping for all things, enduring all things and as never ending (1 Cor 13:4-8) make to feel guilty those who do not patiently and lovingly submit to domestic violence, sexual abuse, or ecclesiastical control for resisting such violence and for having failed their Christian calling. No wonder, that those wo/men and children who take their faith seriously are convinced that resistance against violence is un-Christian and that their suffering is willed by G*d.

It must not be overlooked, however, that such patri-kyriarchal readings of those scriptural texts and Christian traditions which might have originally had an anti-kyriarchal aim are unavoidable in a discursive and institutionalized politics of meaning that seeks to sustain and reproduce patri-kyriarchal cultural relations of submission. Hence, if Christian the*logies and churches should not continue their collusion in kyriarchal violence, they must help to fashion an "ethics and politics of meaning" that can engender resistance to all forms of victimization and foster responsibility for changing structures and discourses that produce suffering, violence, and murder.

As long as Christian the*logy and pastoral practice do not publicly repent their collusion in sexual, domestic, and political violence against wo/men and children, the victims of such violence are forced to choose between remaining a victim or remaining a Christian. However, such an alternative deprives religious wo/men not just of their communal support but also of the belief systems that give meaning to their life. It overlooks that religious systems of meaning collude in but do not produce and sustain the sociocultural practices of "feminine

---

36. Sheila Redmond, "Christian 'Virtues' and Recovery from Child Sexual Abuse," in *Christianity, Patriarchy, and Abuse: A Feminist Critique*, ed. Joanne Carlson Brown and Carol R. Bohn (New York: Pilgrim, 1989), 73.

discipline." When confronted with this either-or choice, victimized religious wo/men are likely to intensify their search for meaning rather than to resort to religious and cultural nihilism.

An alternative feminist the*logical strategy for transforming the impossible either-or choice that confronts religious wo/men who suffer from abuse and violence, I suggest, must focus on wo/men's religious agency and the*logical subjectivity and foster resistance and change. It can do so by exploring the *contradictions* between the religious-cultural kyriarchal politics of "femininity" on the one hand, and the religious-cultural emancipatory radical democratic politics of meaning and self-worth in the eyes of G*d which is inscribed in Christian texts and traditions, on the other. Such a strategy attempts to shift the cultural and the*logical discourses on violence against wo/men and children by focusing on the contradiction between the lived experience of survivors' agency and the discursive the*logical meanings that negate such agency.

Speaking from within religious and cultural communities, discourses, and traditions of meaning, such a critical feminist the*logy of liberation contests the authority of the practices and discourses that advocate the politics of subordination and violence on the*logical grounds. By surfacing the contradiction between the overt and covert aims of cultural and religious practices of "feminine" inscription as well as by providing contesting religious discourses as resources of meaning, it aims to empower those victimized by kyriarchal oppressions and the whole Christian community to believe in a G*d who is with us in our struggles to eradicate violence and to foster self-determination, dignity, and well-being for all.

In the House of the Fathers and Masters

In this last section I want to turn to the social location of our own feminist discourses in the house of the the*logical fathers and masters. I do so in order to avoid the trap of objectification—that is, of speaking only about the suffering and violence of other wo/men on the one hand, or that of "guilt tripping," that is, of blaming each other for experienced violence of domination—on the other. Feminists from all corners of the world have come together not only to explore the global dimensions of violence against wo/men but also to articulate feminist religious-theological strategies of resistance and change. Our discourses have to be careful, however, not to project the struggles against violence only unto other wo/men without dealing with potential violence in our own discourses.

This is a unique opportunity and truly historic moment in the development of feminist liberation the*logy, because our conversation is determined by its unique theoretical location at the intersection of ecumenical, interreligious, postcolonial, and cosmopolitan discourses. As such it participates in the ongoing struggles around the globe for wo/men's religious self-determination, rights and authority. We can build constructively upon the traditions and frameworks of feminist discourses to shape a cosmopolitan radical democratic feminist vision. In short, we have come together from different places around the world to face the challenge of articulating a feminist the*logy of liberation that can contribute to the construction of just families, communities, and societies free from violence.

And yet, as my systemic analysis has sought to show, we still come together in the space ruled by the the*logical fathers and masters and in the house built by them. In *The Handmaid's Tale* the Canadian writer Margaret Atwood has given us a political novel that projects into the future a totalitarian society whose kyriarchal structures and languages are modeled after those of biblical religions.[37] The speaking subject is a woman whose real name and identity are not known. She is a Handmaid called Offred who lives in the Republic of Gilead. Gilead has replaced the United States of America and is ruled by a group espousing an ideology similar to that of the Moral Majority in the pre-Gileadean period of the 1980s. Wo/men have lost their right to property and employment; the black population, called the children of Ham, are resettled in segregated National Homelands; and Jews are repatriated through the Jewish boat-plans. In this biblical Republic, reading and writing are outlawed, the news media is censored and controlled, and everyone is required to spy on every one else.

The kyriarchal stratifications of Gileadean society are marked by a special dress code and color scheme. White wo/men are classified according to their gender functions: The wives of poor men, the Econowives, wear red-, blue-, and green-striped dresses, because they have to fulfill all functions divided among different wo/men in the elite households. "Unwomen" are those wo/men who have been shipped to the Colonies because they are childless, infertile, older wo/men, nuns, lesbians, or other insurrectionist elements. The Wives of the Commanders of the Faithful are blue-clad and their daughters white-veiled. The Wives supervise the household and knit for the Angels, who are a kind of military police force. Those who do household work are called Martha and have to wear a dull green.

Similar to surrogate mothers today, Handmaids function as breeders substituting for infertile Wives, since infertility is not officially acknowledged in husbands. Both Handmaids and Wives are supervised by Aunts. As female overseers, the Aunts are expected to control wo/men in the most cost-effective way for reproductive and other purposes. Moreover, they have the task to resocialize wo/men into the kyriarchal family values of the Republic of Gilead. The Aunts also oversee the Salvaging, the public execution of female offenders who are hanged so that their souls are saved.

I have deliberately recounted Atwood's chilling narrative as a warning to us. If we do not want to function like the Aunts in Atwood's tale we must

---

37. Margaret Atwood, *The Handmaid's Tale* (New York: Fawcett Crest, 1987).

courageously address—and it takes some courage to do so—the sources of violence in our very own feminist the*logical discourses that produce violence of wo/men against wo/men. If I speak of my own experience, I do so not because I wish to summon an individualistic therapeutic response but in order to demonstrate the political valence of our conversations.

In concluding I want to lift up four issues for our discussions.

First, I suggest, we must remain conscious that we all speak not only from a marginal but also from an implicated position. As we all know too well, for centuries Christian wo/men have been excluded from the ranks of ordination, the*logical education and spiritual leadership not only by custom but also by law. Hence, in the context of the global reemergence of the societal wo/men's movements in this century, wo/men in the churches also have organized for change. We have struggled for the rights of wo/men to ordination, sexual self-determination, and the*logical education.

From its inception the wo/men's movements in the churches and in the*logical institutions has been ecumenical in its impact, for all Christian churches and the*logies have inculcated and perpetrated the kyriarchal subordination and second class citizenship of wo/men in spite of their organizational and doctrinal differences. At the same time as wo/men in some churches have achieved ordained status, wo/men in other churches have begun to question ordination as the incorporation into a hierarchical-patriarchal class system. Hence the focus of their struggles has shifted from ordination to feminist ministry, from an equal rights movement to a movement for structural changes.

In addition, wo/men in the United States not only have, in the last forty years or so, achieved access to the*logical education as well as become professional the*logians or scholars in religion in ever greater numbers. They also have articulated feminist/women/gender studies in religion as a different form of the*logical discourse and a new discipline of religious studies. In the process we have produced a growing body of feminist the*logical work that seeks not only to critically deconstruct but also to constructively change Christian scriptural readings, traditions, doctrines, ritual-spiritual practices, liturgical rituals and ecclesial institutions. Whereas some have declared Christian the*logy and church as intrinsically patriarchal, others have reclaimed the religious agency, the*logical authority and ecclesial self-determination of Christian wo/men.

Moreover, in the past years more and more feminists around the world have overcome multiplicative structures of oppressions that obstruct wo/men's access to literacy and education. We have entered professional the*logical education, engaged in feminist discourses, and published the*logical work. Consequently, feminist the*logy increasingly speaks in a chorus of multicultural, ecumenical, and interreligious voices. These voices continue to challenge Eurocentric academic postures of feminist the*logy and religious wo/men's and gender studies. They have pointed out that Christian wo/men have not only been excluded and silenced by Western kyriarchal societies and churches. They also have participated in and mediated religious forms of oppression as missionaries and colonizers.

Feminist the*logical explorations therefore must address the cultural-religious image and cult of the "White Lady" that is not restricted only to white wo/men and its function in perpetrating the multiplicative axes of oppression—gender, race, class, and colonialism—through Christian the*logy and mission.[38] At the same time feminists in religion must create and support post-colonial spaces and autonomous organizations where wo/men from different cultures and different walks of life can articulate and celebrate their religious-cultural-ethnic differences and thereby overcome the kyriarchal divisions and oppositions that dehumanize us. Hence, it is more than disturbing that at this point in time North American gender/women/feminist studies in religion celebrate the relativism of highly acclaimed poststructuralist and postmodern male theorists which are sometimes explicitly antifeminist. This trend is emerging exactly at the moment when a considerable body of critical theoretical work by two-thirds-world wo/men has become available.

Second, by now I am sure, some would want to interrupt me and to point out that they are not feminist and that my continuing use of the qualifier "feminist" smacks of white supremacy, Eurocentric universalism, and Western colonialism. The expectation of such an interruption is not just hypothetical but bespeaks my own frequent experience. For instance, it happened in a recent strategic discussion on whether we should go on to argue for priestly ordination in light of the Pope's statement prohibiting ordination for wo/men or whether we should rather assert and develop feminist ministry.

Although the discussion contrasted patri-kyriarchal ministry with feminist ministry, one of the participants objected to articulating our goal as feminist ministry with the statement "I am not a feminist but a womanist." I observed in response that this objection puts us in a bind because leading womanist the*logians would see it as a co-optation of their naming if we used the term "womanist" for a predominantly Euro-American Catholic wo/men's movement. When I pointed out in addition that in Alice Walker's explication a womanist is defined as a black feminist, my colleague countered that womanist the*logians have long moved past Walker's conception without specifying in what way they did so.[39] As a result we spoke of wo/men in ministry, an expression that is politically "safe."

This incident raises a host of important political questions that we need to discuss openly if our discourses should not end in violence against each other.

---

38. See Kwok Pui-lan, "The Image of the 'White Lady': Gender and Race in Christian Mission," in *A Special Nature of Women?*, ed. A. Carr and Schüssler Fiorenza (London: SCM, 1991), 19-27.

39. See the roundtable discussion C. J. Sanders et al., "Christian Ethics and The*logy in Womanist Perspective," *Journal of Feminist Studies in Religion* 5/2 (1989): 83-112.

For many wo/men of the two-thirds world, the term "feminist" designates the wo/men's movement as a movement of white middle class American wo/men that is conceptualized within a totalizing gender perspective. Especially liberationist wo/men scholars in religion have argued therefore that the qualifier "feminist" should be replaced with a proliferation of names and self-designations such as "womanist," "mujerista," Asian/African/Latin American, lesbian, differently-abled, Christian or Jewish wo/men's perspective. Such a proliferation of self-designations would interrupt the gender discourse of white Euro-American middle class wo/men and positively distinguish the particular social-religious locations and hermeneutical perspectives of these discourses.

However, such a suggestion constitutes not only a practical absurdity, since one cannot possibly name all the multifarious, ever shifting, different situations, perspectives, standpoints, and identities of wo/men. It also overlooks that two quite different types of discourses are at stake here. Whereas feminist/feminism has been articulated in critique of the dominant male system of kyriarchal power, womanist and mujerista[40] the*logy and other ways of "feminist" self-naming have a different address and intent. They seek to distinguish themselves positively from an essentializing gender feminism that mistook the experience of white middle class wo/men as that of all wo/men.

Hence, other feminist theorists of the two-thirds world have argued, to the contrary, for retaining the qualifier "feminist." Abandoning the term "feminism," they point out, would be a "mixed blessing" for wo/men in the two-thirds world. Not only would such a practice give credit for the historical achievements of feminism as worldwide *political* movements to white, Euro-American wo/men alone. It also would relinquish the claim of liberationist feminists around the world that they, as long or even longer than white feminists, have defined and practiced feminism albeit in a different key.[41] Instead of completely abandoning feminism as Western, white, and middle class, these feminist scholars maintain that wo/men of the two-thirds world have always engaged with feminism or the "feminist movement"—to use bell hooks' expression. It is more important for feminists of the two-thirds world, they argue, to be concerned with participating in shaping "and defining feminism than with changing the terminology. . . . Since 'modern day' feminism is still in the process of incarnation, especially at the international level, I question whether the coining of a new term simply retreats from the debate, running the risk of losing sight of the fair amount of universality in wo/men's oppression."[42] Rather than to reify "feminist/feminism"

---

40. See the roundtable discussion Ada María Isasi-Díaz et al., "Mujeristas: Who We Are and What We Are About," *The Journal of Feminist Studies in Religion* 8/1 (1992): 105-26.

41. See Barbara Smith, ed., *Home Girls: A Feminist Anthology* (New York: Women of Color, 1983) and bell hooks, *Feminist Theory: From Margin to Center* (Boston: South End, 1984).

42. Cheryl Johnson-Odim, "Common Themes, Different Contexts: Third World Women and Feminism," in *Third World Women and the Politics of Feminism*, ed. C. T. Mohanty, A. Russo, and L.

as a white supremacist definition by theorizing it in terms of the Western sex-gender system, one needs to destabilize and problematize its meanings.

I do not want to be misunderstood here. I do not argue that feminists of the two-thirds world should stop insisting on their own particular perspective and criticizing White European and American feminist the*logical articulations for their cultural imperialism, white supremacy, and exclusivist monopoly of feminism.[43] Rather, I argue it would be politically fatal for wo/men's liberation movements in biblical religions if we were to restrict "feminism" to white Euro-American wo/men and then to define it in *opposition* to Asian, Latin American, or African wo/men's perspectives and womanist and mujerista the*logy.

To relinquish a common name for our diverse struggles and the*logies would mean to exempt or dull our "feminist" critique of our white fathers' and masters' kyriarchal discourses and institutions. It also would deflect and deconstruct the power of this critique by turning its critical edge against one another. In my experience, elite male scholars have no compunction to deflect the impact of a critical feminist hermeneutics of liberation by pointing out that black wo/men are fundamentalist readers of the Bible or to deflect the critique of the patri-kyriarchal family by arguing that Hispanic wo/men value femininity and family life.

This brings me to my *third* argument: while seeking to avoid the perils of gender essentialism and the pitfalls of feminist universalism, I believe we are now in danger of falling into the trap of national, racial, cultural, religious, or regional essentialist identity politics. Since the personal is political, let me again illustrate my point with reference to my own experience. I still feel very uneasy that I was invited to speak here as a North American representative. Since I participated as an "independent feminist the*logian" in the 1983 male-dominated EATWOT dialogue, I also assumed that I would be invited to the present dialogue on the basis of my feminist the*logical work.

However, the organizational structures of our dialogue are such that only continental representatives can participate. This policy has placed me in a very precarious and awkward position. Since I have lived for the past twenty-five years in the United States but have remained a German citizen, I am not able to represent either North American or European wo/men. In my experience, American feminists see me as a German immigrant representing Euro-American feminism in its "purest" form, whereas German feminists have labeled me as representing American feminist imperialism. In *But She Said*, I have sought to theorize and generalize this experience as applying to the positioning and experience of all feminist liberation the*logians in kyriarchal academy and religion who must remain bilingual resident aliens or alien residents speaking with a foreign accent.

Torres (Bloomington: Indiana University Press, 1991), 316.

43. See also the special section on "Appropriation and Reciprocity in Womanist/Mujerista/Feminist Work," *The Journal of Feminist Studies in Religion* 8/2 (1992): 91-122.

Hence, I suggest that my predicament is not just personal but theoretical and political. If I cannot speak as European, or German, or Bavarian, or even for my home town or family, you also cannot speak as representatives of African, American, or Asian wo/men. To essentialize our different identities in such one-dimensional national/cultural/racial or confessional terms would mean to re-inscribe *structural kyriarchal divisions as feminist differences* and to overlook that they also can sustain the oppressive power relations of the fathers' and masters' house. Hence I would suggest that no one of us should assume to represent here a whole continent but rather that we speak in our very own the*logical voice.

We must talk with each other[44] rather than about each other if we do not want to make the victimizations and struggles of wo/men around the world into the object of our discourses and thereby to re-inscribe kyriarchal class divisions. Instead, I suggest, we must attempt to collaborate in articulating and theorizing a feminist liberationist positionality that can address the global changes brought about by the so-called "new world order" made in the USA.

In this global situation of venture capitalism, poverty, and information highways, feminist Christian movements and the*logical discourses together with other liberationist-democratic movements are challenged to envision a liberating Spirit Center of global dimensions. We must seize the "grace" of the cosmopolitan moment and weave together the heterogeneous strands of feminist discourses into the multi-colored tapestry of a common but different ethical-religious vision. For doing so, we need to steadfastly focus on the wo/men at the bottom of the global kyriarchal pyramid of oppression and honor the subjugated knowledges of every wo/man around the globe. The postcolonial moment demands the transformation of Eurocentric cultural canons and North-American political hegemony. It aims to discover silenced traditions and subjugated knowledges, and seeks to celebrate ethnic-cultural-religious pluralism. This post-colonial moment, however, is in danger of being subverted by the capitalist processes of economic and cultural colonization, religious fundamentalism, ethnic cleansing, and divisive balkanization.

In order to speak to the postmodern situation that relativizes all universal claims to justice and liberation, we must recognize and affirm that we all are privileged. The mere fact that we can engage in a the*logical discourse bespeaks this fact. Only if we relinquish the "ladylike" claim to political innocence, moral purity, helpless victimhood, and spiritual powerlessness will we be able to articulate a the*-ethical vision and intellectual-religious strategy that can undermine and subvert the dehumanizing tendencies of global colonization. In short we must be very careful to break out of our kyriarchally constructed positionality and frame of reference. Otherwise we will not be able to articulate a spiritual

---

44. See the excellent article by Ann duCille, "The Occult of True Black Womanhood: Critical Demeanor and Black Feminist Studies," *Signs* 19/3 (1994): 591-629.

feminist vision that affirms and defends the dignity, self-determination, human rights, and well-being of every wo/man around the globe.

Fourth, liberation the*logies of all colors and persuasions have driven home that it is a sign of oppression and dehumanization not to have a written history and known heritage. Hence, a primary goal of feminist scholars should be to create and safeguard our own the*logical traditions and history of intellectual, social, political, religious struggles. More than a decade ago, the Australian feminist Dale Spender documented how patriarchy works to make disappear from historical consciousness the thought, knowledge, and intellectual work that is produced by wo/men. Consequently, every other generation of wo/men must reinvent the feminist intellectual wheel. Wo/men and not just male scholars foster such a disappearance and silencing of feminist traditions, innovative theories, creative art and the*logical insights. They do so by subscribing to a "double" intellectual standard because "it is still a deeply entrenched conviction that intellectual competence cannot coexist with 'femininity.'"[45]

One can detect such a "double" standard, for instance, in feminist literature which uses established or acclaimed male scholarship for challenging and criticizing feminist work. In religious studies such scholarship takes an apologetic turn when it defends canonical biblical texts, ecclesiastical traditions, or kyriarchal intellectual frameworks over against their feminist critics. Many wo/men scholars, for instance, eagerly give credit to and elaborate on the traditions and theoretical frameworks of their intellectual "masters" or religious "fathers." Yet they do not accord the same treatment to those of wo/men scholars. Rather than proudly continuing or critically correcting existing feminist intellectual traditions and building on their theoretical frameworks, they often do not know, appreciate, or give credit to extant feminist work. In order to claim creativity and originality many wo/men scholars still feel compelled to prove that they are "firsts." They do not recognize that political creativity and originality is only possible if one consciously builds on existing feminist intellectual work in religious studies and firmly locates one's work within ongoing feminist the*logical traditions and discourses.

In her response to my chapter on the*logical education in *But She Said*, Susan Brooks Thistlethwaite has pointed out that many battered and sexually abused wo/men turn to religious or the*logical studies. They/we know all too well the violence that wo/men encounter when we step out of our "feminine" places and roles. They/we therefore are to heed the warning signals given by the fathers and masters of the*logical education, to play by their rules and not to assert feminist questions, arguments, and knowledges. Hence many wo/men academics who have entered the university through the doors opened by feminists are eager to distance themselves from the feminist movement.

---

45. Dale Spender, *Women of Ideas (And What Men Have Done to Them)* (London: ARK, 1983), 27.

Consciously or not, they often function like the Aunts in Atwood's republic, as defenders of kyriarchal epistemology or religious doctrine in order to safeguard the academic or ecclesiastical "privilege" of the "White Lady." Yet such "Aunts" are not necessarily white or female. For instance, several African, African-American, Asian, and Latin American colleagues have told me that they have been censured not only by their male but also by their female two-thirds-world colleagues for teaching, citing, building on, or critically developing my work or that of other white feminists.

Hence every feminist discourse is under pressure to be like Athena, who was born without a mother and sprang full-bodied from the brain of Zeus. Like some battered wo/men who enact the batterers' violence upon their children, so feminist discourses are encouraged again and again to direct the violence they have internalized as femininity against other wo/men rather than against the powerful fathers and masters of the the*logical house. As Audre Lorde has so forcefully pointed out in her poem "Contact Lenses": "Lacking what they want to see makes my eyes hungry. . . . Seeing usually was a matter of what was in front of my eyes, matching what was behind my brain. I see much better now and my eyes hurt."[46]

In my experience, speaking or writing on violence against wo/men tends to evoke violent reactions because it is emotionally unsettling and often hits "close to home." Hence, we must be especially careful not to blame each other for why our eyes and hearts hurt if our work should subvert rather than continue the power of the dehumanizing and death-dealing violence that is kept in place by those kyriarchal structures and discourses that we seek to change.

---

46. Audre Lorde, *The Black Unicorn: Poems* (New York: Norton, 1978), 94.

6

Christian Anti-Judaism

Prejudice and Accountability in Feminist The*logy

The lively discussion about anti-Judaism in Christian feminist the*logy indicates how much even feminist scholarship and the*logy remain caught up in malestream kyriarchal thought patterns that unconsciously re-inscribe their exclusions and limitations, despite feminist scholars' aim to disclose and combat them as oppressive. Therefore, it is necessary to look critically at our own theoretical frameworks and methods of argumentation so that we do not unwittingly re-inscribe and continue old prejudices.[1]

The Rhetorical Site of Feminist Christian-Jewish Dialogue

Defining the rhetorical site of feminist Christian-Jewish dialogue is complicated and many-sided. In order to do so, I need to crystallize three difficulties one encounters when speaking about Christian-Jewish dialogue.

First, feminist the*logians have questioned the established Christian-Jewish dialogue as such.[2] Thus, for example, Judith Plaskow, who has significantly shaped the feminist discussion of anti-Judaism, has fundamentally called into question the established dialogue, which is conducted for its own sake:

---

1. First published as "Christlicher Antijudaismus aus feministischer Perspektive," in *Das christlich-jüdische Gespräch: Standortsbestimmungen*, ed. Christina Kurth and Peter Schmid (Stuttgart: Kohlhammer, 2000), 56-70. I want to thank Linda Maloney for the initial translation of this chapter.

2. From the extensive literature on this subject, I will mention a single collection: Leonard Swidler et al., eds., *Bursting the Bonds? A Jewish-Christian Dialogue on Jesus and Paul* (Maryknoll: Orbis, 1990).

First of all, I am by no means convinced of the meaning of the Christian-Jewish dialogue. To prevent misunderstandings: as a Jewish woman who does feminist theology I have always worked together with Christian and post-Christian women theologians. Together we have formulated a critique of patriarchal religion; engaged, we spoke and argued over how deeply patriarchy is anchored in Judaism and Christianity; together we discussed what it means to rediscover the history of women and make it visible; and we struggled together to integrate the experience of women into our respective traditions. But these are substantial questions that we have in common, and speaking about substance is something entirely different from just talking with each other. In my view dialogue for dialogue's sake leads all too often to dishonesty, defensiveness, guilt feelings, or self-reproach.[3]

In light of this warning, I do not want to foreground anti-Judaism in Christian women's studies;[4] instead, I want to first look critically at Christian anti-Judaism from a feminist the*logical perspective. Such an approach to the topic of this symposium[5] is justified because Jewish and Christian feminists have as their common goal to increase awareness of wo/men's religious-the*logical position as "second-class citizens" in their respective religious communities as well as to critically analyze the kyriarchal ideologies legitimating such second-class citizenship.

It is important to see that it was not women's or gender studies,[6] but feminist the*logy that has articulated the problem of anti-Judaism. For quite some time, Christian feminist the*logians have critically investigated anti-Judaism and anti-Semitism in their own discourses and in those of established the*logy because they work toward the common goal of transforming kyriarchal religious structures. Unlike women's or gender studies, feminist the*logy does not simply have "woman/women" or "gender" as the object of its research. Rather, it seeks to articulate a theoretical-religious perspective and method that can transform

---

3. Judith Plaskow, "Feministischer Antijudaismus und der christliche Gott," *Kirche und Israel* 5 (1990): 9-25.

4. For the German discussion, see Marie-Theres Wacker, "Feministische Theologie und Antijudaismus: Diskussionsstand und Problemlage in der Bundesrepublik Deutschland," *Kirche und Israel* 5 (1990): 168-76; Leonore Siegele-Wenschkewitz, ed., *Verdrängte Vergangenheit, die uns bedrängt: Feministische Theologie in der Verantwortung für die Geschichte* (Munich: Kaiser, 1988); and above all Christine Schaumberger, ed., *Weil wir nicht vergessen wollen: Zu einer feministischen Theologie im deutschen Kontext* (Münster: Morgana, 1987).

5. The symposium, "Standortsbestimmungen im christlich-jüdischen Gespräch," took place in August, near Basel, on 21–23 June 1998. I want to extend my particular thanks to Prof. Stegemann and his assistant, Christina Kurth, for the invitation to this symposium.

6. For gender research, see Theresa Wobbe and Gesa Lindemann, *Denksachen: Zur theoretischen und institutionellen Rede vom Geschlecht* (Frankfurt: Suhrkamp, 1994); Elisabeth Schüssler Fiorenza, "Gender," in *The Encyclopedia of Politics and Religion*, ed. Robert Wuthnow (Washington: Congressional Quarterly, 1998), 290-94; Judith Butler, *Gender Trouble: Feminism and the Subversion of Identity* (New York: Routledge, 1990); and Renate Hof, *Die Grammatik der Geschlechter: "Gender" als Analysekategorie der Literaturwissenschaft* (Frankfurt: Campus, 1995).

kyriarchal[7] structures of oppression. Such oppressive structures either devalue wo/men as second-class citizens and make wo/men's lives difficult, or they extol "feminity or womanhood" as the complementary, heterosexually defined supplement to manhood in order to maintain women's secondary position in society and religion.

Femininity and gender are thus essential factors in sociopolitical and religious-cultural multiplicative kyriarchal structures. However, one must not overlook that discourses of femininity are continually modified by other kyriarchal discourses such as race, class, or imperialism, and are thus defined differently, so that there is no such thing as "woman herself," or a "female nature."[8] Hence, "woman as such" does not exist; there are only many different wo/men. The differences between Jewish and Christian wo/men, for example, are often greater than their differences from the men of their own race, class, religion, or culture. Such differences are also expressed in language that differentiates between "lady," "broad," "woman," "girl," and "maiden" and thereby articulates class differences between wo/men.

On the other hand, andro-kyriocentric language, that is, grammatically masculine generic language[9] conceals wo/men's existence, subsuming them under the generic term "man," which includes wo/men under male terms and speaks, for example, of Christians, Jews, Germans, Americans, or Muslims, without making clear that these terms refer to men *and* wo/men. In order to make these masking mechanisms of language conscious, German-speaking feminists have begun to write "ChristInnen" or "JüdInnen," with a capital "I," or to speak in English of "Christian wo/men" or "Jewish wo/men" instead of simply "Christians" or "Jews," and to insist in their respective communities of worship on religious language that is just.

Second, it is important to consider the context of the Jewish-Christian dialogue. Like liberation the*logians, feminist the*logians emphatically point out that all knowledge and understanding is contextual. For example, I live as a German immigrant in an ecumenical and interreligious cultural university context that is typical of the United States but is essentially different from the confessionally Christian-dominated situation in Switzerland or Germany. I teach in a

---

7. For the introduction and development of this analytic category see especially my books, *But She Said: Feminist Practices of Biblical Interpretation* (Boston: Beacon, 1992) and *Sharing Her Word: Feminist Biblical Interpretation in Context* (Boston: Beacon, 1998).

8. See also the essays in Elisabeth List and Herlinde Studer, eds., *Denkverhältnisse: Feminismus und Kritik* (Frankfurt: Suhrkamp, 1989).

9. Marielouise Janssen-Jurreit, *Sexism: The Male Monopoly on History and Thought*, trans. Verne Moberg (New York: Farrar, Strauss, and Giroux, 1982); Deborah Cameron, *Feminism and Linguistic Theory* (New York: St. Martin's, 1985); Deborah Cameron, ed., *The Feminist Critique of Language: A Reader*, 2d ed. (New York: Routledge, 1998); Dennis Baron, *Grammar and Gender* (New Haven: Yale University Press, 1986); and Casey Miller and Kate Swift, *Words and Women* (Garden City: Doubleday, 1977).

university whose work is not only inter-confessional but also interreligious, while the*logical institutions in German-speaking countries are very strongly influenced by Christian confessional institutions and their doctrinal controls.

In my university context, the concern is not so much with questions that are controversial in the churches, but rather with those that are scientifically controverted and culturally and politically important. Therefore, a critical feminist the*logy of liberation in the United States that is not restricted to confessional schools does not necessarily need to be concerned with ecclesiastical the*logy or matters of "purely" religious meaning. Instead, it can focus on the*logical, cultural, and ideological criticism. Finally, feminist the*logy and religious studies in the United States are found much more frequently as part of the curriculum than they are in Europe.

Hence, it is understandable that often in German-speaking university situations, where very little feminist the*logical knowledge can be presumed, the critical points that have been raised in debates between Jewish and Christian or black and white feminists are easily misunderstood. The critique of the existence of anti-Judaism in feminist the*logy does not imply that feminist the*logy invented anti-Judaism or programmatically promotes it, but only that it often unwittingly reproduces and reinscribes the internalized anti-Jewish prejudices produced by malestream the*logy. This observation is important because of the accusation that despite its goals to the contrary, Christian feminist the*logy has further and more firmly inscribed Christian anti-Judaism in feminist terms. This charge, which has been made by Jewish feminists, has been misconstrued in Germany by churchmen and Christian male scholars as an argument against feminist the*logy as such.[10]

In the public, more liberal discourses of the North American academy the complexity of the situation has prevented such an antifeminist cooptation of Christian-Jewish feminist controversies. However, even in the United States, male scholars still determine not only the*logical knowledge, but also the Jewish-Christian dialogue. Already in 1983, two Jewish feminists, Annette Daum and Deborah McCauley, criticized not only Christian feminist the*logy for its anti-Judaism, but also the institutionalized Jewish-Christian dialogue for its characteristic androcentrism.[11] In the intervening years, the malestream Jewish-Christian dialogue has paid little attention to the important contributions which feminist the*logy could make to its discourses.[12] Although some male scholars

---

10. See, among others, Luise Schottroff, "Passion Jesu—Passion des jüdischen Volkes," *Kirche und Israel* 4 (1989): 97: "It is simply hypocrisy to speak of anti-Judaism in feminist theology and not at the same time [to speak] at least as clearly of anti-Judaism in the dominant theology, for then the problem of anti-Judaism is used to bump off feminist theology."

11. Annette Daum and Deborah McCauley, "Jewish Christian Feminist Dialogue: A Wholistic Vision," *Union Seminary Quarterly Review* 38 (1983): 147-218.

12. For Jewish-Christian dialogue in Germany see also Marianne Wallach-Faller, "Wenn Frauen die männliche Sicht verinnerlichen," in *Streitfall feministische Theologie*, ed. Brita Hübener

have emphasized the importance of feminist, especially Jewish feminist, research for Jewish-Christian dialogue,[13] the majority have passed over the results of the feminist discussion of Christian anti-Judaism in silence.[14]

Moreover, Katharina von Kellenbach's dissertation shows that the discussion of anti-Judaism has had a very different history in German and American inner-feminist discussions.[15] While in North America this discussion has been conducted by Jewish, Christian, and post-Christian feminists and remains embedded in a broad anti-racist social discourse,[16] in the German-speaking realm the debate has taken place primarily between Christian and goddess-feminists because there are very few Jewish feminist the*logical discussion partners around. Defensiveness, hostile images, and guilt feelings, but rarely constructive self-criticism, shape the German-language feminist Christian encounters. The climate that makes the discussion so difficult can best be illustrated by a witty Catholic variant on the story of the woman taken in adultery (John 8:3-10): After Jesus has answered, "let the one who is without sin cast the first stone," he bends down again to write in the sand. Suddenly a stone flies past his head. Jesus looks up and says: "But Mother, how could you?"

In German-language discussions of anti-Judaism, it seems to be hailing stones.[17] This is happening—so my thesis—in order to prove that Christian feminists are guiltless, pure, and unsullied by anti-Judaism.[18] Renate Nestvogel has pointed to the dangers of such an attitude:

---

and Hartmut Meesmann (Düsseldorf: Patmos, 1993), 269-76, and Martin Stöhr, "Die verheissene Einheit steht auf dem Spiel," in *Streitfall*, ed. Hübener and Meesmann., 277-86.

13. See A. Roy Eckardt, "Salient Jewish-Christian Issues Today: A Christian Exploration," in *Jews and Christians: Exploring the Past, Present, and Future*, ed. James H. Charlesworth (New York: Crossroad, 1990), 151-78.

14. For example, Princeton's "Interfaith Institute" over the last ten years invited scholars to discuss "the painful but interwoven history of Jews and Christians" and published the conference papers. Significantly, neither the first nor the second volume contained a single contribution from a woman scholar, let alone a feminist.

15. Katharina von Kellenbach, *Anti-Judaism in Feminist Religious Writings*, AAR Cultural Criticism Series (Atlanta: Scholars, 1994).

16. See the thorough discussion of the American controversy in my book, *Jesus and the Politics of Interpretation* (New York: Continuum, 2000), 115-44.

17. Elisabeth Schüssler Fiorenza, "Die werfe den ersten Stein: Zum strukturellen christologischen Antijudaismus," *Schlangenbrut* 14 (1996): 23-26.

18. See Eveline Valtink, "Feministisch-christliche Identität und Antijudaismus," and Marie-Theres Wacker, "Der/dem anderen Raum geben: Feministisch-christliche Identität ohne Antijudaismus," in *Von den Wurzeln getragen: Christlich-feministische Exegese in Auseinandersetzung mit Antijudaismus*, ed. Luise Schottroff and Marie-Theres Wacker (Leiden: Brill, 1996). However, this collection seems to contain not a single Jewish contribution that puts German Christian feminist exegesis critically under the microscope from a Jewish feminist point of view. Like dominant exegesis, so also the feminist biblical interpretation represented in this volume seems to remain restricted to its own Christian viewpoint. For this problem in general, see the essay by Eveline Goodman-Thau, "Bibelauslegung im Europäischen Kontext," which unfortunately has not been published, as far as I know.

Analogously to the world outside, our inner world, into which we also see only in a limited way, contains much that is rejected and is not recognized as our own. . . . The anxiety of scholars about the discovery of their own racism is, in my observation, frequently neutralized, fended off, excluded, and rationalized by an especially intensive confrontation with and critique of racism in others. To learn to admit one's own feelings would be the first step in dealing with those feelings. . . . If we do not do it, we will always, with our selective vision, suspect them in others, oppose them there, produce hostile images, and thus participate in the hostile, violent forms of this society that we have also internalized in one way or another.[19]

The feminine need to prove oneself guiltless focuses on others' Christian feminist anti-Judaism, but rarely recognizes and promotes Jewish scholars' positive scholarly contributions. For example, during my time as visiting professor at the Humboldt Universität in Berlin in the summer semester of 1997, I learned that a number of German-language publications on feminist Christian anti-Judaism exist. But I could find almost no feminist editions of Jewish source material or translations of Jewish feminist the*logical works and publications that have contributed to an increased knowledge of Jews and Judaism in the first century of our era. Judith Plaskow's book *Standing Again at Sinai* seems to be the single great exception here.[20]

I do not want to be misunderstood: my purpose here is not to avoid a critical confrontation with the structural anti-Judaism in which we all remain caught up throughout our lives. Instead, my concern is to stress that feminists may only criticize the anti-Jewish "splinter" in the work of others when they have critically confronted the problem of the anti-Jewish "beam" in their own eyes.

In short, my interest is in a constructive feminist critique that will make it possible to name the "pathology of structural theological anti-Judaism"[21] and to eliminate anti-Jewish approaches within the*logical intellectual frameworks that legitimate prejudices and dehumanization. The critical confrontation of the structures of prejudice in Christian anti-Judaism must no longer lead to its continuing reified re-inscription in the form of assigning guilt to others. Instead, I argue with Katharina von Kellenbach that we must do everything we can to replace the anti-Jewish discourses of dehumanization with a critical feminist dialogue culture of respect and appreciation.

Third, a further difficulty results from the fact that German-speaking European the*logical scholarship still does not sufficiently discuss the intersection of

---

19. Renate Nestvogel, "'Fremdes' oder 'Eigenes'? Freiräume zwischen Ausgrenzung und Vereinnahmung," in *"Fremdes" oder "Eigenes"? Rassismus, Antisemitismus, Kolonialismus, Rechtsextremismus aus Frauensicht*, ed. Nestvogel (Frankfurt: IKO, 1994), 50.

20. Judith Plaskow, *Standing Again at Sinai: Judaism from a Feminist Perspective* (New York: Harper and Row, 1990).

21. Wolfgang Stegemann, "Das Verhältnis Rudolf Bultmanns zum Judentum: Ein Beitrag zur Pathologie des structurellen theologischen Antijudaismus," *Kirche und Israel* 5 (1990): 26-44.

the various racist structures of oppression.[22] For example, there is little research being done on how religious anti-Judaism, racism, and sexism are intertwined, although they have been linked in German Nazi discourse. Such a discussion would make it clear that the debate on anti-Judaism must remain embedded in a wide-ranging critical discussion of racism.

If such a discussion does not happen, the intra-feminist debate on anti-Judaism in Christian feminist publications risks overlooking the structural-the*logical racist conditioning of Christian anti-Judaism in feminist the*logy, which has often uncritically mediated anti-Judaism, although it certainly did not invent it. While the ideologically mediating role of the*logy is widely recognized, it is not sufficiently considered that the uncritical mediation of anti-Judaism through wo/men is structurally conditioned.

Since in kyriarchal western societies the white, educated "lady" mediates kyriarchal knowledge and makes it "humanely" acceptable, wo/men scholars are always under pressure to fulfill this role. For example, Susanne Heine, who has repeatedly taken the discourses of feminist the*logy harshly to task, has also accused them of "defaming Jews."[23] Heine rightly distinguishes two feminist strands of argumentation in modernity, one of which, namely the romantic discourse on the feminine, has proved to be the gateway to anti-Judaism. However, Heine overlooks the fact that the romantic discourse of femininity and the ideology of the "White Lady" are not produced by feminists but by hegemonic kyriarchal systemic structures of domination. Especially white, educated "women" participate in the re-inscription of kyriarchal oppression by actively fulfilling the role of the "White Lady" in the kyriarchal system of domination and by transmitting its ideology through family, upbringing, school, church, and cultural work.[24]

Therefore, it has fateful consequences for the discussion of anti-Judaism that on the one hand the intersections of the variegated racist structures of oppression are still not adequately discussed, and on the other hand, that the undifferentiated discussion of complicity[25] blocks an adequate structural analysis of wo/men's

---

22. The exception here seems to be Christine Schaumberger. See her essay, "'Das Recht anders zu sein, ohne dafür bestraft zu werden': Rassismus als Problem weisser feministischer Theologie," in *Weil wir nicht vergessen wollen*, 101-22.

23. Susanne Heine, "Die feministische Diffamierung von Juden," in *Der Feministische "Sündenfall"? Antisemitische Vorurteile in der Frauenbewegung*, ed. Charlotte Kohn-Ley and Ilse Korotin (Vienna: Picus, 1994), 15-59. Heine's article is part of the "documentation of a symposium of the Jewish Institute for Adult Education in Vienna" that took place in 1993. Read intertextually, it is shown its limits not only by the subsequent contribution from Hannelore Schröder on the "Antifeminismus und Antisemitismus Otto Weinigers," where Schröder impressively shows that anti-Semitism and anti-feminism are two sides of the same reactionary coin. But she is corrected also by Anita Natmessnig's measured contribution, "Antisemitismus und feministische Theologie."

24. See Gunhild Buse, *Macht, Moral, Weiblichkeit: Eine feministisch-theologische Auseinandersetzung mit Carol Gilligan und Frigga Haug* (Mainz: Grünewald, 1993).

25. Christina Thürmer-Rohr, *Vagabundinnen: Feministische Essays* (Berlin: Orlanda, 1987).

participation in kyriarchal discourses. Especially feminist liberation the*logians from the two-thirds world have repeatedly pointed out how deeply Western feminist ways of thinking are still racially colored and limited by Christian Eurocentrism. In the United States the the*logical discussion of anti-Judaism seems to have taken a different course because the common work between feminists of different cultures and religions is energetically and critically pursued, while in German-speaking countries almost no foreigners or members of other religious communities seem to take part in feminist the*logical discussions.[26]

In the last two decades Christian, Jewish, post-biblical, and pagan feminists in the United States have articulated theoretical structural analyses, and worked toward a feminist transformation of biblical religions. In doing so we have underscored that in all three Abrahamite religions, sacred scriptures and traditions have been formulated and interpreted from the perspective of privileged male clergy. They therefore reflect neither the perspective nor the experiences of wo/men. Religious prohibitions, rituals and pious practices have often legitimated the*logies and ways of behaving that marginalize wo/men and other non-persons, categorize us as "subhuman," and silence, exclude and exploit us. Feminist anti-Judaism discussions must therefore be solidly anchored in the interreligious, postcolonial discourse of anti-racism.

Important Results of the Feminist Anti-Judaism Discussion

In the context of a broad discussion of anti-racism, the exchange between Jewish and Christian feminists on anti-Judaism in Christian the*logy has brought to light some important issues that are significant for the whole Jewish-Christian dialogue. On the one hand, Jewish and Christian feminists have insisted that interreligious dialogue must address foundational topics of interest to all the dialogue partners. Instead of stressing one's own religious identity at the expense of others and instead of producing guilt-provoking criticism, the goal of interreligious dialogue must be the transformation of kyriarchal relationships.

On the other hand, feminist theory has repeatedly argued that we must be careful not to deploy antagonistic dualisms, since these further inscribe kyrio-centric ideologies. Dualistic conceptions that construct Jewish and Christian the*logy monolithically and then set these totalizing constructs antagonistically over against each other legitimate kyriarchal interests. Jewish or Christian the*logy, in the singular, did not exist in the first century and does not exist in the twenty-first. Rather, from antiquity until today there has been a rich variety

---

26. This deficit of dialogue partners also makes it understandable that Marie-Theres Wacker, "Den/dem anderen Raum geben," 265, accuses me of having given back to Jewish feminist dialogue partners a basic the*logical question rather than answering it. Wacker seems to have difficulties in seeing Jewish feminists as dialogue partners with whom one can conduct a critical discussion and debate material questions, and who sometimes can even be contradicted.

of Jewish and Christian the*logies that may not be reduced to an orthodox-monolithic construct.

It must further be seen that structures of domination politically and culturally condition many the*logical differences and religious antagonisms. Therefore a feminist dialogue between Jewish and Christian feminists can succeed only if it rests on the will to collaborate in working toward justice and in deconstructing kyriarchal relationships. In a world in which global injustice and exploitation are steadily increasing, scholars in religion are called upon to articulate spiritual visions and the*logical knowledge that contributes to the creation of a world ethos of justice and well-being for all the inhabitants of the earth and for the earth itself.[27] Therefore religious communities must cease relegating wo/men to the margins of their institutions and discourses. Still more, in order to be able to contribute their own distinctive vision and ethos to such a global spiritual project, religious communities must cease to define their identity through negative distancing from or competition with each other.

Positively, the one G*d of Jews, Christians, and Muslims calls religious people to engage their prophetic-eschatological traditions of equality, justice, liberty, dignity, love, and redemption to support emancipatory forces for a more just world.[28] But biblical religions are only able to do this if they no longer feel compelled to safeguard their identity through hostile images of the other, or to suppress the voices of feminists, exclude them, and reduce them to silence.

Finally, feminist Jewish-Christian dialogues have insisted most emphatically that every interreligious dialogue must take into account the different power relations and respective contexts of the participants. If it is difficult for Christian feminists to appreciate the inequality of power in Christian-Jewish relationships and dialogues, it is still more difficult for the general Christian public. Anti-Judaism has become a "commonplace" because for centuries Christians exercised power over Jews.

But this inequality of power that favors Christians is not immediately recognized. Whenever I mention anti-Judaism in my lectures someone in the audience feels compelled to point out that the situation in the first century of our era was altogether different: At the time of Christian beginnings, it is argued, Christians were in the minority and Jews represented the religious establishment. Those

---

27. Wacker, "Der/dem anderen Raum geben," 265, seems to assume that insisting on a "global" perspective suppresses the problem of anti-Judaism. But I have argued the exact opposite, that only a broad, anti-racist discussion can comprehend and combat the anti-Semitic character of Christian anti-Judaism.

28. For the Christian-Jewish dialogue from the perspective of political the*logy and liberation the*logies, see Dan Cohn-Sherbok, *On Earth as It Is in Heaven: Jews, Christians, and Liberation Theology* (Maryknoll: Orbis, 1978); Marc H. Ellis, *Zwischen Hoffnung und Verrat: Schritte auf dem Weg einer jüdischen Theologie der Befreiung* (Luzern: Exodus, 1992); and the essays in David Tracy and Elisabeth Schüssler Fiorenza, eds., *The Holocaust as Interruption* (Edinburgh: T & T Clark, 1984).

who interrupt me assert further that it was Judaism, as the apostle Paul, himself a Jew, repeatedly attests, which excluded Christians and persecuted them. This Christian apologetic defense overlooks, however, that during the long Christian history, and still today, unequal power and violence between Jews and Christians have been of an altogether different nature than in the first century, when those we call today "Jews and Christians" could not yet be distinguished and lived as minorities under Roman rule.

The inequality of power between Jews and Christians in the past and today must therefore be articulated as a central problem in every interreligious dialogue. One could argue that such inequality of power between Jews and Christians is a typical problem caused by men. It is true that Christian wo/men were for centuries barred by law and custom from public cultural and religious leadership positions in the churches, and were prevented from participating actively in the the*logy that produced Christian anti-Judaism and anti-Semitism. Nevertheless, wo/men are implicated in the long, shameful, and death-dealing history of Christian violence against Jewish wo/men. Therefore Christian wo/men must acknowledge their collusion in the reproduction and communication of Christian anti-Judaism and take responsibility for it.

Christian Anti-Judaism in the Interpretation of Jesus[29]

Following established biblical scholarship and the*logy Christian feminist the*logical discourses have often worked with the antithesis that Judaism corresponds to sexism and Christianity to feminism, because Jesus was seen as a feminist who liberated wo/men.[30] Although Jewish feminists have repeatedly pointed to this anti-Jewish pattern,[31] both scholarly and popularizing studies continue to emphasize Jesus' positive attitude toward wo/men and his negative critique of "Jews," as if Jews were not also wo/men and Jesus was not a Jew. Such arguments draw a picture of "Jesus the feminist"[32] over against the patriarchal background of Jewish religion that was responsible for the "low status" of Jewish wo/men in

---

29. For further elaboration, see my book *Jesus and the Politics of Interpretation* (New York: Continuum, 2000) and my article on "Critical Feminist Historical-Jesus Research," in *Handbook for the Study of the Historical Jesus,* vol. 1., ed. T. Holmén and S. E. Porter (Leiden: Brill, 2009), 509-48.

30. See the essay by Judith Plaskow, "Anti-Judaism in Feminist Christian Interpretation," in *Searching the Scriptures: A Feminist Introduction,* ed. Elisabeth Schüssler Fiorenza (New York: Crossroad, 1993), 117-29.

31. See also Susannah Heschel, "Jüdisch-feministische Theologie und Antijudaismus in christlich-feministischer Theologie," in *Verdrängte Vergangenheit, die uns bedrängt,* 54-103 and Heschel, "Anti-Judaism in Christian Feminist Theology," *Tikkun* 5 (1990): 26-28.

32. This expression was probably shaped by Leonard Swidler, but the same line of argument is found in many popular and even scholarly publications. See Leonard Swidler, "Jesus was a Feminist," *Catholic World* 21 (1971): 177-83, and his book *Biblical Affirmations of Woman* (Philadelphia: Westminster, 1979).

the first century. Although Jewish feminists have continuously pointed out the anti-Jewish tendencies in the texts about Jesus, Christian feminists continue to reproduce such tendencies, often unawares. The stubborn persistence of veiled or open anti-Judaism in popular and scholarly arguments for the liberating uniqueness of Jesus continues to nourish Christian anti-Judaism.

In her publications, Judith Plaskow has repeatedly pointed to the long history of Christian domination and violence and emphasized that in Christian the*logy Jews are either co-opted or demonized. In addition, other Jewish feminists have criticized not only feminist, but also established the*logy and biblical scholarship for asserting Jesus as liberator of wo/men because of the allegedly poor and lowly status of Jewish wo/men.[33] Although biblical scholarship is fairly united today in the agreement that Jesus was a Jew who did not want to found a new religious community or church,[34] this insight has scarcely penetrated popular understandings.

What I experienced many years ago is unfortunately reappearing even more strongly in the wake of neo-racism: When I explained in a lecture on the Synoptic Gospels at a Catholic university that Jesus was a Jew, to my astonishment a lively discussion broke out among the students. "That can't be," they argued. "Jesus was G*d's son, not a Jew." As I added more and more arguments for my position, a student finally said in frustration: "You may be right that Jesus was a Jew, but the Mother of G*d certainly wasn't!"

German Lutheran the*logical students did not react much better when they were confronted, in a lecture on "a Jewish view of Jesus," with the thesis that scholarly the*logical discourses about the historical Jesus are dogmatically colored and often function to legitimate anti-Jewish prejudices. They argued energetically against such a suggestion, which threatened their self-concept and identity as Christians. Christian identity and the image of Jesus are so closely connected at the expense of Judaism, that Jewish feminists rightly ask whether it is even possible to formulate a christology that does not inevitably inscribe anti-Judaism.[35] They emphasize that the Christian politics of identity and meaning making that shapes the anti-Jewish-Docetic image of Jesus, continues to re-inscribe Christian anti-Semitism religiously.

This stubborn persistence of the anti-Jewish image of Jesus in Christian self-understanding has its roots in the texts of the Christian Testament itself—especially in the Gospels—and is often unwittingly further inscribed and fed by subliminal the*logical de-Judaizing tendencies. However, it must be stressed that anti-Judaism is not simply read into the Gospels but is already deeply inscribed

---

33. Judith Plaskow, "Christian Feminism and Anti-Judaism," *Cross Currents* 33 (1978): 306-9.
34. See, for example, Daniel Kosch, "Jesus der Jude—Zehn Thesen," *Kirche und Israel* 7 (1992): 74-82.
35. For this set of problems see my book *Jesus: Miriam's Child, Sophia's Prophet* (New York: Continuum, 1995).

in them. They were written at a time when the Jesus movement—or better, the Jewish Christ (that is, Messiah) movement—emerged historically in the debates and the*logical conflicts with other Jewish groups.

These the*logical conflicts were always already political, inasmuch as religion and politics were not separate entities in antiquity. These conflicts took place in a climate shaped by Roman imperialism. In such a political-the*logical climate, one of the most difficult problems for the Jewish Jesus-people must have been that Jesus had been executed by the Romans as a political rebel. The Gospels, all of which were written after the destruction of Jerusalem by the Romans in the year 70, codified this experience of Jesus as a victim of the Jewish freedom struggles against Rome in anti-Jewish terms in the interest of their own political-imperial contexts.

Critical exegesis has shown how the Gospels shifted the responsibility for Jesus' execution from the Romans to the Jewish authorities and the whole Jewish people.[36] Since those who followed an executed rabble-rouser were suspect in the eyes of the Roman authorities it was compelling to interpret Jesus' execution as a Jewish political misunderstanding. Such a the*logical-political interpretation of Jesus' execution was formulated as an argument in the conflicts with other Jews and with non-Jewish groups. Hence, all four Gospels not only reflect controversies with the dominant forms of Judaism but they also testify to the separation anxieties that shaped early Christian identity. They continue throughout the centuries to re-inscribe Christian identity as in tension and conflict with other identity formations of Judaism.

The Gospels therefore require a critical rhetorical analysis,[37] since a mirror-reading that repeats the rhetoric of the Gospels without critically examining it cannot but continue to re-inscribe Christian identity as anti-Jewish. When Christianity came to power, this apologetic image of Jesus in the Gospels was removed from its originating historical-political, rhetorical situation and minority context. Thus for centuries, it served as a rationale for Christian persecutions of Jewish wo/men, who even today are still held responsible by many for the death of Jesus.[38] Many Jewish wo/men in the United States tell, for example, how when they were children, "Christ-killer" was shouted at them on Good Friday. If the apologetic rhetoric of the Gospels is taught today uncritically as historical fact, or proclaimed liturgically as the word of G*d, Christian identity will continually be recreated and deeply re-inscribed as anti-Jewish identity.

---

36. See Wolfgang Stegemann, "Gab es eine jüdische Beteiligung an der Kreuzigung Jesu?" *Kirche und Israel* 13 (1998): 3-24.

37. For the rhetorics of biblical interpretation as well as the rhetorics of Pauline texts, see my book *Rhetoric and Ethic: The Politics of Biblical Studies* (Minneapolis: Fortress Press, 1999).

38. See also Christina Kurth, "Der Prozess Jesu aus der Perspektive jüdischer Forscher: Überlegungen zum Vorwurf der Schuld der Juden am Tod Jesu," *Kirche und Israel* 13 (1998): 46-58.

The tradition-history of the story of the woman who anointed Jesus as Messiah furnishes a good example of such an ongoing inscription of anti-Jewish, anti-wo/men prejudices.[39] The Gospel of Mark places this story at the beginning of its narrative of Jesus' execution and resurrection.[40] Mark is probably making use here of a traditional story of a wo/man who anointed Jesus' head and named him the Messiah, the Anointed One.[41] A revelatory saying of Jesus links this nameless wo/man's prophetic symbolic action with the proclamation of the gospel throughout the world. The community that continued to tell this story after Jesus' execution knew that Jesus was no longer in its midst.

Either in the course of the handing on of the story or in the redactional phase, three kyriarchally effective interpretations of this wo/man's prophetic symbolic action were introduced. *First,* in the discussion with the disciples, the "poor" are no longer understood as constitutive members of the community, but rather as objects, declared as "others" who deserve alms. *Second,* the symbolic action of the nameless wo/man is interpreted in terms of femininity: she does what is expected of wo/men; she prepares the body of the dying man for burial.[42]

Third and finally, the story was recontextualized in the tradition (cf. Mark and John) as an "example story" that contrasts the action of the wo/man with the deed of Judas, who betrayed Jesus. The wo/man disciple remains nameless while the disciple who betrayed Jesus is named. Contrary to the words of Jesus, the text thereby concentrates attention on the disciple who betrayed rather than on the wo/man disciple. In addition, this interpretation, inasmuch as it names

---

39. See Robert Holst, "The Anointing of Jesus: Another Application of the Form-Critical Method," *JBL* 95 (1976): 435-56, and Klaus-Peter März, "Zur Traditionsgeschichte von Mk 14, 3-9 und Parallelen," *NTS* 67 (1981–82): 89-112.

40. For discussion of the Markan account, see Monika Fander, *Die Stellung der Frau im Markusevangelium unter besonderer Berücksichtigung kultur- und religionsgeschichtlicher Hintergründe* (Altenberge: Oros, 1989), 118-35, and Joanna Dewey, "The Gospel of Mark," in *Searching the Scriptures: A Feminist Commentary,* ed. Elisabeth Schüssler Fiorenza (New York: Crossroad, 1994), 470-509. For Matthew, see the outstanding analysis by Elaine M. Wainwright, *Toward a Feminist Critical Reading of the Gospel according to Matthew* (Berlin: de Gruyter, 1991), 253-83.

41. See my book *In Memory of Her: A Feminist Theological Reconstruction of Christian Origins* (New York: Crossroad, 1983). Incidentally, the methodological considerations for avoiding anti-Judaism in Jesus research that I presented there have been discussed little in the meantime, although they have initiated an entire direction in research that evaluates the Christian Testament as a source for the history of Jewish wo/men. See Amy-Jill Levine, ed., *"Women Like This": Perspectives on Jewish Women in the Greco-Roman World* (Atlanta: Scholars, 1991) and Bernadette Brooten, "Jewish Women's History in the Roman Period: A Task for Christian Theology," *Harvard Theological Review* 79 (1986): 22-30.

42. Hence such a rhetoric may not be interpreted as a sociological-historical description. Against Vernon K. Robbins, "Using a Socio-Rhetorical Poetics to Develop a Unified Method: The Woman Who Anointed Jesus as a Test Case," *SBL Seminar Papers* (Atlanta: Scholars, 1992), 302-19.

the betrayer as Judas, also triggers an anti-Jewish reaction in readers that will be deepened in the course of the Passion narrative.

Although the name of Judas is not suspicious in itself, the context makes it so here. "Judas" stands

> etymologically in relation to "Jew" (*Yéhûdᵃ*; *Ioudaios*); and thus the one who gave Jesus over could be understood by those hostile to him as the quintessential Jew. Augustine holds that as Peter represents the church, Judas represents the Jews (*Enarratio in Ps 108*. 18, 20). . . . This theological prejudice was cemented as anti-Jewish polemic in dramatic literature and art, where Judas was depicted with grossly exaggerated "Semitic" features and his love for money was generalized.[43]

Thus it becomes possible to trace the depoliticizing rhetoric of the Gospel traditions in the course of the reinterpretation of the anointing story, which originally had the potential to be a politically dangerous story. Within this Gospel rhetoric we can trace back early Christian apologetic attempts to present the Christian movement to Roman imperial eyes as politically reliable. This depoliticizing Gospel rhetoric emphasized the anti-Jewish interpretation of the suffering and execution of Jesus[44] and promoted Christianity's political accommodation to Roman kyriarchal structures, an accommodation that opened the door to the Roman imperial cooptation of the gospel.

A Rhetorical Model of Interpretation

This process of kyriarchal reinterpretation in the Gospels has produced the ideological framework that marginalizes Christian wo/men and stereotypes Jewish wo/men. Since it has become historical common sense, it is necessary to enable wo/men to read the Christian Testament critically, to recognize, analyze, and uncouple these existing anti-Jewish and antifeminist frames of reference.[45] Only such a critical feminist reading can, in my opinion, advance the articulation of a Christian self-understanding that no longer needs to define itself through

---

43. Raymond E. Brown, *The Death of the Messiah* (New York: Doubleday, 1994), 1395. See also James Brownson, "Neutralizing the Intimate Enemy: The Portrayal of Judas in the Fourth Gospel," *SBL 1992 Seminar Papers*, ed. Eugene H. Lovering Jr. (Atlanta: Scholars, 1992), 49-60.

44. For a comprehensive bibliography of the passion stories, see Raymond E. Brown, *The Death of the Messiah*, 94-106. For a critical engagement with Brown, see John Dominic Crossan, *Who Killed Jesus? Exposing the Roots of Antisemitism in the Gospel Story of the Death of Jesus* (San Francisco: HarperSanFrancisco, 1996) and Nico Rubeli-Guthauser, "Er starb, und die Gewalt seines Todes wiederholte sich: Ein Neutestamentler appelliert an das öffentliche Gewissen," *Kirche und Israel* 13 (1998): 25-45.

45. For a feminist discussion of models of reading, see Katrin Schwenk, *Politik des Lesens: Stationen der feministischen Kanonkritik in den USA* (Pfaffenweiler: Centaurus, 1996).

negative distancing from Judaism or seek to justify its identity with the*logical masculinism.

In closing, I want to list here four important anti-Jewish patterns of thought, reading screens, or interpretive lenses that often determine the reading of the Christian Testament in anti-Jewish ways.

The *first reading screen* or interpretive lens does not emphasize what Jesus and Judaism have in common but stresses the contrast between Jesus and Judaism. Thus, for example, it is repeatedly asserted, contrary to all scholarly knowledge, that in comparison to the rabbis, Jesus liberated wo/men from their inhuman Jewish conditions.

The *second interpretive lens* works with the Reformation's oppositional construct of law and grace. While rabbinic Judaism degenerated into a religion of laws, it is argued, Jesus preached the love and grace of G*d.

The *third reading lens* insists on Jesus' uniqueness. The more Jesus is seen as a Jew, the less unique he appears to be. If Jesus preached nothing but ordinary Judaism, it seems that Christianity is deprived of any basis for its claim to be a unique and universal religion.

The *fourth reading lens* therefore insists that Jesus abolished Judaism and founded the church as the new Israel in its place. Jesus fulfilled and superseded the sacred Scriptures of Judaism; they have become now the Old Testament. This reading lens can be seen in the expression "Jewish-Christian tradition," which suggests that there is only one single tradition. Christianity and Judaism are not two independent religions that have the Hebrew Bible as their common heritage. Thereby Judaism is dissolved into Christianity.

In light of these Christian anti-Jewish reading lenses, which serve as screens for meaning making, biblical scholarship may no longer present its hermeneutical discourses about Jesus in the Christian Testament as "scholarly," descriptive, and value-free. Instead, scholars must make it clear that the Gospels are rhetorical discourses so that not only the hermeneutical lenses with which they are read but also the rhetoric of the text itself, becomes problematized. Not a positivistic, but only a rhetorical self-understanding of biblical scholarship, I argue, can keep before our eyes the question of our historical Jewish biblical roots in a way that does not end in Christian imperialism and exclusivity.

In such a rhetorical model of interpretation, Christian identity need no longer be derived from the kyriarchal anti-Jewish forms of expression and their socio-cultural contexts of the past. Instead, Christian identity, like any other religious identity, has to be negotiated anew in light of the (messianic) *basileia* of G*d and its vision of justice and well-being for all without exception. Biblical scholarship and the*logy can no longer afford to neglect its participation in the construction of cultural and religious identity discourses. Instead, it must learn to reflect critically in different sociopolitical contexts on the oppressive or liberating functions of its scholarly interpretations and historical reconstructions.

Only when Christians cease to proclaim anti-Jewish scriptural texts as the word of G*d, when we celebrate positively Jesus' Jewishness, respect Judaism as an independent religion, and learn to understand Judaism and Christianity in Alan Segal's image as "twins" whose common mother is the Hebrew Bible[46] will it be possible to articulate Christian identity in such a way that it no longer exists at the expense of Judaism or any other religious community.

---

46. Alan F. Segal, *Rebecca's Children: Judaism and Christianity in the Roman World* (Cambridge: Harvard University Press, 1987). I am aware that other Jewish scholars reject this metaphor and insist that the equation of the Hebrew Bible with the Old Testament by Christianity is already an appropriation of Jewish scripture and tradition. But this discussion has scarcely been approached or critically treated in German-speaking feminist discourse on anti-Judaism.

PART III

Catholicism as a Site of Feminist Struggles

7

Public Discourse, Religion, and Wo/men's Struggles for Justice[1]

Man enjoys the great advantage of having a god endorse the code he writes; and since man exercises a sovereign authority over women it is especially fortunate that this authority has been vested in him by the Supreme Being. For the Jews, Mohammedans, and Christians, among others, man is master of divine right: the fear of God, therefore will repress any impulse towards revolt in the downtrodden female.[2]

De Beauvoir's observation that male power and authority has been encoded in civil and religious law and sanctioned as divine right echoes the indictment made by nineteenth-century suffragists such as Elizabeth Cady Stanton and has become a "common sense" understanding in contemporary feminism. Religion has been seen solely as patriarchal and repressive, whereas law, education, and politics have not been abandoned as sites of feminist struggles, although their oppressive character has been recognized as well. Rather, this recognition has spurred feminists not only to criticize but also to reform and transform these cultural discourses.

However, feminists have not extended the same consideration to religion. The first part of de Beauvoir's statement has spawned a new field of research, feminist studies in religion, which has shown that all discourses of Western culture

1. First published in *DePaul Law Review* 51 (Summer 2002): 1077-1101. I want to thank Rev. Craig B. Mousin for inviting me and especially for patiently prodding me to revise the lecture for publication. I also am grateful to my former assistant Dr. Laura Beth Bugg for polishing my text.
2. Simone de Beauvoir, *The Second Sex* (New York: Knopf, 1953), 621.

have been shaped by biblical religion, especially Christianity.[3] However, her conviction that wo/men in religion "lack any impulse toward any revolt" has resulted in the widespread feminist assumption that anyone engaged in religion cannot be a true feminist. Hence, societal feminist groups and Christian feminist groups seem often to work in parallel on similar issues but don't seem to know much about or reinforce each other's projects.

This seems to be the case because like de Beauvoir's negative assessment of religion, feminist theory not only has been inclined to eliminate religion from its projects of reform but also has tended to deny the feminist agency of wo/men in religion. Consciously or not, de Beauvoir's conclusion that the "downtrodden" religious female will not revolt against such divinely sanctioned oppression is still shared widely by academic feminists. It has framed the discussion in exclusivist terms and, in consequence, has been disastrous for contemporary feminism's relation with biblical religions, since it denies the feminist agency of wo/men who remain loyal members of Judaism, Christianity or Islam. If wo/men who remain active members in biblical and other religions suffer from "false consciousness," it is surmised they cannot really be true feminists.

Religion and the Reform of Society

As noted previously, Jewish feminist the*logian Judith Plaskow has pointed to the widespread suspicion in women's studies that anyone interested in religion must be either co-opted or reactionary, and she has argued that such feminist suspicion is not justified.[4] Much of the work of feminist studies in religion has been generated by and for grass roots wo/men in and outside organized religions that search for a feminist spirituality and politics of meaning for their lives. Conversely, feminist scholars in religion for the most part have continued to be practically involved and to participate either in traditional religious groups, in wo/men-church groups, or in Goddess and spirituality movements that have critically challenged and enriched biblical articulations and religious formations.[5]

First, a similar argument that feminists ignore religion to their detriment was already made in the nineteenth century by Elizabeth Cady Stanton who advanced a multidimensional political argument. In an article published in the *Woman's Tribune* on February 7, 1891, she maintained a fourfold segmentation of the American social order into the areas of family, society, politics, and religion. By comparing

---

3. For legal studies, see Angela L. Padilla and Jennifer Winrich, "Christianity, Feminism, and the Law," *Columbia Journal of Gender and Law* 1/1 (1991): 67-116.
4. See also Michelle Lelwica, "From Superstition to Enlightenment to the Race for Pure Consciousness," and the responses by Amy Richlin and Martha Ackelsberg in *JFSR* 14/2 (1998).
5. Judith Plaskow, "We Are Also Your Sisters: The Development of Women's Studies in Religion," *Women's Studies Quarterly* 20/1 (1993): 9-21.

these four domains to the four strands of a rope, Cady Stanton articulated a complex vision of women's oppression. "Here then is a fourfold bondage, so many cords tightly twisted together, strong for one purpose. To attempt to undo one is to loosen all. . . . To my mind, if we had at first bravely untwisted all the strands of this fourfold cord which bound us, and demanded equality in the whole round of the circle, while perhaps we should have had a harder battle to fight, it would have been more effective and far shorter."[6]

As for Simone de Beauvoir, so also for Elizabeth Cady Stanton: religion is an important strand in the rope of patriarchal oppression. Although in Cady Stanton's view every form of religion has degraded women, it is especially biblical religion, she argued, that has kept women in subjection throughout the centuries. Religion is an element in public policy and in the process of wo/men's socialization. It makes hetero-sexism and the other instruments of dehumanization such as race, class, ethnic and national prejudice appear to be normative and ordained by G*d. Religion shapes not only individuals but also the law and all other public policy issues.

However, unlike de Beauvoir, Cady Stanton argued that no serious reform of society in the interest of women's emancipation will be successful if one does not seek to advance the reform of biblical religion at the same time. If suffragists believe that they can neglect the revision of the Bible and the reform of religion because there are more pressing political issues at stake, Cady Stanton insists, then they do not recognize the impact of religion and the Bible upon society and especially on the lives of women.[7]

Because biblical religion has a great impact on wo/men's lives and shapes American culture, Cady Stanton argued, wo/men must study religion and interpret the Bible differently since it has shaped the traditional cultural role of wo/men. The traditional biblical worldview ascribed separate, specific, and immutable social roles to wo/men in the private realm of the home as well as in the public and cultural realm. It required the subordination and/or complementarity of wives to husbands in the home and of wo/men to men in the wider society. Such subordination is based on the view of wo/men as the property of men. Male ownership is justified in and through the story of Genesis 3 as the consequence and punishment for wo/men having brought sin into the world. These basic patriarchally or better kyriarchally[8] determined assumptions of wo/men's subordinate status as second class citizens are inscribed in the Scriptures and replicated in legal and political culture.

---

6. Mary D. Pellauer, *Toward a Tradition of Feminist Theology: The Religious Social Thought of Elisabeth Cady Stanton, Susan B. Anthony, and Anna Howard Shaw* (Brooklyn: Carlson, 1991), 23.

7. Elizabeth Cady Stanton, *The Original Feminist Attack on the Bible: The Woman's Bible*, ed. Barbara Welter (New York: Arno, 1974). See also the collection of essays and commentaries in *Searching the Scriptures: A Feminist Introduction*, vol. 1, and *A Feminist Commentary*, vol. 2 (New York: Crossroad, 1993), which I initiated and edited in celebration of the centennial anniversary of *The Woman's Bible*.

8. For the elaboration of kyriarchy see the introduction to this volume.

They compel wo/men to be submissive to and compliant with male violence. They foster guilt feelings and self-blame in wo/men who have been sexually abused, battered or raped.

In publishing the *Woman's Bible*, Cady Stanton sought to interrupt the conservative trend in the Suffrage Movement and tried to force the National American Woman's Suffrage Association (NAWSA) to engage in a public discussion of this conservative social trend with its narrow political focus on the ballot rather than on complete emancipation from the "woman's sphere,"[9] as the feminine ideology of the "White Lady" or of "true womanhood" was called in the nineteenth century.

In response to those who contended that a suffragist critique of religion and the Bible was a waste of time or a political mistake, Cady Stanton argued that one cannot reform one area of society without reforming all the others at the same time. Since "all reforms are interdependent," one cannot attempt to change the law, education and other cultural institutions without also seeking to change biblical religions. In addition, she insisted, it is important that suffragists interpret the Bible and redefine religion, since religious authority is and has been used against women struggling for emancipation. Not only men but also wo/men have internalized its misogynist religious teachings as divinely revealed.

Cady Stanton and her collaborators on the *Woman's Bible* utilized historical-critical the*logical scholarship to free wo/men from such false beliefs by proving that the Bible is the word of men who have projected their own selfish interests onto it. Texts that speak negatively about wo/men are either mistranslated, misinterpreted, or antiquated relics of past time, or not true because they contradict the principles of reason and science. Since throughout the centuries men were also the Bible's authoritative interpreters, wo/men must now claim their right to biblical interpretation and the*logical articulation.

In short, against the advice and opposition of her suffragist friends, Cady Stanton asserted the political importance of wo/men's biblical interpretation and religion. Hence, she deserves our respect and honor, although we must not forget that she also was shaped by the limitations set by her race and class privileges and could not quite overcome them. As Toni Morrison so forcefully has argued, racial, and I would add misogynist and heterosexist, ideology does not just have "horrific results on its objects" but also on the mind, imagination, and behavior of the masters who perpetuate it.

Just like other Anglo-Saxon suffragists and social reformers, Elizabeth Cady Stanton was very much determined and limited by her social status and class position. To support her argument that elite wo/men's suffrage would buttress the numbers of Anglo-Saxon voters, she resorted to anti-immigrant sentiments and

---

9. For this interpretation see Kathi L. Kern, "Rereading Eve: Elizabeth Cady Stanton and *The Woman's Bible*, 1885–1896," *Women's Studies* 19 (1991): 371-83.

anti-Catholic prejudice. When she exhorted American wo/men of wealth and refinement, she did not shy away from appealing to ethnic and racial prejudices, "If you do not wish the lower orders of Chinese, Africans, Germans, and Irish, with their low ideas of womanhood, to make laws for you, demand that woman, too, shall be represented in the government."[10]

Moreover, unlike Clara Colby, for instance, Cady Stanton did not concern herself with labor problems and the different needs and struggles of African American and Native American wo/men. Finally, the *Woman's Bible* uncritically repeats many of the anti-Jewish patterns and stereotypes prevalent in Christian popular and scholarly discourse of its time. However, Cady Stanton was right in insisting that to reject biblical religion as totally patri-kyriarchal would mean to give up on the reform of a very important part of society.

African American wo/men had already stressed the importance of religion as a source of empowerment and vision for change in the nineteenth century. In contrast to that of elite white women, the point of departure for African American wo/men was not primarily either the struggle for women's individual emancipation and personal self-development or the indictment of biblical religion. Rather, African American wo/men heard and read the Bible and used the Christian symbol-system in the context of their experience of slavery and liberation. Womanist ethicist Katie Cannon has pointed out that in the last century racial slavery was the sociopolitical context not only of Afro-American but also of white malestream biblical interpretation. She identifies three ideological constructs that made it possible for white Christians to justify chattel slavery of Africans. As property, slaves were not seen as fully human, as Africans they were classed as heathen savages to be saved through enslavement, and as Christians, white or black, they were expected to believe that slavery was divinely willed in the Bible.[11]

Within this context of slavery and in resistance to it, African wo/men used the Bible and Christian religion as a "language" to express their hope for justice and as a "matrix" for the transformation of the self-understanding and self-esteem of those who had suffered from institutionalized enslavement. As with white suffragists and black men, African American wo/men sought not only to resist the oppressive elements of Christian religion and the Bible but also to gain valorization and authentication from them.

However, unlike white wo/men and black men, African American wo/men spoke from a doubly disadvantaged location. As blacks they had to address white audiences who doubted the human capacity of African Americans for learning and religious salvation. As wo/men they had to address audiences, black and

---

10. As quoted by Barbara Hilkert Andolsen, "Daughters of Jefferson, Daughters of Bootblacks," *Racism and American Feminism* (Macon: Mercer University Press, 1986), 31.
11. K. G. Cannon, "Slave Ideology and Biblical Interpretation," *Semeia* 47 (1989): 9-24.

white, who questioned both their ability to exercise authority and the legitimacy of their speaking in public.

To do so, African American wo/men such as Sojourner Truth, Amanda Berry Smith, Jarena Lee, Julia Foote, Maria Stewart or the Quaker Elizabeth (of whom we know only her baptismal name), derived their religious authority not primarily from the Bible and church teachings but from mystical experiences in which they encountered G*d or Jesus directly. It was this confidence in the privileged nature of their relationship with the divine that allowed African American wo/men to claim their own authority and to transcend the limits imposed upon them by the kyriarchal gender-race-class system of slavery.

The struggles of both African American and Anglo-Saxon wo/men in the nineteenth century demonstrate that the struggles of wo/men in religion for their full citizenship are not just inner-church or purely intra-religious issues. Rather, they neeed to be understood in terms of their sociopolitical location and function in an international context of globalization. We should not forget that religious ideas and discourses are embedded in sociopolitical situations and sustain or combat certain trends and aspirations of their societies. As Gregory Baum has observed, thinking is inevitably marked and molded by its historical location: "Ideas will have a relation to the existing social reality; they either draw attention to the unjust conditions that cause human suffering or, conversely they withdraw the mind's attention from these problems and their human consequences."[12]

In the face of global cultural and religious fundamentalisms,[13] feminists in religion contend that the*logical debates on, for example, wo/men's ordination are not only of significance for religious communities. Rather, the*logical discourses are always already implicated in structures of domination. The*logical discourses collude in the production and maintenance of systems of knowledge and media-discourses that either foster exploitation and oppression or contribute to a praxis and vision of emancipation and liberation. Hence it is critically important that feminists study religion not just as an oppressive discourse but also as a possible resource of power and strength in wo/men's lives.

Second, if feminists in law, education, or politics do not want to lose the gains that were made for wo/men in the past four decades, they have to learn how to distinguish between different forms of religion rather than to reject religion out of hand as oppressive. They need to learn how to support wo/men's struggles for justice within religious communities. They also must study feminist the*logical discourses in order to better understand the mindsets, belief-systems and social behavior of religious wo/men who are their students, clients, or defendants. As

---

12. Gregory G. Baum, "Remarks of a Theologian in Dialogue with Sociology," in *Theology and the Social Sciences,* ed. Michael Horace Barnes (Maryknoll: Orbis, 2000), 11.

13. For the fundamentalist tendencies in Roman Catholicism see John Darcy May, "Catholic Fundamentalism? Some Implications of Dominus Jesus for Dialogue and Peacemaking," in *Dominus Jesus,* ed. Michael J. Rainer (Münster: LIT, 2001), 112-33.

the feminist philosopher Caroline Ramazanoglu has pointed out, millions of women appreciate religion as a source of meaning for their lives. Hence, she argues, feminists cannot afford to disregard the fact that religion still remains "the dominant factor in the personal identity and cultural location of millions of women around the world. If religion is one of the most important and immediate factors which enables a woman to know who she is, and to give meaning to her life, an international feminist movement cannot afford to ignore religion."[14]

In a similar fashion the Pakistani feminist Farida Shaheed has argued that Muslim feminists must operate within the religious belief system of Islam if they are to be effective. Feminist teachers, lawyers, or activists cannot and should not make religious wo/men choose between feminism and their personal religious beliefs if they want to effectively advocate legal, economic or any other type of reform. In short, "[A] women's movement needs to be perceived as rooted in the cultural reality of the society in which it operates. . . . [D]iscriminatory laws sanctified through Islam cannot be effectively countered with arguments which deny or discard Islam."[15] The same observation could be made with respect to Judaism, Christianity, Hinduism, or Buddhism.

Feminists in biblical religions have played a major role in wo/men's struggles for justice. We have developed feminist the*logies and studies in religion on the basis of our involvement in a feminist movement that seeks to change relations of domination and subordination. Hence, from the outset, feminist the*logy and studies in religion have made an explicit connection between feminist critique and social change.

Wo/men's the*logical voice and religious authority has been developed in and through critical reflection on experience, consciousness-raising, and the articulation of feminist the*logy as a critical the*logy of liberation committed to feminist struggles for changing and transforming biblical religions.

At a time when public discourses again deploy biblical religion for denying women's basic rights of sexual self-determination, economic equality, and full citizenship, it is crucial for feminists to recognize the interconnectedness of all wo/men's struggles for liberty, equality, and well-being with wo/men's struggles in biblical religions for authority and full citizenship in churches, synagogues, and mosques.

Third, feminist theorists have consistently overlooked feminist movements in biblical religions when discussing the Second Wave of feminism, although fundamentalist right-wing movements have made religion again central to public discourse. Since many white feminist scholars still tend to be convinced that religion is the prime enemy that keeps wo/men in oppressive situations, they have neglected

---

14. Caroline Ramazanoglu, *Feminism and the Contradictions of Oppression* (London: Routledge, 1989), 151-52.

15. Farida Shaheed, "The Cultural Articulation of Patriarchy: Legal Systems, Islam, and Wo/men," *South Asia Bulletin* (1986), 12-13.

to study feminist the*logies and religious studies. Hence feminist work in religion has had very little impact on their own critical analysis, theories, and transformative practices. Societal feminist movements and theorists have not been able, therefore, to articulate bodies of knowledge and strategies for successfully counteracting the impact of fundamentalism on society, politics and law.

Presently the struggle against wo/men's second class citizenship, for instance, centers in Roman Catholicism and some Protestant churches, especially those in the two-thirds world on the question of the non-ordination of wo/men and the right of wo/men to determine their sexuality and reproductive powers, whereas in liberal Protestant churches it focuses on the issue of same sex marriages or the ordination of homosexuals. However, I do not want to suggest that only Christian religion and the*logy are such sites of feminist struggles. To the contrary, similar but different issues are raised by feminists in Judaism, Islam, Buddhism, or Hinduism. In consequence, not only biblical religions but also other major world religions are undergoing intense critical scrutiny by feminists. All religious belief systems and institutional practices are experiencing the growing pains of feminist re-visions.[16]

Nevertheless, like the first wave so also the second wave of the societal white wo/men's movement, has continued to neglect or reject religion as totally oppressive and self-alienating to women. Hence, the work of feminist scholars in religion as well as of religious activists has not been sufficiently recognized and utilized as a resource in feminist struggles for justice. Since cultural feminist theorists generally seem not to know much about feminist theories and struggles in religion, or, if they do, are only aware of the critical assessment of religion, they are not able to build on the work of religious feminists and to reinforce each other's projects for transformation. Hence, they are not able to cause a ripple effect of change and to strengthen the powers of resistance and renewal. Nor are they able to support their struggles with religious resources that have inspired and shaped the struggles for justice.

Fourth, the liberal feminist rejection of religion as repressive and as "false consciousness" has also affected the work of feminists in religion. It has sparked divisions between biblical and post-biblical feminists, between Jewish/Christian feminists and the Goddess movement, and between feminist the*logies as confessional and feminist studies of religion as objective academic studies. In the feminist discourses of the nineteenth and twentieth centuries, this feminist either/or attitude towards religion has been symbolized by two biblical images, that of Eden/home and that of exodus/margins. These images suggest that wo/men in religion have only an either or choice. Either affirm religion as good because it is one's home[17] and family, to whom one owes absolute loyalty, or move out of

---

16. See the excellent contributions in Paula M. Cooey, William R. Eakin, and Jay B. McDaniel, eds., *After Patriarchy: Feminist Transformations of the World Religions* (Maryknoll: Orbis, 1991).

17. For an excellent problematization of the feminist desire for home, see Laura Levitt, *Jews and Feminism: The Ambivalent Struggle for Home* (New York: Routledge, 1997).

religion into the desert of marginality and the promised land of radical feminism, leaving behind slavery and bondage with the fleshpots of Egypt. Because post-biblical feminists have judged biblical religions to be intrinsically oppressive and totally misogynistic, apologetic feminists have defended them as basically liberating and intrinsically good for wo/men.

Whereas, for instance, the wo/men's ordination movements in Christianity and Judaism have affirmed their desire for religion as home and have claimed equal rights for the daughters of the house with the sons of the house, post-biblical feminists have called for the exodus of women from the bondage of patriarchal churches and institutionalized religions into the "other world" of feminist spirituality. However, more recent critical feminist thinking has sought to transform this either/or exclusivist choice between feminism and religion into a dialectic between oppression and struggles for justice.

For instance, the feminist literary critic Susan Gubar has pointed to the rich critical work of Jewish feminists in religion writing during the 1970s, 1980s, and 1990s that has "analyzed particularly vexed areas of Judaism for wo/men," but she confesses she did not read them. "By an accident of birth, I was a Jewish feminist, but by virtue of that very fact I could not conceive of becoming a feminist Jew, a label that would have struck me as a contradiction in terms."[18] In the process of reasoning out this contradiction, Gubar, however, reformulates it not in terms of an either/or choice but in terms of "both and" when she points out, "For many feminist critiques, moreover, Jewish devotion to the text and education has been supplemented by the equally long history in Judaism of a strong commitment to each individual's social responsibility. . . . Yet exactly such a concern about social and political justice would underscore the exclusion of wo/men from, in Ostriker's words, the 'questions and answers twining minutely like vine around the living Word.'"[19]

This jarring contradiction between wo/men's exclusion from the word and the Torah's call to social justice, Gubar concludes "may have spawned not only the feminist movement in Judaism but feminism itself as well as feminist scholarship."[20] In preparing for her article she sent a questionnaire to leading feminist theorists and found confirmed what she suspected all along, that Jewish experience and thought have "profoundly shaped the evolution of feminist thinking in our times. Still, even now the vexed relationship between Judaism and feminism seems to mean that the pleasure I and many of my contemporaries can receive from our heritage will always be mixed with sorrow, the pride with

---

18. Susan Gubar, "Eating the Bread of Affliction: Judaism and Feminist Criticism," in *People of the Book: Thirty Scholars Reflect on their Jewish Identity*, ed. Jeffrey Rubin-Dorsky and Shelly Fisher Fishkin (Madison: University of Wisconsin Press, 1996), 18.

19. Susan Gubar, "Eating the Bread of Affliction," 27.

20. Ibid.

grief, the joy with anger, sweetness with bitterness, honey on the tongue with tears in the eyes."[21]

In a similar fashion, Islamic feminists like the Sisters in Islam Forum in Malaysia[22] are developing discursive strategies that claim both their religious heritage and their rights as Muslim wo/men to freedom, justice, and equality. "The most important feature of contemporary Muslim wo/men's struggle for rights is that they reject the proposition that they cannot be *both* free and equal with men *and* good Muslims at the same time. This they deny. On the contrary, they insist that a woman becomes an authentic Muslim when she has achieved freedom and equality as an individual citizen [emphasis added]."[23]

A Radical Democratic Imagination: The *Ekklēsia* of Wo/men

In my own work, I have sought to overcome the dualistic feminist alternative "either religious or feminist" by seeking to conceptualize a vision that could both include and transcend the understanding of religion either as home or as exodus. For doing so I built on the discussions of radical democracy in feminist political theory[24] and on critical legal studies[25] that seek to reconceptualize legal discourses as a site of political struggles. By introducing the radical democratic notion of the "*ekklēsia* of wo/men" as an alternative religious symbolic concept to "exodus" and "paradise/home," I sought to reframe theoretically the feminist either/or binary which re-inscribes the dualistic divisions between religion and culture, religion and democratic rights, or religious and secular wo/men's movements.

As discussed in previous chapters, *ekklēsia* is best translated as "democratic congress" of full decision making citizens. Democratic equality, citizenship, and decision-making power are constitutive for the notion of *ekklēsia*. However, since the Greek word "*ekklēsia*" is also determined by a Christian language context and is usually translated as "church," I prefer not to translate it, so that the term can function as a signifier that must be actively decoded in order to know

---

21. Ibid., 15.

22. www.sistersinislam.org.my.

23. Mahnaz Afkhami, Greta H. Nemiroff, and Haleh Vazir, *Safe and Secure: Eliminating Violence against Wo/men and Girls in Muslim Societies* (Baltimore: SIGI, 1998), 7. See also Miriam Cooke, "Multiple Critique: Islamic Feminist Rhetorical Strategies," in *Postcolonialism, Feminism, and Religious Discourse*, ed. Laura E. Donaldson and Kwok Pui-Lan (New York: Routledge, 2001), 142-60.

24. See for instance, Seyla Benhabib, ed., *Democracy and Difference: Contesting the Boundaries of the Political* (Princeton: Princeton University Press, 1996) and Chantal Mouffe, ed., *Dimensions of Radical Democracy* (London: Verso, 1992).

25. See for instance Mary Frug, *Postmodern Legal Feminism* (New York: Routledge, 1992) and Martha Minow, *Equality and the Bill of Rights* (Ithaca: Cornell University Press, 1992) and *Identities* (New Haven: Yale University Press, 1991). See also H. Markus, R. Shweder, and M. Minow, eds., *The Free Exercise of Culture* (New York: Russell Sage Foundation, 2001).

what the Greek word actually means. Theoretically, the symbolic concept of the *ekklēsia* of wo/men seeks to develop a "democratics" as the horizon for feminist struggles both in religion and society at large. I have borrowed the term "democratics" from Chela Sandoval, who has theorized it as one of the methods of the oppressed:

> With the transnationalization of capitalism when elected officials are no longer leaders of singular nation-states but nexuses for multinational interests, it also becomes possible for citizen-subjects to become activists for a new decolonizing global terrain, a psychic terrain that can unite them with similarly positioned citizen-subjects within and across national borders into new, post-Western-empire alliances. . . . The new countrypeople [of this imagined community] who fight for egalitarian social relations under neocolonial postmodernism welcome citizenry to a new polity, a new homeland. The means for entry is "the methodology of the oppressed," a set of technologies for decolonizing the social [and religious] imagination. These technologies. . . . are all guided by democratics, the practitioners commitment to the equal distribution of power. . . . Love as social movement is enacted by revolutionary, mobile, and global coalitions of citizen-activists who are allied through the apparatus of emancipation.[26]

As a white, Christian wo/man I am somewhat hesitant, however, to claim "love" as a revolutionary force and as an "oppositional social action as a mode of 'love' in the postmodern world." Although I am well aware that numerous U.S. third-world feminists have eloquently written about the power of prophetic love in struggles for justice,[27] I cannot forget the function of "romantic love" in the oppression of wo/men, nor the anti-Jewish Christian valorization of the "God of love" over the "Old" Testament "God of justice." To mark the oppressive history and negative potential of love I would prefer to speak of "just love" or "loving justice." In consequence, the democratics of the *ekklēsia* of wo/men must be equally informed by the following insight of Patricia Hill Collins:

> Rather than being seen as yet another content area with Black feminist discourse, a concern with justice fused with a deep spirituality appears to be highly significant to how African-American women conceptualize critical social theory. Justice constitutes an article of faith expressed through deep feelings that move people to action. For many Black feminist thinkers, justice transcends Western notions of equality grounded in sameness and uniformity. Elsa Barkley Brown's discussion of African American women's quilting (1989) points us in the direction of conceptualizing an alternative notion of justice. In making their quilts Black women weave together scraps

---

26. Chela Sandoval, *Methodology of the Oppressed* (Minneapolis: University of Minnesota Press, 2000), 183.

27. Audre Lorde, bell hooks, Toni Morrison, Cornel West, June Jordan, Gloria Anzaldúa, Maria Lugones, Merle Woo, Alice Walker—to name only a few.

of fabric from all sorts of places. Nothing is wasted, and every piece of fabric has a function and a place in a given quilt. . . . [T]hose who conceptualize community via notions of uniformity and sameness have difficulty imagining a social quilt that is simultaneously heterogeneous, driven toward excellence, and just.[28]

Like Cady Stanton's image of the "fourfold cord" or Hill Collins' concept of "the social quilt," so the democratics of the oxymoronic construct *ekklēsia* of wo/men" seeks to name a feminist space where citizen-subjects fight for justice and egalitarian relations that recognize the unique difference of each and every one. This feminist space is one where the so-called "secular" and "religious" wo/men's movements can be conceptualized not as opposites or never-meeting parallels, but as a radical democratic, spiritual decolonizing space and feminist public, as a "congress" of diverse wo/men's groups and feminist movements working together for transformation of both society and religion.

If, just as legal or political feminist discourses, religious feminist discourses and movements were recognized as common feminist sites of political struggles not only over gender differences, but also over other forms of domination such as racism, colonialism, or capitalism, then the split between societal and religious, between biblical and post-biblical feminisms could be overcome in the diverse struggles for religious and political rights, the equalization of power, and changing relations of domination in and outside religion. To crystallize my points:

First, "*ekklēsia* of wo/men" is not only a feminist symbolic construct intended to overcome the dualistic split between religious and societal wo/men's movements and a democratics for decolonizing the cultural and religious imagination, but also a descriptive historical term developed in terms of my own Christian liberationist the*logical framework. Still, it could also easily be elaborated in terms of other religious egalitarian visions. In early Christian literature the expression "*ekklēsia*" is the very name for the Christian community. (The word "synagogue" has a similar valence and means the "congregation of the people of God.") The very self-description of the early Christian communities was a radical democratic one.[29] The *ekklēsia* understood as the force field of divine Wisdom-Spirit is a "new creation," in which the Spirit empowered people are all equal but not the same. They all share in the multifaceted gifts of divine Wisdom-Spirit, all without exception: Jews, Greeks, Barbarians, wo/men and men, slaves and free, those with high social status and those who are nothing in the eyes of the world.[30]

Only when one realizes how fundamental this radical democratic spirit was to the self-understanding of the early Christian communities can one appreciate the

---

28. Patricia Hill Collins, *Fighting Words: Black Women and the Search for Justice* (Minneapolis: University of Minnesota Press, 1998), 248-49.

29. This is not unusual. Most organizational sociologists point out that most religions have such an egalitarian self-understanding in the beginning.

30. See Elisabeth Schüssler Fiorenza, *In Memory of Her*, 160-99.

break in Christian self-understanding that took place when the church adopted the administrative organizational structures and legal institutions of the Roman empire, which were monarchical-hierarchical.[31]

Although the word *ekklēsia* is usually translated in English as "church," the English word "church" derives from the Greek word *kyriakē*, that is, belonging to the lord/ master/ father, but not from the Greek term "*ekklēsia*." The translation process, which has transformed "*ekklēsia*/congress" into "*kyriake*/church," indicates a historical development that has privileged the kyriarchal/hierarchical form of church. Hence, the rendering of the Greek word *ekklēsia* with "church" promotes a Christian self-understanding that is derived from the kyriarchal model of household and state in antiquity, which were governed by the lord/master/father of the house, to whom freeborn wo/men, freeborn dependents, clients, and workers as well as slaves were subordinated as his property.

I will illustrate such a kyriarchal understanding with reference to my religious-social location—the Catholic community. The Roman Catholic Church is determined by hierarchical structures, represented by men, and divided into a sacred two-class system of the ordained and the laity, connoting second-class citizenship of the laity. It is ironic that in defense of the Roman imperial structures that crucified Jesus, the hierarchy has insisted in the nineteenth century, over against democratic forces within the church, that monarchy is the G*d-given order, and in this century that the Roman Catholic church is not a democratic community. Hence, wo/men have no rights to full citizenship and church office.

Whereas in the nineteenth century the Roman Catholic hierarchy defended monarchy as the governmental form willed by G*d for society, in the twentieth century official church teaching has advocated human rights and democratic freedoms in society but insisted that these do not apply to the church. For instance, Pope Leo XIII rejected all "modern liberties," the freedom to worship, the separation of church and state, freedom of speech and the press, the liberty of teaching and the freedom of conscience, because the people were the "untutored multitude."[32] While Pope Leo recognized that there is true equality insofar as we are all children of God, he denied that there is any equality in society and culture. "The inequality of rights and of power proceeds from the very Author of nature, 'from whom all paternity in heaven and earth is named.' "[33] He pointed out that "the abilities of all are not equal, as one differs from another in the powers of mind or body, and there are much dissimilarity of manner, disposition and character." Hence, he argues,

---

31. Elisabeth Schüssler Fiorenza, "A Discipleship of Equals: Ekklesial Democracy and Patriarchy in Biblical Perspective," in *A Democratic Catholic Church: The Reconstruction of Roman Catholicism*, ed. E. C. Bianchi and Rosemary Radford Ruether (New York: Crossroad, 1992), 17-33.

32. Charles E. Curran, "What Catholic Ecclesiology Can Learn from Official Catholic Social Teaching," 105.

33. Pope Leo XIII, "On Socialism," in *The Church Speaks to the Modern World: The Social Teachings of Leo XIII*, ed. E. Gilson (Garden City: Doubleday, 1954), 193.

"it is most repugnant to reason to endeavor to confine all within the same measure and to extend complete equality to the institutions of civil life."[34] Here difference is not understood as giftedness but construed as inequality. While the present pope no longer upholds these anti-democratic sentiments for society, he still maintains them for the Roman Catholic church by insisting on the non-ordination of wo/men and forbidding any public discussion of it.

Second, the expression *ekklēsia gynaikōn, the ekklēsia of wo/men,* is a linguistic tool and the*logical means of conscientization. It seeks to bring into public consciousness the masculine overdetermination of *ekklēsia* in malestream political discourses and religious representations. Since the signifier "woman" is still used to draw exclusive boundaries in societal democracies and biblical religions, it is important to mark linguistically the difference between democracy and church as Roman kyriarchal institution and as *ekklēsia,* the congress of decision-making citizen subjects. The *ekklēsia* of wo/men is a means of conscientization that articulates a radical democratic imagination.

Because of the elite male embodiment of ancient and modern democracies, one needs always to qualify *ekklēsia* with *wo/men* if one wants to speak of radical democracy in church and society. Qualifying *"ekklēsia"* with *wo/men,* seeks to lift into consciousness that church, society, and religion are governed by elite men who have been exclusive of wo/men and other servant-people for centuries. Thus the notion of the *"ekklēsia* of wo/men" seeks to enunciate a vision that connects wo/men's struggles in biblical religions with global, societal and political movements for justice, freedom, and equality. These movements have emerged again and again throughout the centuries, I submit, because of the disparity between the professed vision of radical democratic equality in church and society and the actual reality of domination and subordination, which they experienced every day.

Third, the image of the *ekklēsia* of wo/men seeks to forge a link between the societal and religious women's liberation movements and to overcome their dualistic split into religious and secular. If dehumanizing and misogynist religious values and mindsets inform cultural assumptions about wo/men and public policy, then it is important to articulate radical democratic religious values and visions to replace this kyriarchal ethos in the public imagination. *Ekklēsia* of wo/men articulates a vision of radical equality for creating a world of justice and well-being. It wants to name the vision of justice and salvation which feminist movements seek and in which biblical religions share.

Such a rearticulation of biblical religions in terms of radical democratic equality is necessary if religion is to become an influence and power for radical democracy. The *ekklēsia* of wo/men seeks to realize this vision of G*d's renewed creation by working for a radical democratic society which does not have any hungry, strangers, or outcasts but cherishes the earth and struggles in solidarity

---

34. Pope Leo XIII, "On Freemasonry," in *The Church Speaks to the Modern World,* 130.

with those who are oppressed by racism, nationalism, poverty, neo-colonialism, and heterosexism.

Wo/men are *ekklēsia*, the assembly of free adult citizens who have the right and duty to decide our own and our children's religious future. *Ekklēsia* as the decision-making assembly of full citizens insists on the ancient Roman and medieval maxim: That which affects all should be determined by every one (or in Latin: *quod omnes tangit, ab omnibus judicatur*). In and through struggles for change and liberation the vision of the *ekklēsia*, of G*d's life-giving and transforming power for community, becomes experiential reality in the midst of structural sin, of the death dealing powers of oppression and dehumanization.

Thus it is misleading to translate this contradictory expression, "*ekklēsia* of wo/men," as "wo/men-church," because in the process of translation, "*ekklēsia*" tends to lose its radical democratic meaning. While the translation "wo/men-church" makes the connection between wo/men and church, it is not able to hold together the meaning of "*ekklēsia*" as both democratic assembly and as church, as political and as religious. As a result, the intended radical political valence of the term is lost. Yet, the goal in qualifying and circumscribing "*ekklēsia*" with the term "wo/men" has been precisely to raise into public consciousness the fact that neither church nor society are what they claim to be: *ekklēsia*, that is, the democratic congress of equal decision-making citizens who are wo/men.

The qualification of *ekklēsia* with the term "wo/men" does not only serve as a linguistic tool for indicating how a diversified and pluriform non-dualist wo/men's movement is to be imagined. It also seeks to signify the multiple forms in which the *ekklēsia* of wo/men is lived today in order to presage the rich diversity of the radical democratic *ekklēsia* of the future. Wo/men are not the same nor do they have an essence in common that makes them different from men. There are as many differences between wo/men and within wo/men as there are between men and wo/men. Wo/men are not just determined by gender, but also by race, class, ethnicity, culture, age, sexual preference, and religion. Identity is not stable, but changes over the course of time. Hence the oxymoron "*ekklēsia* of wo/men" should not be understood in the cultural terms of femininity as promoting the ideal of the "White Lady," but as modeling a plurivocal feminist movement for change. As Hedwig Meyer–Wilmes has observed, "One could even say that the *ekklēsia* of wo/men is a postmodern concept. . . . It takes for granted the achievements of modernity: it is grounded in an egalitarian view of structures, a multiplicity of [liberatory] images and a concern to make the *ekklēsia* visible in different [social] formations."[35]

Fourth: The radical equality of the *ekklēsia* of wo/men is the*logically grounded in the conviction that all wo/men are created in the image of G*d, each

---

35. Hedwig Meyer-Wilmes, "The Diversity of Ministry in a Postmodern Church," in *The Non-Ordination of Wo/men*, 80.

and every human being is precious in Her eyes, and that all have received multi-faceted gifts and powers. In all our differences wo/men represent the divine here and now because women are made in the divine image and likeness. Every one is made in the image of divine Wisdom, who has gifted and called every individual differently. The divine image is neither male nor female, white or black, rich or poor but multicolored, multi-gendered, and more.

As a richly gifted people, the *ekklēsia* of wo/men presages a world-community in which religious, racial, and class but also heterosexual markers no longer signify and legitimate status differences and relations of kyriarchal domination and subordination. As a pilgrim people the *ekklēsia* of wo/men may fail again and again, but it continues to struggle, to live in fullness and to realize its calling to be the radical democratic society in process.

However, when I first began to theorize the *ekklēsia* of wo/men as an alternative image and a mediating radical democratic biblical symbol, I was unaware that the suffrage movements already had employed the symbol of democracy as a religious-biblical symbol in its struggle for justice. Mary Pellauer's dissertation on the religious thought of Elizabeth Cady Stanton, Susan B. Anthony, and Anna Howard Shaw has made a convincing case that these leading suffragists spoke of democracy in religious terms.[36] Although they choose quite different political and religious paths, Pellauer argues that their struggles against misogyny and for justice are positioned within an ethos shaped by the conjunction of their socio-political analysis and their religious-moral perspective. She points out that Anna Howard Shaw can even speak of the "gospel of democracy."

> The democracy of the gospel must permeate the democracy of our land and we must learn that as the hand cannot say to the foot, or the ear to the eye—"I have no need of thee." Neither can the educated say to the uneducated—"I have no need of thee"; nor the rich to the poor—"I have no need of thee." Each has need of the other; each must live and grow together, or else the survivors must be chained to the diseased and corrupt body of the outcasts. We cannot separate ourselves from them.[37]

The dissertation of Karen Baker-Fletcher makes a similar case for the African American educator and suffragist Anna Julia Cooper. Baker-Fletcher points out that equality and freedom were not simply physical states for Anna Julia Cooper but political-spiritual realities.[38] Cooper believed that democratic progress was "a shadow mark of the creator's image" derived "from the essential worth of humanity." Cooper envisioned a future for humanity governed by the

---

36. Mary D. Pellauer, *Toward a Tradition of Feminist Theology: The Religious Social Thought of Elisabeth Cady Stanton, Susan B. Anthony, and Anna Howard Shaw* (Brooklyn: Carlson, 1991).

37. Quoted in ibid., 260.

38. Karen Baker-Fletcher, *A Singing Something: Womanist Reflections on Anna Julia Cooper* (New York: Crossroad, 1994).

principles of equality, freedom and democracy that were ontological universal aspects of human nature. She asserts "that progress in the democratic sense is an inborn human endowment—a shadow mark of the creator's image, or if you will an urge-cell, the universal and unmistakable hallmark traceable to the Father of all."[39]

Like her white compatriots, Anna Julia Cooper understood democracy in religious terms. However, Cooper broadens the suffragist ethos of struggle for full citizenship when she insists that democratic equality and freedom are G*d-given, inborn ontological capacities of every human being regardless of race, sex, class, and country. Against theories that claimed democracy, equality, and freedom as the property of the superior races of western European civilization,[40] Cooper insists that these were inherent in the fact of being human and hence could never be suppressed. The key metaphor for G*d in Cooper's religious discourse according to Baker-Fletcher is a "Singing Something" that in every nation cries out for justice. As Baker-Fletcher puts it, "What makes one human is one's inner voice, the voice of equality and freedom that is directly traceable to God. The voice of God, in this sense, sings through the human spirit and calls humankind to action, growth, development, and reform. There is movement involved in the act of vocalization."[41]

While the notion of the *ekklēsia* of women is theorized quite differently and speaks to a different rhetorical situation and historical context,[42] it nevertheless is a part of and continues this radical, democratic, nineteenth-century suffragist tradition. This submerged feminist intellectual tradition of radical democratic religious agency and emancipatory biblical interpretation, in which my own work is rooted, has claimed and continues to claim the authority and right of wo/men to interpret experience, Bible, tradition, and religion from their own perspective and in their own interests.

---

39. Anna Julia Cooper, "Equality of Races and the Democratic Movement," privately printed pamphlet (Washington, D.C., 1945), 5, quoted by Baker-Fletcher.

40. Like other Anglo-Saxon suffragists and social reformers, Elizabeth Cady Stanton was very much determined and limited by her social status and class position. She not only expressed anti-immigrant sentiments by arguing that the suffrage of women of her own class would increase the numbers of Anglo-Saxon voters, but she also appealed to ethnic and racial prejudices when she exhorted: "American women of wealth and refinement, if you do not wish the lower orders of Chinese, Africans, Germans, and Irish, with their low ideas of womanhood to make laws for you, demand that woman, too, shall be represented in the government." Quoted by Barbara Hilkert Andolsen, "Daughters of Jefferson, Daughters of Bootblacks," *Racism and American Feminism* (Macon: Mercer University Press, 1986), 31.

41. Baker-Fletcher, *A Singing Something*, 192-93.

42. For a discussion of this theoretical context, see Anne Phillips, *Engendering Democracy* (Cambridge: Polity, 1991); Judith Butler and Joan W. Scott, eds., *Feminists Theorize the Political* (New York: Routledge, 1992); Joan Cocks, *The Oppositional Imagination: Feminism, Critique, and Political Theory* (New York: Routledge, 1989); and Mary Lyndon Shanley and Carole Pateman, eds., *Feminist Interpretations and Political Theory* (University Park: Pennsylvania State University Press, 1991).

This tradition has insisted that equality, freedom, and democracy cannot be realized if wo/men's voices are not raised, not heard, and not heeded in the struggle for justice and liberation for everyone, regardless of sex, class, race, nationality, or religion. Although this feminist tradition of wo/men's religious authority and agency remains fragmented and has not always been able to completely overcome the limitations and prejudicial frameworks of its own time and social location, its critical knowledge and continuing vibrancy nevertheless remains crucial for contemporary radical democratic struggles in society and religion.

8

Wo/men and the Catholicity
of The*logy

Karl Rahner has argued that the most important event of the Second Vatican Council was the manifestation of the world-church where for the first time bishops of Asia, Africa, Latin America, and the Pacific Rim acted together with the pope as equals when articulating and deciding the the*logy of the Council.[1] Rahner rightly criticized the Eurocentrism of Roman Catholic the*logy[2] and church but he did not recognize its andro-kyriocentrism.[3]

Yet, one must not overlook that the Second Vatican Council's representation of world-catholicism was totally male, since wo/men were not among the bishops of the emerging world-church. The absence of wo/men from the ranks of bishops is not an historical accident but the result of systemic discrimination and legal exclusion; it is due to the structural sin of sexism and misogyny and its the*logical rationalizations. As long as wo/men are excluded from church leadership and governance not

---

1. See Karl Rahner, "Basic Theological Interpretation of the Second Vatican Council," in *Concern for the Church: Theological Investigations*, vol. 20 (New York: Crossroad, 1981), 77-89, and "The Abiding Significance of the Second Vatican Council," 90–102. A different version was published as "The Struggle for the Catholicity of Theology," *Bulletin ET: Zeitschrift für Theologie in Europa* 12 (2001): 207–28.

2. For an exploration of the task of the*logy, see Claude Geffre and Werner Jeanrond, eds., *Why Theology? Concilium* 6 (Maryknoll: Orbis, 1994).

3. By stressing andro-kyriocentrism, I do not want to detract from the postcolonial critique of Eurocentrism that has indicted the "European mode of military-missionary expansion." This military missionary expansion according to Jan Nederveen Pieterse "was projected outside Europe during the Crusades, which produced Europe's first overseas colony, the Kingdom of Jerusalem. . . . Christianity thus appears historically as part of the politics, the civil institutions, and the cultures of empire." See Jan Nederveen Pieterse, ed., *Christianity and Hegemony: Religion and Politics on the Frontiers of Social Change* (New York: Berg, 1992), 3-4.

just by custom but also by law, the catholicity of the world-church is jeopardized. Hence, the exclusion of wo/men from full *ekklesial* citizenship with all rights and responsibilities is not just a "woman question" but a fundamental the*logical problem.[4] The world-church lacks the fullness of the catholicity of *ekklēsia* if half of its members are systematically excluded and discriminated. Today this lack of catholicity is even more obvious because other Christian churches have welcomed wo/men as official ministers, priests and bishops with full rights and responsibilities.

True, in the past forty years or so Catholic wo/men have engaged in the study of academic the*logy in ever greater numbers and have become acknowledged as leading the*logical scholars. They have created feminist the*logy[5] and wo/men's studies in religion[6] as a new academic discipline that has produced significant research and scholarship. However, this scholarship has had only minimal impact on ecclesiastical discourses and policy in Roman Catholicism. To my knowledge feminist the*logians are still not invited as consultants to bishops' conferences, Vatican congregations or papal commissions. We still experience silencing and exclusion. Not just for me but for many others the experience of becoming a catholic the*logian has been and still is an experience of struggle:[7] the struggle to find our own the*logical voice, the struggle for its integrity and truthfulness, the struggle to articulate a different vision of catholicity and the*logy, the struggle with a kyriarchal tradition and doctrinal discourse that on principle has excluded wo/men as the*logical authorities and increasingly speaks the language of silencing, control and violence.

Consequently, the struggle for the catholicity of the*logy is not just a struggle for wo/men's ordination. It is also the struggle for freedom of thought, intellectual independence and personal integrity, for *eleutheria* and *parrhēsia*, for the free and uncensored speech of citizens of which St. Paul speaks. Such freedom is the *sine qua non* for the practice of the*logical catholicity. This struggle for a

---

4. I presented this paper at the Congress of the European Society for Catholic The*logy. The concluding lecture by Cardinal Lehman eloquently discussed Catholicism's realization in a European context but was not prepared to adequately address my question as to the fundamental problem of wo/men's exclusion from full ekklesial citizenship and its destructive consequences for the catholicity of the*logy and church.

5. For a general introduction to American Christian feminist the*logy, see Anne M. Clifford, *Introducing Feminist Theology* (Maryknoll: Orbis, 2001). See also my book *Wisdom Ways: Introducing Feminist Biblical Interpretation* (Maryknoll: Orbis, 2001). For feminist the*logy in an international context, see Shawn Copeland and Elisabeth Schüssler Fiorenza, eds., *Feminist Theology in Different Contexts* (Maryknoll: Orbis, 1996) and my collection *The Power of Naming: A Concilium Reader in Feminist Liberation Theology* (Maryknoll: Orbis, 1996). See also Anne Jensen and Maximilian Liebmann, eds., *Was verändert Feministische Theologie? Interdisziplinäres Forum zur Frauenforschung* (Münster: LIT, 2000).

6. See *The Journal of Feminist Studies in Religion*, which Judith Plaskow and I cofounded in 1985. See also Darlene M. Juschka, *Feminism in the Study of Religion: A Reader* (New York: Continuum, 2001).

7. See my book *Discipleship of Equals: A Critical Feminist Ekklēsia-logy of Liberation* (New York: Crossroads, 1993).

different catholic the*logy has as its goal a catholicity that speaks with *parrhēsia* in many tongues and idioms.[8] Consequently it seeks to introduce into hegemonic the*logical discourse the religious experiences and questions of wo/men and other marginalized peoples.

For the full catholicity of the*logy and of the world-church is only possible if and when all without exception have the opportunity to participate in the discourses that shape Christian identity and mission.[9] Thus I have argued throughout my work that the recognition of wo/men as full *ekklesial* citizens with all rights, privileges, and duties demands a new articulation and self-understanding of the*logy and church. It requires an articulation of catholic identity not as sameness but as diversity and rich giftedness in the power of divine Spirit-Wisdom.

In order to elaborate this thesis, I will first discuss what I mean by catholicity and indicate what is at stake in the struggle for the catholicity of the*logy. Then in a second step I will go on to elaborate the struggle for the catholicity of the*logy and the world-church as a long-lasting ongoing struggle between two opposing the*logical discourses on catholicity. The first is the Roman imperial discourse[10] of control and exclusion, which is expressed in the rhetoric of recent Vatican edicts and censure. Since this discourse understands Roman Catholic identity as sameness and truth as univocal and positively identifiable, it seeks to control the*logical thought and work.

The other is the radical democratic discourse of *ekklesial* diversity that understands catholic identity as an open-ended, all-inclusive, shifting identity that is constantly being renegotiated. I will exemplify this kind of discourse with a Pastoral Letter from the Asian Bishops Conference. Both discourses, that of Roman Catholicism and that of *ekklesial* Catholicism, can claim Scripture and tradition as their authority and source and both are encoded in the documents of the Second Vatican Council.

In addition, I will point out that the notion of the *ekklēsia* of wo/men calls for a different catholic praxis and the*logical imagination that can bring about change and envision transformation. I am privileged to experience such a catholicity daily because of my institutional location in a non-Catholic institution that ironically provides a truly catholic context. At Harvard University Divinity School

---

8. See Francis Schüssler Fiorenza, "Pluralism: A Western Commodity or Justice for the Other?," in *Ethical Monotheism, Past and Present: Essays in Honor of Wendell S. Dietrich*, ed. Theodore Vial and Mark Poster (New York: Oxford University Press, 2001), 278–306.

9. Even the discourses that are aware of the problematic character of mission seem not to have yet recognized this point. See, for example, Ralph Pechmann and Martin Reppenhagen, eds., *Mission im Widerspruch: Religionstheologische Fragen heute und Mission morgen* (Neukirchen-Vluyn: Aussat/Neukirchener, 1999) and Theodor Ahrens, *Zwischen Regionalität und Globalisierung: Studien zur Mission, Oekumene, und Religion* (Amersbeck bei Hamburg: Verlag an der Lottbek, 1997).

10. By this I mean a discourse that is shaped by the rhetoric and values of empire, the Roman Empire as well as subsequent imperial powers of domination.

more than fifty religious denominations and persuasions are represented in the student body but not in the faculty. Not only Roman Catholic students from different social and international locations, but also Lutheran, Baptist, Episcopalian, Presbyterian, Black Church, Quaker, Methodist, Seventh Day Adventist, Evangelical, Pentecostal, American Indian, Muslim, Jewish, Buddhist, Atheist, Wicca, Unitarian, Hindu, Greek Orthodox, and Mormon students can be found debating together in seminars and lectures and engaging in a critical exploration of biblical texts, feminist the*logy, critical radical democratic theory, or ethics and dogmatic the*logy.

Not only students' different religious universes but also their variegated cultural locations make for the catholicity of our the*logical reflections and discussions. Here the catholicity of the*logy is practiced, a catholicity that speaks with many voices and searches for truth in many different locations. Such catholicity celebrates multiplicity, equality, and freedom. It requires freedom of inquiry and public argument, a freedom that is more and more lacking within Roman Catholic institutions. It necessitates that one acknowledge the catholicity of other churches and religions. It calls for a the*centric[11] or pneumatocentric rather than a christocentric or ecclesiocentric understanding of Christian identity.[12]

Finally, in a fourth step I point out that the struggle for the catholicity of the*logy is not just an inner-church quarrel but functions within the global struggles supporting or diminishing a more just and equitable world. In these struggles "wo/men" and "the feminine" have become important cultural and religious signifiers in fundamentalist and radical egalitarian religious discourses.

In short, it will not come as a surprise that I argue at the heart of the struggle for the catholicity of the*logy and the realization of a world-church is the question of wo/men's social, political, cultural and religious authority, full citizenship and creative leadership that galvanizes both societal and religious, Roman and ekklesial, catholic discourses. Just as the question of the catholicity of church and the*logy is an eminently feminist the*logical one, so also the exclusion of wo/men as ecclesial subjects from tradition, the*logy and church office is not a "woman's question" but a fundamental ecclesialogical one. Hence, I argue that the*logy is only able to adequately develop a critical catholic consciousness if and when it develops a feminist consciousness.

The Struggle for the Catholicity of The*logy

The feminist sense of catholicity still comes to the fore in the dictionary definition of the term. The *Shorter Oxford Dictionary* characterizes catholicity as

---

11. See Paul Knitter, *One Earth and Many Religions: Multifaith Dialogue and Global Responsibility* (Maryknoll: Orbis, 1995).

12. See James Provost and Knut Walf, *Catholic Identity Concilium* 5 (Maryknoll: Orbis, 1994), for a discussion of identity.

the quality of having sympathies with or being all-embracing; broad-mindedness and tolerance. The term catholicity is derived from the Greek word *katholikos* (*kath' holou*),[13] which is the equivalent of global (*kath' holon tēs gēs*) or ecumenical (relative to the *oikoumenē*). According to Robert Schreiter catholicity means "wholeness,"[14] in Peter Schineller's view it is brought about by inculturation,[15] and for Siegfried Wiedenhofer it is "Ganzheit und Fülle durch Austausch und Kommunikation."[16] Rather than emphasize wholeness and inculturation, I would underscore the meaning of "catholic" as global and ecumenical, as social-religious complexity and multi-vocal reality, as "all-embracing," "broadminded," or "universal." However, such universality must not be conceptualized in hegemonic kyriarchal but in radical democratic feminist terms.

Feminist and post-colonial critics[17] have pointed out that the claim to "universality" has tended to be articulated as a claim of dominance. Universality (or catholicity) is a kyriarchal term. The Western kyriarchal rhetoric of universality has engendered ideological mystifications such as the following:

1. Kyriocentric theory and the*logy has claimed to be universal and catholic although they express the experience and theorize the worldview of a very few elite educated (clergy) men. They speak of humanity or democracy in universal terms although they have limited it to a specific group of people.

2. Kyriocentric theory and the*logy have claimed to be universal, although they have made their own culturally limited experiences and Eurocentric horizons paradigmatic for all of humanity. Their claim to universal knowledge mystifies their particular or regional perspective and social location and thereby serves the interests of domination.

3. Kyriocentric discourses of universality and catholicity actively exclude the "others," that is all wo/men and subjugated or marginalized men, from intellectual theories, history and communal practices. This exclusion of the "others" of elite educated propertied men is not just accidental but was formulated in the interest of their domination and exploitation.

---

13. Avery Dulles, *The Catholicity of the Church* (Oxford: Clarendon, 1985).

14. Robert J. Schreiter, *The New Catholicity: The*logy between the Global and the Local* (Maryknoll: Orbis, 1997), 219. However, he does not explicitly address the feminist critique of this concept.

15. Peter Schineller, "Inculturation as a Pilgrimage to Catholicity," *Concilium* 204 (1989): 98-106.

16. Siegfried Wiedenhofer, *Das katholische Kirchenverständnis: Ein Lehrbuch der Ekklesiologie* (Graz: Styria, 1992), 279.

17. See Nancy Fraser, *Justice Interruptus: Critical Reflections on the "Postsocialist" Condition* (New York: Routledge, 1997); Leila Gandhi, *Postcolonial Theory: A Critical Introduction* (New York: Columbia University Press, 1998); Uma Narayan, *Dislocating Cultures: Identities, Traditions, and Third-World Feminisms* (New York: Routledge, 1997); and R. S. Sugirtharajah, *Asian Biblical Hermeneutics and Postcolonialism: Contesting the Interpretations* (Maryknoll: Orbis, 1998).

4. These kyriocentric claims to universality have functioned to legitimate Western imperial expansionism and colonization and to justify dehumanization, exploitation, cultural annihilation and religious demonization. Hence, the discourses of Christian mission must be scrutinized as to their participation in Western political imperialism, cultural absolutism, and religious colonialism.

A radical democratic feminist discourse, in turn, seeks to correct this kyriarchal understanding of universality and catholicity and to define the meaning of the word "catholic" as expressing the following:

1. Catholic means both theoretical and practical openness to all peoples, cultures and religions *as equals*. This requires opposition to religious sectarianism and individualistic identity formations that define the self over against the other who is understood in negative terms. Positively, it asks for the development of a radical egalitarian spirituality that is ecumenical, interfaith, and cosmopolitan.
2. Catholicity requires openness to truth and values wherever they are encountered. It seeks to revalorize the cultural and religious heritage of the "others" who have been excluded and exploited. Hence, a spirituality that is able to appreciate the "other" is called for.
3. Catholicity entails the ability to bridge divisions, generations and historical chasms. Thus a critical catholic feminist the*logy and political spirituality strives to break down the divisions that separate nations and religions from each other and to articulate religious visions that foster a world-ethos that seeks for the well-being of every one without exception.
4. Catholicity asks for the recognition that unity is not uniformity but solidarity in diversity. In order to articulate catholicity as pluriform diversity religious and the*logical discourses must shift their focus from christological discourses that have legitimated Western imperialism to pneumatological discourses that celebrate the multifaceted gifts of divine Wisdom Spirit, who creates and sustains global relations of justice and well-being and inspires the realization of a truly cosmopolitan world-church.

In short, such a critical feminist understanding of universality and catholicity can foster social-religious plurality and global connectedness linking radically different local churches and variegated cultures. It is engendered by a radical democratic spirituality that envisions an all-embracing inclusive reality in which all people are truly equal but not the same; an *ekklesial* culture where differences are respected and people are truly free, where socioreligious responsibility rather than individualistic self-absorption prevails; a society and world-church which is truly just and in which status and power inequalities—especially the vast gulf between well-to-do and impoverished people—are recognized for what they are.

A radical democratic the*logical vision of catholicity has its roots not only in classical Greco-Roman culture but also in the vision of Israel's prophets and of the early Christian movement's calling for a society and church in which G*d's justice and peace is already partially realized today but will become full reality in the future. This kind of catholicity is deeply embedded in Scripture and church history, and has inspired the vision of the church articulated at the Second Vatican Council. Today it is invigorated by attention to the radical democratic spiritual visions of other cultures and religions.

However, throughout Western philosophy and the*logy another discourse on catholicity/universality seems to have been operative in Roman Catholic the*logical debates and Western political philosophy, a discourse that is sustained by the exclusion and vilification of the "other." This discourse of domination and "othering" is an inheritance of the Roman empire and Western philosophy but it is also found in other cultural and religious totalitarian regimes, neo-colonial practices and authoritarian structures.

Political feminist theorist of culture Page duBois[18] has pointed out that in Greco-Roman society and tradition two different understandings of truth and universality prevailed. The logic of imperial domination produced a discourse of truth that was singular, universal, unitary, abstract doctrinal and accessible only to a very few. It has engendered torture and violence in both Greco-Roman antiquity and in contemporary society. It has shaped exclusivist identity formations that project all evil and negativity onto the others who are not like us. It also has shaped the the*logical discourse of orthodoxy and heresy that has served imperial interests.

Rebecca Lyman among others has argued that when second century authors gave *hairesis* a technical meaning they did so in order to define the the*logical opinions of others as unacceptable and dangerous, as false and intrinsically alien. This discourse of heresy has decisively shaped Christian the*logy and community as absolutist and exclusivist.

> Eventually the characteristics of heresy became a negative norm for orthodoxy by contrasting multiplicity to unity, intellect to spirit or sect to church. Certain the*logical teachings were therefore classified under labels that were increasingly abstracted and cited as types in contrast to orthodox ideas. Through this intellectualization of the*logical conflict as *hairesis* the concrete situation of the conflict . . . was effectively hidden beneath a label which condemned, excluded and distanced the idea or person from orthodox life and teaching. . . . Classifications and labels therefore were an essential part of the rhetorical strategy in ancient conflict.[19]

---

18. Page du Bois, *Torture and Truth* (New York: Routledge, 1990).
19. Rebecca Lyman, "A Topography of Heresy: Mapping the Rhetorical Creation of Arianism," in *Arianism after Arius: Essays on the Development of Fourth-Century Trinitarian Conflicts,*

In contrast, the logic of democracy, that is, the notion of equal power among members of a community, produces an understanding of truth as a multiple polyvalent assembly of voices, as a process, a dialectic ongoing dialogue. The truth of democracy and difference, duBois argues, is produced in struggle and debate; it is a praxis rather than a purely mental activity, and it is concrete and historically relative to its sociopolitical location. Truth is not handed down from on high but it is found between people as they struggle for justice and liberation and face the challenges of everyday life with hope and dignity. These two logics of truth, that of imperial domination and that of radical equality, are also inscribed in the the*logical self-understanding of church. This "church" is characterized by sacred structures of domination (*hieros* and *archein*), represented by men only, and draws its boundaries of identity in and through the exclusion of wo/men from the sacred, both through the non-ordination of wo/men and through celibacy.[20] Its ethos is control and obedience, positivist legalism and authoritarian exclusion. It is divided into a two-class system, that of the ordained and that of the laity, connoting second-class citizenship for those who are not clerics. In recent times it has been identified with the pope and the hierarchy as personifying the Roman Catholic church.[21]

The struggle for the catholicity of the*logy is about these two different logics of truth, that of radical democracy and that of Roman exclusion and control. One the*logical direction uses the Roman discourse of control and censure with its claims to absolute truth and its demands for absolute submission of the intellect to Roman Catholic papal and curial decrees; the other engages the ekklesial discourse of catholicity, which is inclusive and appeals to the pluriform gifts of divine Wisdom Spirit.

These two discourses understand catholicity quite differently and are in grave conflict with each other, a conflict that seems on the whole to affect the clergy more than the people of G*d. Sociological surveys have shown that ordinary Catholics usually do not pay much attention to the edicts coming from Rome because they do not speak to the problems facing them. Only those who still claim active Catholic citizenship, groups such as Women-Church, *Wir sind Kirche*, or the Women's Ordination movement stand up to the present onslaught of Roman intellectual monarchism, and they do so for the sake of the catholicity of the church. They hold the Roman hierarchy accountable on grounds of their the*logical birthright to be church, the pilgrim people of G*d.

However, one must not understand the struggle between these two discourses as an absolute typological dualism. Rather, these two discourses are interrelated and condition each other; they are articulated in a typological fashion in order to underscore the issues at stake in the variegated struggles for

---

ed. Michael R. Barnes and Daniel H. Williams (Edinburgh: T and T Clark, 1993), 47.

20. See the chart in my book *Discipleship of Equals*, 226.

21. See Paul Collins, *Papal Power: A Proposal for Change in Catholicism's Third Millennium* (London: Fount, 1997).

a world-church. In her study *Gender, Religion, and "Heathen Lands,"* Maina Chawla Singh has shown, for instance, how the discourses on wo/men's suffrage and that on "missionary women" have conditioned each other and interacted with each other in shaping the the*logy and practice of Protestant missions in the last two centuries.

> Thus, while prompted by the specific context of church governance and exclusion in directing their work first toward women and children in general, and then toward their "heathen sisters," North American women found a niche and a new recognition. The zeal for rescuing their "heathen sisters from the "evils" of their culture became for missionary women a strategy to address their own exclusion from church organization. Such endeavors for the "downtrodden" female other were therefore embedded in issues of gender, identity, autonomy and power.[22]

Equally, the two very different discourses on catholicity and universality—which I will discuss in the following sections—permeate and shape each other. In characterizing these two discourses, I do not have particular people in mind but institutional discursive structures. Members of the hierarchy and of the Vatican as well as of the general Catholic public, women as well as men, can position themselves in one or the other of these discourses. Moreover, their positioning in one of these discourses is not fixed but can shift from occasion to occasion, and debate to debate. Hence, accountability and critical reflections on one's ideological location in the discourses of power is called for in every instance.

The Logic of Domination

The Second Vatican Council sought to mitigate if not change some of the monarchical structures and to abandon the imperial rhetoric of Roman Catholic exclusivism that found its culmination in the anti-democratic discourses of Vatican I and its antimodernist ethos. However, as political scientists tell us, it is not easy to switch from authoritarian rule to a politics of radical ecclesial change towards the evangelical fullness of catholicity. Liberalization is not democratization. Authoritarian regimes can sometimes afford to introduce small changes without risking the loss of power.

It is this period of flux, heterogeneity, and change envisioned by Vatican II that the discourses of the Congregation of the Doctrine of the Faith seek to bring under control by returning to the rhetoric and measures of the inquisition, a rhetoric that was explicitly rejected by Vatican II. The renewal of Vatican II sought to balance the monarchic rule of the papacy with the aristocratic collegiality of the hierarchy and to embed both forms of organization with a democratic

---

22. Maina Chawla Singh, *Gender, Religion, and "Heathen Lands": American Missionary Women in South Asia* (New York: Garland: 2000), 10.

understanding of the church as the people of G*d. However, it attempted to do so without the structural institutional changes necessary to overcome the church's Roman imperial inheritance. The logic of imperial domination is still at work in the Vatican's notion of catholicity, which seeks to establish its universal control through doctrinal definition, censure and silencing.

As liberation historians have pointed out, in early Christianity the Pax Christi was gradually identified with the Pax Romana, and Christianity became an imperial religion. The state promoted ecclesiastical interests, clergy became a privileged class, and the church adopted imperial structures and discourses. Like the Roman emperor, the pope is called *pater patrum* and *pontifex maximus*. Like that of the Roman empire the constitution of the church is a combination of monarchic and aristocratic government with a veneer of democracy. Like the Roman empire the Roman church has become an expansionist universal power that has exploited the economy and culture of the "subjugated provinces," that is, the local churches.

In modernity, colonialism, in which colonization and mission actively coincided, modeled itself after its Roman predecessor. Like that of Roman imperialism, the Church's universal mission has in the past used force, mediated colonialism, and promulgated Eurocentrism, and still goes on to eliminate or appropriate the cultural and religious resources of its "subordinates." Military and mission, the gun and the Bible, the sword and the cross went, and still often go, hand in hand.

Like the Roman empire, the Roman church extends its administrative control to all those living in its territory. The discussions on the relations between the universal church and the local church are determined by this Roman framework of domination. The insistence of the declaration *Dominus Iesus*[23] on the exclusive salvific universality of Roman Catholicism to the exclusion of other Christian churches and world religions is a defense of the Roman imperial but not the *ekklesial* form of catholicity. Hence, Rome speaks in monologue, it commands and decrees from on high, and penalizes those who dissent.[24]

---

23. For a critical discussion, see Michael J. Rainer, ed., *"Dominus Iesus" Anstössige Wahrheit oder anstössige Kirche? Dokumente, Hintergründe, Standpunkte, und Folgen* (Münster: LIT, 2001).

24. In its Article of Comment on the Notification of the Congregation for the Doctrine of the Faith pertaining to the book of J. Dupuis (*Toward a Christian The*logy of Religious Pluralism*, published in L'Osservatore Romano, Feb 27, 2001, and translated by NCR and posted on NCR Online/documents on March 5, 2001) the CDF defends the authoritarian rhetorics of *Dominus Iesus* in the following statement: "The clear declarative/assertive tone of a magisterial document— typical of a declaration or of a notification of the Congregation for the Doctrine of the Faith, analogous to that of doctrinal decrees of the former Holy Office—intends to communicate to the faithful that it is not a case of debatable arguments or disputed questions. . . . It would certainly be wrong to hold that the declarative/assertive tone of the Declaration *Dominus Iesus* or of the present Notification are regressive steps backward in comparison to the literary genre and the expositive and pastoral nature of the magisterial documents of Vatican Council II and afterward. It would,

Still, it has been less recognized that these Roman discourses of orthodox Truth are also highly gendered. They are full of references to the hierarchy as sons and fathers, to the church as mother and she, and to the people of G*d as men of faith. Since Rome has categorically refused to change exclusive androcentric language in the liturgy and has overturned the recommendations of several bishops' conferences for the adoption of non-gendered liturgical language, such androcentric language that linguistically excludes wo/men is no longer conventional but deliberate. It maintains the status quo and limits our vision for as Heidegger declared, "the limits of our language are the limits of our worlds."

The use of the feminine[25] for the church serves to symbolically exclude and obliterate real wo/men, since according to Vatican teaching Christ and the church can be represented by men only. It reinforces the colonial discourses of domination in which "the feminine" signifies both the subordination and exploitation of wo/men and of all those who are non-persons: slaves, heathen savages, homosexuals and impoverished peoples, all of whom are seen and treated as "feminine" other. Or "the feminine" is used to express the Romantic glorification and idealization of the female which is expressed in Goethe's "das ewig Weibliche zieht uns hinan," that is, the eternal feminine draws men heavenward.

It is ironic that the church adopted the same Roman imperial structures which were responsible for the crucifixion of Jesus. Because Roman Catholicism remains caught up in these very same hierarchical imperial structures, the Roman bureaucracy has continued to insist that the church is not a democratic community. Whereas in the nineteenth century papal discourses defended monarchy as the governmental form willed by G*d not only for the church but also for society, in the past century papal encyclicals have advocated human rights and democratic freedoms in society but insisted that these do not apply to the church. However, moral authority cannot be claimed for something that one does not practice. To claim that radical democratic and evangelical values such as equality, justice, and freedom do not need to be practiced in the Roman Catholic Church but only by society means to engage in the Roman imperial discourses of control, violence, and domination.

---

however, be equally wrong and unfounded to retain that after Vatican II the declarative/assertive type must be abandoned or excluded from the authoritative interventions of the Magisterium."

25. See for instance Cardinal Joseph Ratzinger, *Church, Ecumenism, and Politics* (New York: Crossroad, 1988), 20: "The Church is not some piece of machinery, is not just an institution, is not even one of the usual sociological entities. It is a person. It is a woman. It is an other. It is living. The Marian understanding of the Church is the most decisive contrast to a purely organizational or bureaucratic concept of the Church. We cannot make the Church: we have to be it. . . . It is only in being Marian that we become the Church. In its origins the Church was not made but born. It was born when the intention 'Let it be to me according to your word' awoke in the soul of Mary." Here it becomes evident how naturalistic feminine language is used to avoid a discussion of radical egalitarian structures and for inculcating an ethos of submission and obedience.

The Logic of Radical Democracy

In order to engender the radical democratic renewal of Roman Catholicism it is necessary that the struggle for *ekklesial* catholicity does not deteriorate into sectarian dualistic opposition and mutual condemnation. Resistance to religious colonization requires not only the*logical and organizational change but also a change of the imagination. Feminist and postcolonial theorists have pointed out how extremely difficult it is to reject values and practices by which one is deeply shaped. It requires both a critical recognition of the imagery of domination and an imaginative creation of a new form of consciousness and a new way of life.[26] Hence, the struggle for the catholicity of the*logy must be understood as the intellectual and spiritual struggle for a different ekklesial imagination.

Although Vatican II was not a wholehearted attempt of radical democratic structural change but sought only to introduce limited reforms, it must not be overlooked that—inadequate as such liberal reforms were—they also opened up space for *ekklesial* debates and struggles of renewal. In the past forty years Catholic liberation the*logies and *ekklesial* reform movements have thought to make use of these spaces of reform as sites of struggle. They have achieved far-reaching changes because such a transitional process is beyond the control of those in power. Change can be checked for a while but this cannot be done indefinitely.

The egalitarian discourses and reform movements of the *ekklēsia* understand church as the democratic assembly[27]and congress of full decision-making citizens. The word "synagogue" has the same valence and also means the "congregation of the people of G*d." In Pauline literature the expression *ekklēsia* is the very name for the Christian community. This self-description of the early Christian messianic communities who gathered in the name of Jesus was a political-democratic one. Just as the *basileia* vision of the Jesus movements bespeaks an alternative political-religious imagination to that of the Roman empire (*basileia*), so also does the self-designation *ekklēsia* of the Christ movements.

Moreover, this language still presupposes the embeddedness of the church in the traditions of Israel as the people of G*d. *Ekklēsia* is the actual democratic assembly of G*d's people, who are the Jewish people.[28] Only when one realizes

---

26. See for example, Jan Nederveen Pieterse and Bhikhu Parekh, eds., *The Decolonization of Imagination: Culture, Knowledge, and Power* (London: Zed, 1995).

27. See John W. de Gruchy, *Christianity and Democracy* (Cambridge: Cambridge University Press, 1995), who explores the need for global democratization and Christianity's contribution to it.

28. This understanding of *ekklēsia* is rooted in the people of G*d who concretely assemble in the *ekklēsia*. In his discussion of *ekklēsia* and the people of G*d, Ratzinger follows a German form of exegesis that is not aware of its anti-Jewish horizon. Consequently, he ends up affirming christological exclusivism and Christian superiority: "In the New Testament the term 'people of God' is not a description of the Church, but it can *only* denote the *new Israel* (emphasis added) in the Christological reinterpretation of the Old Testament and thus by means of its Christological transformation. In the New Testament the normal term for church is the word ecclesia, which in the Old Testament denotes the assembly of the people through being summoned by the word of

how fundamental this radical democratic spirit was to the self-understanding of the early Christian communities can one appreciate the threat to Christian self-understanding that happened not only when, early on, Greco-Roman discourses of submission were introduced in the Christian Testament by early Christian writers, but also when the church adopted the administrative organizational structures of the Roman empire, structures which were monarchical-hierarchical. Hierarchalism, exclusivism, domination and anti-Jewish supersessionism go hand in hand.

In contrast to the Vatican's rhetoric of imperial decree and punishment for non-compliance, which promotes a global catholic monoculture, lived *ekklesial* catholicity speaks with compassion, freedom, and persuasive power.[29] Such a rhetoric is found, for example, in the final statement of the Seventh Plenary Assembly of the Asian bishops conference, which gathered January 3–13, 2000, in Samphran, Thailand. The Asian bishops' statement is entitled "A Renewed Church in Asia: A Mission of Love and Service." They begin with a reference to the words of the prophet Joel, "I shall pour out my spirit on all humanity," and thereby clearly mark the inclusive and dynamic catholicity of their vision with its reference to the oppressive structures of globalization.

The Asian bishops acknowledge that "the dawn of the new millennium is a time of crisis," but they do not react with fear and control. Rather, they go on to insist that "a time of crisis, as Scripture and the whole history of the Church shows us, is a time of new beginnings, new movements," and they observe "seven movements that as a whole constitute an Asian vision of a renewed church." These movements are: (1) the movement towards a Church of the Poor and a Church of the Young; (2) the movement toward a truly local church; (3) the movement toward deep interiority and a deeply praying community; (4) the movement toward an authentic community of faith, which in Asia is a movement toward Basic Ecclesial Communities; (5) the movement toward a new sense of mission in which "the Church has to be a compassionate companion and partner of all Asians, a servant of the Lord and of all Asian peoples in the journey toward full life in G*d's kingdom"; (6) the movement toward empowerment of men and women. The bishops insist that the church cannot be a sign of the Kingdom and of the eschatological community if the fruits of the Spirit to wo/men are not given due recognition, and if wo/men do not share in "the freedom of the children of God"; and finally, (7) "the movement toward active involvement in generating and serving life. The Church has to respond to the death-dealing forces in Asia."

God. . . . It is used because in it is included the idea that it is only through the new birth in Christ that what was not a people has been able to become a people." Cardinal Joseph Ratzinger, *Church, Ecumenism and Politics*, 18.

29. See Felix Wilfred, *Asian Dreams and Christian Hope: At the Dawn of the Millenium* (Delhi: ISPCK, 2000).

In concluding the section on Renewal, the bishops affirm a the*logy of the Spirit that has motivated religious reform movements throughout the centuries and throughout the world:

> For us in Asia, to renew the church is to be open to the mystery of the Spirit, to welcome the arriving presence of the God of surprises who will capture our hearts in wonder. We need therefore to be more than mere workers of renewal. We need to have the creative imagination of poets and artists, of wonderers and dreamers as befits those who are gifted by the Spirit of God. . . . Discerning and knowing God, communing with God through contemplative experience, the Church experiences the mandate of *missio Dei* as ongoing, as dynamically interacting with the complex realities of Asia.

This Asian the*logy is Spirit-centered, socially located, and ekklesially catholic. Its rhetoric is concrete, inclusive, and filled with grace and hope. It articulates a vision of all-embracing love that does not seek to dominate and control. It thereby contributes to the enunciation of a different ekklesial imagination that can inspire action for change and movements of renewal.[30]

However, the rhetoric of the Asian bishops does not directly address the injustice of ecclesiastical structures. For instance, when speaking about the problems of wo/men as one of many problems, the bishops address "widespread discrimination," "violence and abuse of wo/men," and the cultural prejudices and traditions sustaining such violence in the family and in Asian societies and cultures. Yet they do not address such church practices as clergy abuse, the exploitation of wo/men church workers or their exclusion from the official magisterium.

Although the Asian bishops affirm that Jesus' "great sensitivity and respect for wo/men are an invitation for a deep conversion for our church and society," they do not adamantly reject but tacitly accept the Roman politics of exclusion and silencing promoted in recent Vatican documents. Hence, the Asian bishops' rhetoric still reflects the cultural common-sense assumption that men represent the church in general and wo/men are just a special case. Because of this andro-kyriocentric assumption in the*logical discourses, the catholicity of *ekklēsia* understood as a radical democratic congress of fully entitled, responsible decision making citizens has never been fully realized either in church history or in Western democracy.

First, as discussed in previous chapters, in order to raise into consciousness the masculine over-determination of catholicity in malestream the*logical discourses and ecclesiastical representations I have coined the expression *ekklēsia gynaikōn,* the *ekklēsia of wo/men,* as a linguistic and the*logical means of conscientization. Since

---

30. Although the bishops do not want to construct a dualistic and idealist worldview, they are in danger of constructing Asianness or the "Asian soul" in an essentialist fashion. For a feminist critique of essentialism, see the writings of the Indian theorist Uma Narayan, who works in the United States.

the signifier "woman" is still used to draw the exclusive boundaries of Church, it is important to mark linguistically the difference between church as Roman kyriarchal institution and church as *ekklēsia*, as the people of G*d. This is justified because official Roman documents still speak of the church as "mother," "she," and "sister," making it common sense that an all-male hierarchy can identify church with itself and still speak of the church in feminine terms, although the hierarchy consists only of fathers, sons and brothers.

Second, feminist historical research has shown that the*logical emphasis on divine Wisdom-Spirit has allowed for the flourishing of the *ekklēsia* of wo/men. Like Jesus (Lk 4:1) those who constitute *ekklēsia* are "filled with the Holy Spirit." The expressions "full of the Holy Spirit," "full of the Holy Spirit and faith," or "full of the Spirit and Wisdom" are all found in Acts. According to Paul, those who are elect and called, those who are *ekklēsia*, "live by the Spirit." They are Spirit-filled people—pneumatics (Gal 5:25). Both wo/men and men are gifted by the Spirit. Justin can still assert in the second century that among the Christians all wo/men and men have received charisms from Holy Wisdom-Spirit.[31] This Spirit-equality of the *ekklēsia* is summed up in the words of the prophet Joel in Acts 2:17f:

> I will pour out my Spirit upon all flesh and your sons and daughters shall prophesy. . . . Yes, and on my male and female slaves . . . I will pour out my Spirit and they shall prophesy.

The *ekklēsia* understood as the force-field of divine Wisdom-Spirit is a "new creation," the Spirit-empowered people who are all equal because they all share in the gifts of divine Wisdom-Spirit, all without exception: Jews, Greeks, Barbarians, wo/men and men, slaves and free, those with high social status and those who are nothing in the eyes of the world.[32]

We still can glimpse such a Spirit-filled realization of *ekklēsia* in the polemics of Irenaeus against the followers of Marcus.[33] Their church order and pneumatic self-understanding seem to have been still very much like those found in 1 Corinthians and Acts. In the group of Marcus every initiate was assumed to have received the direct inspiration of the Holy Spirit. Whenever the congregation met, its members drew lots. This is a traditional Jewish practice used to divine the will of G*d, which was used in Acts to determine the succession of Judas. By means of the drawing of lots members of the Marcus-group were designated variously for performing the role of elder, overseer, reader, expounder of the Scriptures, teacher, or prophet. All members, both wo/men and men, slaves and free, were eligible for performing such functions, which changed from meet-

---

31. *Dialogue with Trypho*, 88.
32. See Elisabeth Schüssler Fiorenza, *In Memory of Her*, 160-99.
33. *Adversus Haereses* 1.13, 1-6.

ing to meeting. The drawing of lots and the communal character of Spirit-filled leadership appears close to what we know about the gatherings of the *ekklēsia* in the first century.

While critical biblical scholarship has shown that the functions of apostles and prophets were interchangeable in the Christian Testament, feminist historical scholarship has discovered that there were wo/men apostles in the beginning of Christianity. Yet, Catholics do not know about them because Mary of Magdala, who was still called in medieval Catholic the*logy "the apostle to the apostles," was turned by the Western church into a whore and sinner, while Junia was lost in androcentric language and grammatical manipulations. Moreover, critical early Christian research has pointed to the preeminence of prophetic leadership, and feminist historical scholarship has elaborated the significance of the notion of prophetic succession for wo/men's leadership in the early church. While the Christian Testament never identifies a presider of the Eucharist, non-canonical writings such as the Didache understand the prophet as such a eucharistic presider.

Wo/men were among the prophetic leaders of the Pauline communities. Luke characterizes Mary, and Elizabeth, as well as Anna, as prophets. He mentions the four prophetic daughters of Philip (Acts 21:9), whose fame according to the church historian Eusebius was so great that the Provinces of Asia derived their apostolic origin from them.[34] The apocryphal Acts of Paul and Thecla mention wo/men prophets like Stratonike, Eubulla, Phila, Artemilla, Nympha, and Myrta. The Montanists as well as many other Christian groups stressed the authority of the Spirit. According to Origen they appealed to the following wo/men prophets: the daughters of Philip; Deborah; Miryam, the sister of Aaron; Hulda; and Anna, the daughter of Phanuel. Didymus maintains that the Montanist wo/men prophets taught and prophesied in the *ekklēsia*, and Firmilian knows of a prophetess in Asia Minor who in 235 C.E. converted many laypeople and clerics. Epiphanius mentions a number of groups who held a prophetess in great honor. They argued that Eve was the first to eat from the tree of knowledge in order to the*logically justify the admission of wo/men to the clergy. As precedent for their practice they referred to Miriam, the sister of Aaron, to the four prophet daughters of Philip, and to Gal 3:28: "They had wo/men bishops and presbyters, since as they said they did not discriminate with regard to sex, got to be in accord with the statement of Paul: In Jesus Christ there is neither male and female."[35]

This clearly articulated leadership and succession of wo/men prophets in ancient the*logy is universal but also ecumenical. It claims not only the suc-

---

34. *Ecclesiastical History* III.39.7-17.

35. Epiphanius, *Panarion* 49.2-3. See J. K. Coyle, "The Fathers on Wo/men and Women's Ordination," *Eglise et Theologie* 9 (1978): 51-101:77.

cession of early Christian prophets but also that of Israel's wo/men prophets. In contrast, the rhetoric of "apostolic succession" is exclusive not only of wo/men but of all non-orthodox Roman forms of Christian and religious experience. The knowledge about the importance of wo/men's prophetic and apostolic leadership for the realization of *ekklēsia* has fallen victim to the heresiological struggles of ancient Christianity that are still ongoing today. The labeling of other Christians as standing in the "demonic succession of false prophets" provides the historical location for the Vatican's insistence on the construct of apostolic succession. This rhetoric neglects the fact that apostolic succession, just like prophetic succession, is a the*logical construct that emerges in the heresiological debates of the second century.

Third, the ecumenical experience shows that the ordination of wo/men is not just a political and administrative pastoral question but an eminently the*logical one that goes to the heart of the catholicity of the church. *Ekklesial* equality in catholicity is the*logically grounded in both creation and in baptism and the gifts of the spirit. The *ekklēsia* of wo/men is called and elect, holy in body and soul, gifted with the Spirit-Sophia. In the words of 1 Peter, we "are a chosen race, a royal priesthood, a holy nation, God's very own people." As a richly gifted people we are the body of Christ, that is, the messianic corporation in whom religious, racial, and class but also heterosexual markers no longer signify and legitimate status differences. As a pilgrim people the *ekklēsia* of wo/men may fail again and again but it continues to struggle, to live in fullness and to realize its calling to be a discipleship of equals. As the discipleship of equals we are church, the *ekklēsia* of wo/men in process. As Hedwig Meyer-Wilmes observes, "One could even say that the *ekklēsia* of wo/men is a postmodern concept of the church. It takes for granted the achievements of modernity: it is grounded in an egalitarian view of structures, a multiplicity of ecclesiological images and a concern to make the church visible in different formations of ministry."[36]

This understanding of catholicity is positioned in the the*logical discourse of *ekklēsia* and Wisdom-Spirit; it envisions the world-church as a reciprocal community of support, a dynamic alliance of equals. It is the catholicity of grace flourishing in the all-embracing atmosphere of divine Wisdom-Spirit in which we live and move. Its principle and horizon is the Holy Spirit who creates community in diversity, commonality in solidarity, equality in freedom and love, a world church that appreciates the other precisely as the other.

Such a catholicity means not only fullness of being, all-encompassing inclusivity, but also dynamic multiplicity and the convergence of many different voices. It is foreshadowed in the image of Pentecost where people from different regions

---

36. Hedwig Meyer-Wilmes, "The Diversity of Ministry in a Postmodern Church," in *The Non-Ordination of Wo/men*, 80. See also her "Ist Öffentlichkeit öffentlich? Kritische Anmerkungen zum Öffentlichkeitsbegriff aus feministisch-theologischer Sicht," in *Wieviel Theologie verträgt die Öffentlichkeit?*, ed. Edmund Arens und Helmut Hoping (Freiburg: Herder, 2000), 113-26.

and cultures could understand the gospel of the Spirit in their own languages, an image that invites us in the power of the Spirit to struggle for the fullness of catholicity, for the *ekklēsia* of wo/men. *Ekklesial* catholicity thus is a pneumatological category. At stake in the struggle for the catholicity of the*logy and church is this prophetic freedom and rich giftedness by the Spirit.

Global Contextualization

The struggle for wo/men's full citizenship and the all-embracing catholicity of the*logy and the world-church, must be understood in terms of its sociopolitical location and function in an international context of globalization. Hence, a radical egalitarian the*logy opens up to critical inquiry the contesting political interests, cultural-religious imaginations and theoretical frameworks that determine not only the articulations of the*logians but also the pronouncements of the hierarchy.

However, to make Vatican declarations and inner-church movements the central site of struggle for the catholicity of the*logy easily neglects the social-political reality in which they are embedded and which they indirectly shape. To see them as purely ecclesiastical quarrels draws attention away from the implication of the Roman church in exploitation and from the possibilities that globalization engenders.

Economic globalization[37] was created with the specific goal of giving primacy to corporate profits and values, installing and codifying capitalist market values globally. It was designed to amalgamate and merge all economic activities around the world within a single model of global monoculture. In many respects wo/men are suffering not only from the globalization of market capitalism but also from sexual exploitation instigated by such market capitalism.

Since nation states are no longer in control of globalization, social political theorists such as Hardt and Negri have pointed out that it may be more appropriate to understand globalization in terms of empire. Insofar as the nation-state is replaced by multinational corporations its globalizing economic, cultural and political forces form a polycentric empire.[38] The danger of this shift from nation state to international corporation is that democratic government no longer can be exercised and the system of global capitalism is not held democratically accountable. However, such globalization also presents possibilities for more radical

---

37. See Jan Nederveen Pieterse, ed., *Christianity and Hegemony*, 11-31. See also Paul E. Sigmund, "Christian Democracy, Liberation Theology, the Catholic Right, and Democracy in Latin America," in *Christianity and Democracy in Global Context*, John Witte Jr., ed (Boulder: Westview, 1993), 187-207.

38. Michael Hardt and Antonio Negri, *Empire: A New Vision of Social Order* (New York: Harvard University Press, 2001). See also my book *But She Said: Feminist Practices of Biblical Interpretation* (Boston: Beacon, 1992), 102-33.

democratization world-wide. It also makes possible the interconnectedness of all being and the possibility of communication across national borders on the basis of human rights and justice for all.

The*logical discourses and religious communities either spiritually sustain the exploitation of global capitalism or they engage the possibilities for greater freedom, justice and solidarity engendered by the technological market forces of globalization. World religions either support the forces of economic and cultural global dehumanization or they abandon their exclusivist tendencies and together envision and work for a catholic spiritual ethos of global dimensions; either they provide radical democratic spiritual values and visions that celebrate diversity, multiplicity, tolerance, equality, justice and well-being for all or they foster fundamentalism, exclusivism and the exploitation of a totalitarian global monoculture.

If Catholicism should contribute to the fashioning of a radical democratic catholic-global ethos, then the struggle for the catholicity of the*logy must remain conscious of its global location and develop spiritual practices and forms of Christian community that can contribute to justice and well-being for all. For that reason catholic the*logy needs to insist on its intellectual and spiritual freedom to articulate ekklesial paradigms of how to live in diversity, tolerance, and respect for those who are not like us.

Feminist and postcolonial theorists have drawn attention to two crucial theoretical issues in emancipatory struggles: On the one hand they have pointed out that cultural and religious essentialism fashions identity discourses of sameness rather than of rich diversity.[39] Hence, they have criticized the christocentric discourses that define Christian identity in terms of exclusivist and male supremacist Eurocentric identity.[40] On the other hand, they have argued that emancipatory struggles need to imagine alternatives to the structure of domination and envision discursive communities that are not simply idealized political or religious fantasies but already have been partially realized in history.[41] Consequently they have sought to redefine Christian identity and mission in the*centric or pneumatocentric terms.

For that reason, one cannot insist enough that the radical democratic equality and catholicity of the *ekklēsia* of wo/men is not simply idealized fantasy but has been realized in the practices and visions of catholic movements of divine Wisdom-Spirit. The*logically they are grounded in the fact that all human

---

39. See Uma Narayan, "Essence of Culture and a Sense of History: A Feminist Critique of Cultural Essentialism," in *Decentering the Center: Philosophy for a Multicultural, Postcolonial, and Feminist World*, ed. Uma Narayan and Sandra Harding (Bloomington: Indiana University Press, 2000).

40. See my books *Jesus: Miriam's Child and Sophia's Prophet* (New York: Continuum, 1994) and *Jesus and the Politics of Interpretation* (New York: Continuum, 2000).

41. See for instance Alison M. Jagger, "Globalizing Feminist Ethics," in *Decentering the Center: Philosophy for a Multicultural, Postcolonial, and Feminist World*, Uma Narayan and Sandra Harding, eds. (Bloomington: Indiana University Press, 2000), 1-25.

beings are created in the image of G*d and that all of creation is given in their care. The *missio Dei*, the *mission of G*d*, seeks for the dignity and wellbeing of all of creation.

Ekklesial catholicity, I argue, is a theocentric and pneumatological category. At stake in the struggle for the catholicity of the*logy and a world-church is the prophetic freedom and rich giftedness by the Spirit. The open cosmic house of divine Wisdom, which has no walls and barriers to the flow of the Spirit images such a full *ekklesial* catholicity and inviting mission.

> Wisdom has built Her house
> She has set up Her seven pillars. . . .
> She has mixed Her wine,
> She also has set Her table.
> She has sent out Her wo/men ministers
> to call from the highest places in the town . . .
> "Come eat of my bread
> and drink of the wine I have mixed.
> Leave immaturity, and live,
> And walk in the way of Wisdom." (Proverbs 9:1-3, 5-6)

Divine Wisdom's inviting table, with the bread of sustenance and the wine of celebration, is set in a cosmic temple with seven pillars that allow the spirit of fresh air to blow through it. In this radical open space of divine Wisdom-Spirit, Catholic the*logians will be able to envision the catholicity of the world church as a multi-voiced, multicultural, multigendered, and multi-religious radical democratic Spirit movement for the well-being of all. Only if Catholic the*logy remains positioned in the open global space of divine Wisdom will it be able to sustain its rich catholicity and to maintain its intellectual freedom.

9

An Open Letter to Miryam IV, Successor of Peter and Mary of Magdala

When I was invited, by the editors of an Italian volume on the agenda of a new pope, to write an article on "Feminism and the Papacy in the Third Millennium," I decided to delineate in the form of a fictive letter the issues and problems the newly elected successor of John Paul II would have to face. Tongue in cheek, I suggested that the new leader of Catholicism would be not only a woman but a feminist who chose the name Miryam IV. The following is the imaginary letter addressed to her.[1]

Dear Friend of divine Wisdom,

It took me a long time to find the proper way to address you: Holy Father, Your Holiness, Pontifex Maximus, Pater Patrum, Pope, Servus Servorum Dei—none of these titles seemed quite right. Among these traditional titles, Servus Servorum Dei seemed to fit. But when I remembered the many Filipina sisters working as unpaid servants of the "servants" of G*d in the hospitals and seminaries of the West, it also sounded hypocritical.

To indicate a different "service" than that of exploited labor, I contemplated the address *minister*—a title given by divine Wisdom to those sent out to proclaim Her good news and to invite all to Her open house and table (Prov. 9:1-6). But this title referred to the non-ordained in post–Vatican II Roman Catholicism. Moreover, "minister" sounded too Protestant or reminded one too much of a political office, such as, for example, "Prime Minister." Equally arrogant seemed "Your Holiness!" After all the weighing and pondering of an appropriate address,

---

1. First published in Italian as "Lettera aperta a Miriam IV, la successore di Pietro e di Maria di Magdala," in *L'agenda del nuovo papa: Dai cinque continenti ipotesi sul dopo Wojtyla*, edited by Luigi De Paoli and Luigi Sandri, (Rome: Riuniti, 2002), 115-40.

I finally settled on *friend*, a name given in Scripture to the children of divine Wisdom and to the followers of Jesus' vision of a world of justice and peace. I hope you will like it and make it your own: Wisdom Friend, Miryam IV.

Papa Feminista

Yet, after I had found an address satisfactory to the demands of etiquette and theological rhetoric, I was at a loss as to what I actually could say to you about the issues and problems you face as new pope in the third millennium. Writing to you as a "friend," I became acutely aware of the pitfalls and dangers ahead of you. What could one hope for? Should I congratulate or commiserate with you, since being elected pope promises to be more a crown of thorns than a bed of roses? The best of the best would not be able to change an encrusted administrative system of mind-control and Eurocentrism such as the Vatican bureaucracy, an institution that has managed to again shut all the doors and windows that were opened only a little bit by Pope John XXIII and the Second Vatican Council.

Dominus Jesus[2]—that is, Lord, Emperor, Slave-master, Father—and not the carpenter of Nazareth and fisherman from Galilee seems to be at the heart of the Roman papalism that you have inherited. Remembering the threat of religious violence against theologians who have shown intellectual integrity, especially remembering the measures against those advocating the ordination of wo/men to the full office of priestly ministry as bishops, one may rightly and helplessly ask: What is a feminist pope to say? What could a good Catholic who is a feminist do in such a retrograde situation?

When contemplating the most recent Vatican rhetoric and the cruel measures of the last papacy against liberation theologians and the faithful at large, the story of the emperor who has no clothes comes to mind. The emperor, so the story goes, paraded around without a shred of clothing. All bystanders pretended not to see. No one had the courage to tell the truth until a child in the assembled crowd called out: "The emperor has no clothes!" This story has become in my view a fitting parable interpreting the desperate measures of the Vatican bureaucracy to keep the faithful from becoming fully responsible adult citizens of the church.

Those in the Vatican and beyond who are suffering from the fear of Dostojewski's Grand Inquisitor seem desperately to want to enforce legally what they cannot reason out the*logically. Lacking arguments, kyriarchal government (that is, proper to the Lord, Slave-master, Father) always has to resort to force. The means of censure and violence are familiar. Lacking the worldly power of the

---

2. For a critical discussion of the by-now-notorious Vatican document *Dominus Jesus,* see Michael J. Rainer, ed., *"Dominus Jesus" Anstössige Wahrheit oder anstössige Kirche? Documente, Hintergründe, Standpunkte, und Folgen* (Münster: LIT, 2001), and page 170 above.

Lord to torture dissidents and to burn them at the stake, the Grand Inquisitors of today can only resort to the violent measures of silencing and exclusion. Facing the threat of religious violence against those advocating the ordination of wo/men to the full office of priestly ministry as bishops,[3] many Catholic feminists have asked: Why should we care at all about Roman Catholicism and its oppressive structures?

But despite the repression of the Vatican bureaucracy, those like you who have been called to priestly ministry continued to act on this call, celebrating the Eucharist, serving the poor, teaching the young, blessing the hopeless, and building up the community. You did this not in order to show the hierarchy up but in order to serve the Catholic people. If you had just wanted to be ordained at any price and to join the clergy, there were plenty of churches that would have welcomed you and all those Catholic feminists who had been called to ordained leadership in a renewed Catholic church.

Seemingly taking the Holy Father, Pope John Paul II, at his word when he said that he did not have the authority of Scripture and tradition to ordain wo/men as priests, feminist the*logians began to look for a way out of this quagmire and to ask: "What about cardinals?" Let's obey the papal decree, we suggested years ago, and declare a moratorium on demands for ordination as deaconesses or priestesses. Instead, let us get ready for the next conclave when feminist cardinals will elect the new successor not only of Peter but also of Mary Magdalene! Maybe it will be one of us feminists! If s/he can't symbolize Christ as his Vicar, we were confident that s/he would very convincingly represent divine Wisdom in all Her splendor.

Tongue in cheek I wrote that, if that were to happen, I would love to serve the church as head of the CDF (my acronym for the Latin Congregatio Doctorum Feministarum!) in order to abolish once and for all the technologies of the Inquisition, although I had no desire to become the successor of Cardinal Ratzinger. If *Commonweal* is correct that Pope John Paul II once called himself a "papa feminista," I pointed out, the next pope will be a feminist! So I wrote to you in 1998. However, being of little faith I did not imagine that this could actually happen. Nor did I pray to Holy Wisdom that it should happen.

But, to quote a saying of my grandmother: Der Mensch dachte und Gott lachte! (roughly translated, "human beings planned and G*d laughed"). Unexpectedly, the Women's Ordination Conference International gave up their campaign for deaconesses and organized a campaign for the appointment of wo/men as cardinals. The office of cardinal, they argued, was instituted to provide a court for the pope. Hence, cardinals are called the princes of the church!

---

3. For a record of this development see my books *Discipleship of Equals: A Feminist Ekklēsialogy of Liberation* (New York: Crossroad, 1992) and *The Non-Ordination of Wo/men and the Politics of Power* (London: SCM, 1999), which Herman Haering and I edited together.

No ordination is required either by Scripture or tradition for this important office, since there is no evidence that the institution of cardinalship goes back either to Jesus or to the apostles. True, it has a long malestream tradition, but this tradition is of the male hierarchy's making. Equity, however, would demand—so we argued—that all cardinals should be feminists as long as bishops must remain masculinists, that is, subscribing to the misogynist notion that only men can represent the divine.

Although the men in the Vatican pointed out that it was church practice since medieval times to require that cardinals must be priests, they could no longer ideologically legitimize their prejudice with reference to Christ and the apostles. The election and appointment of wo/men as cardinals finally got rid of the misogynist virus that has afflicted the Roman Catholic Church for centuries and has led to its paralysis today. Cardinalship for wo/men opened up the only democratic means available in Roman Catholicism to wo/men who were able to determine the election of the new pope and thereby the future of the church.

Now that the miracle has happened and the first feminist pope has been elected, I am not so sure any longer! Should we have organized to abolish the papacy altogether rather than to become cardinals? True, we have a feminist successor of John Paul II, but how can s/he change an encrusted patriarchal imperial system that is almost two millennia old and of which s/he is a part? Plagued by such grave doubts, I picked up in an airport bookstore a novel entitled *The Accidental Pope*, which Ray Flynn, the former mayor of Boston and United States ambassador to the Vatican, wrote together with the novelist Robin Moore.[4] Doris Kerns Goodwin endorses the book as "a suspenseful, provocative, lively tale of Vatican intrigue and U.S. State Department guile."

The tale is simple and was written before John Paul II asked all his cardinals to resign their office and to make way for the appointment of wo/men cardinals. It imagines that the cardinals—all men—who are gathered for the conclave are deadlocked between three candidates: the Camerlengo of the conclave, the Primate of Ireland, and an African cardinal. To get the conclave unstuck, the Primate of Ireland tells an edifying tale about a friend who is a fisherman on Cape Cod. In the next round of ballots, the cardinals, to their great surprise and laughter, unwittingly elect this fisherman from Cape Cod as the next pope. Bill Kelley is an ex-priest, widower, and father of four almost-grown children. After great consternation the cardinals decide to play along with "this joke of G*d" and pro forma to ask Bill Kelly to become the next pope, certain that he will not accept the election. But because of a vision of the blessed Mother, Bill Kelly unpredictably accepts the office, becomes Pope Peter II, and the Roman church has its "First Family" albeit without a "First Lady."

---

4. Ray Flynn and Robin Moore, *The Accidental Pope: A Novel* (New York: St. Martin's, 2000).

Since I looked to the novel for stretching my imagination, I became more and more disappointed and depressed the further I got into it. In this tale, traditional theology sustains its hold on the Catholic imagination: The ex-priest fisherman can become the Holy Father because he is not really a genuine "layman" but as the cardinals argue, "once a priest—always a priest." They insist that he become again a cleric in good standing and take care to legitimize this accidental election by ordaining him bishop of Rome and by citing Scripture and tradition. For Scripture teaches that the first Pope, Saint Peter, was a married fisherman whose mother-in-law was healed by Jesus, and tradition knows of married popes with scandalous family histories. Both the understanding of ordination as induction into the class of clergymen, the traditional notion of family, and the church's teaching on celibacy are left intact.

Moreover, in this novel the U.S. ambassador to the Vatican is a member of Opus Dei and the new Pope is devoted to the "mystery" of Fatima and its anticommunist message. While Our Lady of Fatima protected Pope John Paul II during a near fatal attack by a communist assassin, Pope Peter II dies from a virus transmitted by a Slavic female doctor who hates Americans and is part of the conspiracy to extend the new Russian hegemony to Africa through the Orthodox Church. The alliance of the Roman Catholic Church with the imperial state, Western anti-communism, and its justification through kyriarchal theology is not broken but reenacted in and through the election of an American pope.

After finishing the book, I realized that reality had turned out better than fiction. Yet I asked myself what advice one could give to the newly elected successor of John Paul II, if even the Catholic imagination remains in Babylonian or, better, Roman captivity and is unable to envision a different leadership for the church in service to the world. Will it be possible for any human being, male or female, married or celibate, ordained or lay, to lead the church out of its captivity to Roman imperial mindsets and masculinist structures? Should we even have envisioned and desired a feminist pope? Is a papa feminista not an oxymoron, a contradiction in terms? Will not anybody be co-opted by the institution of the Roman papacy even if, like you, s/he has been a bona fide feminist Christian? Would it not be better to do away with the papal office altogether? Can anyone, even if sent by G*d, overcome the last centuries of ecclesiastical monarchy that climaxed in the dogma of papal infallibility?

The Vicar of Christ continues to represent Christ in the image and likeness of the Roman emperor, as King of Kings and Lord of Lords. For it is laudable but not enough to confess the past sins of the church, as Pope John Paul II has done, while continuing to practice them in the present. It is not enough to claim the equality of all believers while still praying to a G*d who is Lord of Lords, Almighty, Warrior King. True, today's heretics are no longer burned at the stake, but they still are denied the name of the true church of Christ. True, the hierarchy no longer calls to crusades and holy wars against the infidels, but Islam and other religions are still deemed to be inferior to Christianity. True, the most recent popes have rejected anti-Semitism, but they continue to spread anti-Judaism as the word of G*d in and through the proclamation of anti-Jewish Scripture texts. True, the church has repented its racism and colonialist collaboration, but it still treats two-thirds-world churches and their leadership as second-class citizens. True, the church has rejected sexism and misogyny as sins, but it continues to justify its exclusively male leadership in and through a dual-nature theology that legitimates the exclusion of wo/men from its sacred power and leadership. Not only does the hierarchy not ordain Roman Catholic wo/men but it also does not recognize the ordination of so many wo/men priests and bishops in other churches.

In the face of such grave ills and institutionalized failures, a deep sense of despair and lethargy overcame me. Are not those correct who claim that an egalitarian and just Catholicism is impossible and insist that Roman masculine imperialism is constitutive of Roman Catholicism? If one were able to take away the church's Roman imperial structures, would it still be Catholicism? Who was I to persuade someone who was created in Rome's imperial image and likeness to abandon Roman imperialism? Even if the person, woman or man, black or white, African or Asian, gay or straight, young or old, would share my theological vision of Catholicism, s/he would have to abandon it in order to stay in power and to do her/his work effectively.

Yet, I could not get out of my mind the story of Jonah, who refused to go and proclaim G*d's call to repentance to the Ninevites. Even though he was swallowed up by a whale and miraculously escaped it alive, Jonah still did not want to acknowledge G*d's mercy and power for change. Like Jonah, I was tempted to flee; like Jonah, I was convinced that I could not say anything to you, the newly elected one, that could bring about the conversion of the Roman church. Like Jonah, I doubted the power of divine Wisdom's saving grace.

A Feminist Catholic Vision

As I questioned and agonized about what to tell you regarding the future well-being of G*d's people in and outside of Catholicism, Christianity, and other religions, as I argued with G*d and despaired over the affairs of the church that I loved, I had a dream! A messenger of divine Wisdom appeared in all Her glory and said: "Peace be with you! Fear not, ye of little faith, I bring you good tidings. Divine Wisdom loves Her people and sends Her message of abundant grace to Her faithful friends. She invites all without exception: 'Eat of my bread and drink of my cup and walk in the ways of wisdom.'"

And the messenger of the Living One left me puzzling over the meaning of this communication for you, the newly elected successor of John Paul II. What did this announcement made by divine Wisdom mean? Was Wisdom-Spirit commissioning you to go on a pilgrimage around the world, walking incognito from place to place, eating and drinking with G*d's people, befriending and asking them what to do?

Did it mean that you should open the doors of the Vatican, set the tables, and send the Vatican's bishops and cardinals into the streets and byways of the world to invite the poor and the hungry, the maimed and the mentally ill, the old and the young, people of color and "white trash," common men and wo/men rather than the rich and the powerful, the members of Opus Dei, and the managers of the Vatican bank and the heads of states? Or was Her call addressed to all the people of G*d, calling their elected representatives to come and to dine in the splendor of the Vatican so that you could consult with them on the affairs of the church and the world? Or did it mean that divine Wisdom wanted you to invite the church's scholars and theologians, missionaries and aid-workers, priests and ministers, doctors and nurses, experts and consultants to the Vatican for an international symposium on the needs and dreams of all the people of the world, who are G*d's people?

What did this message mean? I thought and thought, asked and asked, but could not come up with one correct answer. Exhausted, I fell asleep again. Now I was back in the time when I was a student in Würzburg and I heard all the church bells of the city ringing to announce the election of the newly elected Pope John XXIII. And his shrewd face of loving-kindness appeared before my inner eye: "Aggiornamento! Open the windows and doors and transform the church into the open house of divine Wisdom, into a cosmic cosmopolitan temple without any walls and fortifications, so that the Spirit of G*d can blow through it with new life-giving power!"

When I woke up, the insistent call of John XXIII and all the saints remained fresh on my mind. This message seemed to be clear: Go and tell Miryam IV: Continue the work that I have begun, John seemed to say. Lead the church out of its bondage and captivity to imperial powers and oppressive traditions. In G*d's eyes nothing is impossible! Take heart, divine Wisdom will grant you the freedom to articulate a new vision of Catholic identity with integrity and courage. This will be possible if you, "Friend of divine Wisdom," will situate your work not in hierarchically controlled institutions but among the people of G*d. In order to do so, you must insist on intellectual freedom and integrity. As Mary of Magdala faced down Peter, so you must withstand the Roman exclusivist rhetoric of absolutism and censure. To articulate a truly Catholic theological vision of church leadership in a feminist voice, a vision that can make a difference, however, will not be possible without struggle.

Catholicity is not simply a denominational name[5] but is best envisioned as a radical democratic project of feminist praxis and vision.[6] If, as the newly elected Pope Miryam IV, you will proclaim as your very own program such a critical feminist understanding of universality and catholicity, you must gather around you feminist theological advisors from all walks of life who will help you

---

5. For an Anglican reflection on Catholicism see Jeffrey John, ed., *Living the Mystery: Affirming Catholicism and the Future of Anglicanism* (London: Darton, Longman, Todd, 1994).

6. See also Rebecca S. Chopp, "A Feminist Perspective: Christianity, Democracy, and Feminist Theology," in *Christianity and Democracy in Global Context*, ed. John Witte Jr. (Boulder: Westview, 1993), 111-30.

articulate such a radical, democratic, Catholic spirituality. Because of your own experiences of struggle and faithfulness to your feminist calling, you are able to bring into ecclesiastical discourses the religious experiences and questions of wo/men and other marginalized peoples.

The Vision of the Three Miryams

Such a spiritual vision and giftedness is already practiced around the world today. An email message from India reflecting on a symposium I have attended aptly expresses it:

> *These days . . .*
> *We heard voices on behalf of the oppressed*
> *Living in garbage heaps and city slums*
> *Little children, rag-pickers in search of food*
> *Who lack education, denied of Child's Rights!*
>
> *Women toiling in the homes, in the mills*
> *Nurturing life, their work uncounted! Unrecognized!*
> *Women battered! Women selling their bodies!*
> *Patriarchal sites, denying woman's Dignity and Rights.*
>
> *Mechanized boats! Foreign trawlers,*
> *Plundering resources of earth and sea!*
> *Aqua Culture destroying soil and lives,*
> *Peoples' Movements, Fisherfolks' Rights.*
>
> *Migrant workers, migration of peoples*
> *In search of work in mega cities . . . ever more cities!*
> *Abandoning their villages, exploited by TNCs*
> *Peoples' struggles for life! Hear their cry for Life!*
>
> *Oppressed of the land, deprived of land*
> *Dalits of the countryside, Tribals of the hill country*
> *Here the pain of exclusion, age old*
> *There the exploitation ever on the rise!*
>
> *We groaned, we pondered, we questioned*
> *Our response as church to these survival rights!*
> *We sought openings to move out in compassion*
> *To transcend death-dealing forces with hope for life!*
>
> *A call to rebirth our earth and bring forth a new dawn!*[7]

---

7. Conclusions of the Ishvani Kendra Silver Jubilee Colloquium, "The Church in Mission: Universal Mandate and Local Concerns" (October, 24–27, 2001).

As I read this message, the round face of Dr. Martin Luther King Jr. appeared before my mind's eye and I heard his famous words, "My eyes have seen the promised land." To give up on the dream of Jesus—the messenger of divine Wisdom, a dream for the restoration of G*d's world of justice and love—I realized would not just mean to abandon the newly elected pope to the powers of domination and evil but also to betray the church glimpsed in the words of my sisters and brothers in India and other parts of the world.

Then I heard a voice like the murmur of many waters and the blowing of many winds:

> Go and tell my beloved, my chosen one:
> I have brought you up from the land of Egypt
> And redeemed you from the house of slavery;
> And I sent before you Moses, Aaron and Miryam. (Micah 6:4)

> I will save you and you shall be a blessing.
> Do not be afraid but let your hands be strong . . .
> These are the things that you shall do:
> Speak the truth to one another,
> Render in your gates judgments that are true and make for peace.
>   (Zech 8:13-16)

Suddenly, I found myself transported to one of the feminist liturgies that are celebrated around the world. In this sacred feminist space I saw the wo/men form a circle around you, the newly elected messenger of divine Wisdom, dancing and chanting: "Behold, the follower of Christ, the messenger of divine Wisdom! S/he has chosen the name of Miryam IV because s/he is the successor of the three Miryams of Holy Scripture: S/he will walk in the footsteps of Miryam, the sister of Moses, who has led her people out of slavery. S/he will listen to the experience of Miryam, the mother of Jesus, who as a young wo/man chooses to bear and nurture a child out of wedlock. S/he will follow Miryam of Magdala, who as the first witness to Jesus' execution and resurrection was sent to proclaim the good news as apostle to the apostles. S/he is the first one to lay claim to the cathedra of Miryam who, as the Magdalene, has been maligned throughout the centuries as the 'great sinner and whore.'"

And then I saw Miryam, the sister of Moses and Aaron, of Jesus and John, of Peter and Paul, of Mohammed and Buddha, of Shiva and Pelé, appear regally clothed in the magnificent black beauty of Bahia, calling us to struggle:

> Yehoyah calls us to serve Her in the wilderness
> Yehoyah summons us to freedom.
> She will bear us on eagle wings
> To a place where freedom swells up like a mighty river,
> Where joy rises like a swiftly flowing stream.[8]

---

8. The poem is by Lynn Gottlieb, *She Who Dwells Within: A Feminist Vision of a Renewed Judaism* (New York: Harper Collins, 1995), 112.

Then I heard a great outcry and lament from the four corners of the earth: "Comfort, O comfort my people! Lead them out of bondage, hunger, and despair so that they can enjoy our wonderful earth with its beautiful mountains, streams, lands and seas. Go and tell the newly elected leader of Catholicism: Like Miryam, the sister of Moses, you are to lead the peoples of the earth out of capitalist bondage, which has engendered unspeakable poverty, and despair around the world. Remember and do not forget the world's poverty and despair!"

Go and denounce this great atrocity and abomination: Eighty countries have per capita income lower than a decade ago. In 1960 the income gap between the fifth of the world's people living in the richest countries and the fifth in the poorest countries was 30 to 1, in 1998 it was 74 to 1. From 1995 to 1999 the world's two hundred wealthiest people doubled their net worth to $1,000 billion, whereas three billion people presently live on two dollars or less a day. Two billion people suffer from malnutrition, including fifty-five million in industrial countries. Neoliberalism is evoking a future where a handful of the world's most well-to-do families may pocket more than 50 percent of the world's ninety trillion dollars in securitized assets (stocks, bonds, and so on). As of 1996 the biologically productive area needed to produce the natural resources we consume and to absorb the carbon dioxide we emit was 30 percent larger than the area available. Relentlessly raising global temperatures are bound to create catastrophic conditions worldwide and the poor of the world will be the hardest hit.[9]

And then I heard a commanding voice crying out in lament: "Rescue, rescue my people from those who exploit and dehumanize them, from those who ravage the earth and kill the spirit." And I saw Miryam, the mother of Jesus, the mater dolorosa, weeping and saying, "Like my son, G*d's children are crucified again and again, day in and day out by the new empire called global capitalism." This "new world order" spanning the globe lives by the principle: Maximize financial returns and profits as much as possible and everything will turn out fine. The predictable results of the neoliberal economic model made in the United States are socially unjust, politically destabilizing, culturally destructive, and ecologically unsustainable.

And I heard another voice of thunder: "Save my people from those who commit sexual abuse and bodily victimization, from those who heap heavy moral burdens on my people, burdens that they do not want to carry themselves." The Roman rhetoric of absolute truth-claims made by your predecessors, and their condemnation of sexual self-determination, artificial birth-control, and the use of condoms to prevent the spread of HIV, must be seen in this context of global exploitation and the people's struggles against it. Hence, your predecessors in the

---

9. According to the *United Nations Human Development Program Report of 1999*. See Jeff Gates, "Modern Fashion or Global Fascism," *Tikkun* 17/1 (Jan/Feb 2002): 30-32.

papacy have not been able to seize the possibilities for a more radical, worldwide democratization that also is made possible by the forces of capitalist internationalization. They have not been able to make visible the interconnectedness of all being and the possibility of communication and solidary organization across national borders in the interest of human rights and justice for all.

This was the voice of Miryam of Magdala. "I, Miryam, the apostle to the apostles, join both the sister of Moses and Miryam, the Mother of Jesus, in commanding you, who bear our name: Go and teach the priests and doctors of the church these basic truths:

"Theological discourses and religious communities either spiritually sustain the exploitation of global capitalism and the dehumanization of G*d's people or they engage the possibilities for greater freedom, justice, peace, and solidarity engendered by the technological forces of globalization.

"World religions either support the forces of economic and cultural global dehumanization or, by abandoning their exclusivist tendencies, they are able to envision and work together for shaping a spiritual ethos of global dimensions. Either they preach radical, democratic spiritual values and visions that celebrate diversity, multiplicity, tolerance, equality, justice and well-being for all, or they foster fundamentalism, exclusivism, and a totalitarian global monoculture.

"Hence I, Miryam, the apostle to the apostles, call you: Go and preach the words of Saint Matthew to your brothers, the bishops, cardinals, and priests who heap burden after burden upon my people and say to them: 'You tie up heavy burdens, hard to bear, and lay them on the shoulders of others; but you yourselves are unwilling to lift a finger to move them. . . . Woe to you, for you tithe mint, dill, and cumin, woe to you for you lock people out of G*d's sacred realm of well-being because you are obsessed with sexual sins, but you have neglected the weightier matters of G*d's law: justice and mercy, and faith. It is these you ought to practice.'

"But do not preach this message of censure to the people! Rather, gather together the people of G*d from all the ends of the earth, from all the different religions, races, classes, and genders, for the great day of the Holy One, blessed be S/he, has dawned. She has called you to guide the nations in peace and justice, to care for the earth and its inhabitants with equity and tender love, to celebrate sexuality as the creative power of life and to proclaim and institutionalize the loving kindness of the Holy One, blessed be She, as the anti-globalist praxis commanded to every one.

Keeper of the Rainbow Covenant

"We the three Miryams send you, who bear our name, to create a Spirit-Wisdom center of cosmic dimension for the healing of the earth and its creatures. Go and preach the gospel of salvation saying: 'Each and every one is made in Holy

Wisdom's image of dancing justice and hence precious in Her eyes.' And fear not! You will not be overcome by the powers that are, by intellectual co-optation and spiritual corruption, as long as you pray with all the friends of divine Wisdom:

> My spirit is one with you, Great Spirit
> You strengthen me day and night
> To share my very best with my sisters and brothers.
> You whom my people see in all of creation
> And in all the peoples of the world
> Show your love for us.
> Help me to know like the soaring eagle the heights of knowledge.
> From the four Directions,
> Fill me with the virtues of Fortitude, Generosity, Respect, and Courage
> So that I will keep my people walking in the path of Understanding and
>   Peace.[10]

"Henceforth, you, the new representative of World-Catholicism, will no longer be called Vicar of Christ but 'Keeper of the Rainbow Covenant.' Divine Wisdom empowers you to call into being a 'rainbow coalition' of all the outcast and wretched of the earth, of all those who struggle for justice and desire happiness for each and everyone. And a multicolored rainbow shall be the sign of the covenant that divine Wisdom has made with the world and all its inhabitants.

"In this radical open space of divine Wisdom-Spirit, you together with all the justice-loving religious leaders of the world shall be able to envision and foster the well-being of divine Wisdom's 'Rainbow Alliance' as a multi-voiced, multicultural, multi-gendered, and multi-religious radical democratic Spirit practice and movement for the well-being of all. And you, Miryam IV, friend and prophet of divine Wisdom, are called to proclaim and sustain this covenant, treasuring, articulating, and using all the powers of spiritual wisdom, holy courage, and religious community accumulated in all the religions of the world throughout the ages."

And then I saw Miryam, the sister of Moses, Miryam, the mother of Jesus, and Miryam, the apostle to the apostles, clasping hands with you, Miryam, Keeper of the Rainbow Covenant, who were now leading the dance of G*d's saving grace. And all the wo/men went out after you with tambourines, dancing and singing.

> May G*d be gracious to us and bless us and make Her face to shine upon
>   us,
> That your way may be known upon earth, your saving power among the
>   nations.
> Let the peoples praise you, O Holy One, let all the peoples praise you.

---

10. Lakota Prayer.

Let the nations be glad and sing for joy, for you judge the peoples with
equity
And with justice and love guide the nations upon earth.
Let the peoples praise you, O G*d, let all the peoples praise you.
The earth has yielded its increase; G*d our G*d has blessed us.
May the Holy One, Blessed be She, continue to bless us.
Let all the ends of the earth revere Her![11]

---

11. Ps. 67 with feminist adaptation.

PART IV

Feminist The*logy

Re-Visioning the Divine

10

Mariology, Gender Ideology, and the Discipleship of Equals

Mariology, or the teaching about Mary, has been of great interest to feminist the*logians, both Roman Catholic and Protestant.[1] In this essay I seek to explore the hardships and difficulties of a feminist journey into the intellectual territory of hegemonic Mariology and I will do so using the the*logical notion of the *discipleship of equals*[2] as a critical lens and frame of reference.[3] What do I mean by discipleship of equals? Discipleship means to follow either a great leader or a compelling idea or vision. To be equal does not mean to be the same but it means that in our diversity we all have equal standing and dignity. Hence, discipleship of equals cannot mean to follow a great leader, be it Jesus or Mohammed, but it means to follow and enact a vision. The vision that compelled Jesus as one among many in the discipleship community of equals was the vision of the *basileia tou theou*, of G*d's different world of justice and love.

In order to approach the topic, I will begin by discussing the cultural and religious construct of Mary as the *eternal feminine*. Then, I will sketch the attempts to demythologize and historize Mary in order to assess their power for realizing the discipleship community of equals. I argue that the ideal-typical approach that seeks to recover the historical Mary as type of the church still re-inscribes

---

1. See Mary Marcella Althaus-Reid and Lisa Isherwood, "The Virgin Mary: Many Images, Many Interests," in *Controversies in Feminist Theology* (London: SCM, 2007), 63-80.

2. See my books *Discipleship of Equals: A Critical Feminist Ekklēsia-logy of Liberation* (New York: Crossroad, 1993) and *Grenzen überschreiten: Der theoretische Anspruch feministischer Theologie* (Münster: LIT, 2004).

3. Published in Portuguese as Elisabeth Schüssler Fiorenza, "Mariologia, ideologia de gênero e o discipulado de iguais," in *Maria entre as mulheres*, ed. Maria Cecília Domezi and Mercedes Brancher (São Paulo: Paulus, 2009), 27-53.

the sex-gender system. Instead one must seek to recover a glimpse of the historical woman Mary of Nazareth in order to integrate her into the discipleship community of equals. Finally, in order to transform Mariology, it is necessary to transform our speaking about G*d by displacing the kyriarchal images and icons of Mary. At the same time we need to reintegrate into the divine the G*ddess traditions that were coopted by Mariology.[4]

Mary and the Eternal Feminine

Feminist the*logians largely agree in their criticism of the malestream image of Mary and of kyriarchal Mariology. Feminist criticism has unmasked the images and symbols of hegemonic Mariology as the religious projection of a celibate, male priestly hierarchy—a projection which has ideologically legitimized male domination in church and society. Malestream Mariology has done so in the past and still continues to do so today. In holding up to wo/men the image of the perpetual virgin and sorrowful mother Mary, churchmen are preaching a model of femininity that ordinary wo/men cannot imitate. Mary, as the completely desexualized "plaster being from the grotto of Lourdes"[5] and as the symbol of humble obedience, serves to religiously inculcate the dependency, subordination, and inferiority of wo/men.

Feminist the*logians have pointed out that malestream Mariology and the cult of Mary devalue wo/men in four ways. They do so *firstly* by emphasizing virginity to the detriment of sexuality, *secondly* by unilaterally associating the ideal of "true womanhood" with motherhood, *thirdly* by religiously valorizing obedience, humility, passivity, and submission as the cardinal virtues of wo/men,[6] and *fourthly* by constructing an essentialized gender complementarity that sustains the structural oppression of wo/men.

Mary, the pure, self-sacrificing, humble handmaiden of the Lord and patient mother full of sorrows, is preached to wo/men as the model that must be imitated but can never be quite reached. Mary, the beautiful virgin and merciful mother, is an expression of modern masculine desire for the eternal feminine which is projected into heaven. Mary, the powerful Queen of Heaven and Earth, also expresses modern nationalist desires of ruling since her images and titles are rooted in medieval feudal society.

---

4. See my book *Jesus: Miriam's Child and Sophia's Prophet* (New York: Continuum, 1994), which focuses on Mariology, language about the divine, and Goddess traditions.

5. Dorothee Sölle, "Maria ist eine Sympathisantin," in *Sympathie: Theologisch-politische Traktate* (Stuttgart: Kreuz, 1978), 56.

6. Demosthenes Savramis, "Die Stellung der Frau im Christentum: Theorie und Praxis unter besonderer Berücksichtigung Marias," in *Mariologie und Feminismus*, ed. Walter Schöpsdau (Göttingen: Vandenhoeck, 1985), 29.

The image of the servile, obedient, self-sacrificing, and sexually inexperienced "handmaiden of the Lord" who is projected into heaven as the eternal feminine cannot but serve kyriarchal interests. In short, malestream Mariology continues to inscribe a sociocultural image of the feminine that sanctifies the marginalization and exploitation of wo/men. Hence, Mary cannot be an inspiring and liberatory model for wo/men either as the feminine yet subordinate human being[7] or as the divinized—but not quite divine—Madonna.

Indeed, it is overlooked that these ideologizing and mythologizing forms of kyriarchal Mariology often go hand in hand with a conservative politics of ecclesiastical and societal restoration that is contrary to the vision of the discipleship of equals. It is no accident that the classic mariological dogmas were articulated at a time when the Greco-Roman imperial form of Christianity became institutionalized and historically operative: "The images of heavenly rulers developed parallel to secular imperial iconography. The imperial Christ, already the norm in the time of Constantine, was followed after the Council of Ephesus in 431 by the empress-like Mary."[8]

Hence, imperial, feudal, and bourgeois social conditions were the root and horizon of medieval Mariology and cult.[9] Such politically conservative tendencies have also influenced the articulation of Mariology in modern times. Barbara Corrado Pope, for instance, has documented that the "century of Mary" opened with the dogma of Mary's immaculate conception and climaxed in the dogmatic proclamation of Mary's assumption into heaven by Pius XII in 1950. It propagated a defensive anti-modernist and anti-communist attitude. Its conservative, backward looking nostalgic politics yearned for the traditional order of monarchy and was afraid of social upheavals.[10]

In the twentieth century, mythologizing tendencies in Mariology have fostered a conservative-restorative and aggressive anti-communist politics.[11] Just as in the sixteenth century, when the rosary was prayed against the Turks, and in the nineteenth century, when it was prayed against the atheists, so too during the days of the "Cold War" it was recited for the conversion of the Soviet Union. A similar social- and ecclesiastical-reactionary political tendency also comes to

---

7. Kari Elisabeth Borresen, "Männlich-Weiblich: Eine Theologiekritik," *Una Sancta* 35 (1980): 325-34.

8. Helga Sciurie, "Maria-Ecclesia als Mitherrscherin Christi: Zur Funktion des Sponsus-Sponsa Modells in der Bildkunst des 13. Jahrhunderts," in *Maria, Abbild oder Vorbild: Zur Sozialgeschichte mittelalterlicher Marienverehrung*, ed. H. Röckelein, C. Opitz, and R. Bauer (Tübingen: Diskord, 1990), 120.

9. Ursula Nilgen, "Maria Regina—Ein politischer Kultbildtyp?" *Römisches Jahrbuch für Kunstgeschichte* 19 (1981): 1-33.

10. Barbara Corrado Pope, "Immaculate and Powerful: The Marian Revival in the Nineteenth Century," in *Immaculate and Powerful: The Female in Sacred Image and Social Reality*, ed. Clarissa W. Atkinson, Constance H. Buchanan, and Margaret R. Miles (Beacon, 1985), 173-201.

11. See the report of Richard N. Ostling, "The Search for Mary: Handmaid or Feminist?" *Time* (Dec 30, 1991): 62-66.

the fore in the post-Vatican II restoration of kyriarchal church structures and the revalorization of kyriarchal Mariology.[12]

Elisabeth Gössmann has criticized feminist the*logy, saying that it has one-sidedly focused on hegemonic kyriarchal Mariology[13] and not paid sufficient attention to the long tradition of wo/men's the*logical reflection on and religious veneration of Mary. Her work has documented that unlike malestream Mariology, wo/men have developed a very positive image of Mary throughout the centuries. For instance, whereas malestream Mariology has underscored the opposition between Mary and Eve,[14] wo/men's mariological reflections have sought to establish a relation between both representations, by seeing Mary as Eve's daughter.

Any feminist the*logy, Gössmann argues, which does not recognize and take into account that wo/men have articulated a different tradition of Mariology is guilty of the same the*logical oversight and forgetfulness that determines the knowledge production of malestream the*logy. Yet, those mariological wo/men's traditions that are still accessible to us must also be critically interrogated as to whether and how much they dare to allow one to move beyond doctrinally and/or culturally set limits.[15]

Feminist attempts to rearticulate *Mariology* as liberating *Marialogy*, I suggest, can gain more than simply information from the wo/men's mariological tradition. By studying this tradition we can become conscious of our own epistemological limitations and the ways they are politically determined by kyriarchal power structures. Such consciousness-raising is necessary because even feminist studies remain caught up in the kyriocentric horizon and preconstructed frame of meaning, which is determined by hegemonic cultural and religious notions of femininity.

Feminists today, like their foresisters, remain enmeshed in kyriarchal constraints set by societal and ecclesiastical structures of domination. Any Mariology

---

12. See the very important article by Natalia M. Imperatori-Lee, "Mother Superior, Mother Inferior? Mary in the Thought of Hans Urs von Balthasar," *Listening* 44/2 (2009): 129-43.

13. Elisabeth Gössmann, "Reflexionen zur mariologischen Dogmengeschichte," in *Maria, Abbild oder Vorbild*, 19-36; Gössmann, "Mariologische Entwicklungen im Mittelalter: Frauen-freundliche und frauenfeindliche Aspekte," in *Maria für alle Frauen oder über allen Frauen?*, ed. E. Gössmann and D. R. Bauer (Freiburg: Herder, 1989), 63-85.

14. See the critical analysis of Eva Schirmer, *Eva-Maria: Rollenbilder von Männern für Frauen* (Offenbach: Laetare, 1988).

15. With reference to the Beguines, see Martina Wehrli-Johns, "Haushälterin Gottes: Zur Mariennachfolge der Beginen," in *Maria, Abbild oder Vorbild*, 147-67. However, one must not forget that the "women tradition" was always suspected of heresy and under surveillance by the inquisition. See Segl, "Die religiöse Frauenbewegung in Südfrankreich im 12. und 13. Jahrhundert zwischen Häresie und Orthodoxie," in *Religiöse Frauenbewegung und mystische Frömmigkeit im Mittelalter*, ed. Dinzelbacher and D. R. Bauer (Köln: Bohlau, 1988) and Johannes Thiele, "Die religiöse Frauenbewegung des Mittelalters: Eine historische Orientierung, " in *Mein Herz schmilzt wie Eis am Feuer: Die religiöse Frauenbewegung des Mittelalters in Porträts* (Stuttgart: Kreuz, 1988), 9-34.

formulated from the perspective of wo/men, therefore, must with the help of systemic feminist analysis consciously seek to explore its entanglement with kyriarchal structures and kyriocentric ideologies, in order not to reproduce them unconsciously. For instance, even an astute the*logian such as Leonardo Boff, one of the leading liberation the*logians in Latin America, does not escape, but the*logically re-inscribes the bourgeois-romantic and cultural-archetypal myth of femininity.[16] In modern times, this myth has legitimized not only the otherness, inferiority, deficiency, and second-class status of all wo/men but also that of oppressed men, who were categorized as "feminine."

In a very perceptive article "Holy Guadalupe . . . Shameful Malinche?" Nancy Pineda-Madrid[17] has shown how deeply engraved the feminine dualism of Guadalupe, the good wo/man, and Malinche, the bad wo/man, is engraved in the psyche and imagination of many Latina/os, especially Mexicans, both men and wo/men. This dualism harkens back to the emergence of feminine dualistic thinking in the Christian tradition's Mary-Eve construct and has its roots in Spain's imperialism and Mexico's nation making. Guadalupe/Virgin Mary encourages wo/men to self-sacrifice and self-effacement in order to become spiritually superior, a superiority that is the result of submission and sexlessness: Marianismo promotes self-sacrifice and thus erodes the self-esteem of wo/men. Mary's purity is contrasted with Malinche, who stands for the traitorous indigenous whore with tempting sexual proclivities who is a vilified sacrificial victim of her people. To quote the late Argentinian feminist the*logian Marcella Althaus–Reid:

> In Latin America, the whole social structure of patriarchalism rests upon the pillars of Mariology, which is a powerful tool for perpetuating of what Paolo Freire calls 'the naive consciousness' of women in Latin America. Such naive consciousness is the product of oppression and through a process of domestication perpetuates the Latin-American stereotypes of womanhood. The main characteristics of this type of consciousness are resignation, passivity and a lack of critical capacity to analyze the situation of oppression.[18]

In short, Mariology sustains the cultural sex-gender system and religiously internalizes it. It does so not only in terms of gender but also in terms of race, nationalism, and class. Hence, mariological discourses that understand themselves as feminist must again and again critically scrutinize the sociopolitical locations and implications of their the*logical reflection. Mariology that constructs Mary

---

16. Leonardo Boff, *The Maternal Face of God: The Feminine and Its Religious Expressions* (San Francisco: Harper and Row, 1987).

17. Nancy Pineda-Madrid, "Holy Guadalupe . . . Shameful Malinche? Excavating the Problem of 'Female Dualism,' Doing Theological Spadework," *Listening* 44/2 (2009): 71-87.

18. Marcella Althaus–Reid, "When God Is a Rich White Woman Who Does Not Walk: The Hermeneutical Circle of Mariology and the Construction of Femininity in Latin America," *Theology and Sexuality* 1 (1994): 56.

as the pure "White Lady" not only diminishes the agency of wo/men but also has coopted G*ddess traditions. It constructs not only the dualism between wo/men and wo/men but also between wo/men and men. Mary, the Queen of Heaven, is not quite divine because divinity is male defined; she thereby inscribes the pattern of subordination as a feminine divine-human pattern. Hence, in the following section I want to focus on feminist work that seeks to demythologize her image by humanizing and historicizing Mary, the wo/man of Nazareth. However, in so doing, feminist the*logies are in danger of re-inscribing powerlessness as cultural femininity and sustaining divine omnipotence as cultural masculinity.

Searching for the Historical Mary[19]

The approach of the Protestant Reformation abandoned Mariology and insisted on a return to the sources of Holy Scripture emphasizing the centrality of Christology.[20] It engendered a thorough criticism of the church's mariological cult and thereby eliminated any reference to a female figure in heaven. Such criticism of Mariology went hand in hand with the abolition of the ideal of virginity and its monastic institutionalization. But Protestant rejection of Mariology has tended to further the kyriarchalization of the*logy and church, insofar as the Reformation did not critically problematize either kyriarchal marriage relations and views on sexuality nor improve the position of wo/men in the ministry of the church.

The elimination of Mary and the saints from the spiritual cosmos of the*logy and church had the—probably unintended—consequence that wo/men no longer appeared in the religious symbolic cosmos nor in the public of the*logy and church. This concentration upon a male determined christology and kyriarchal the*logy threatens to turn Protestantism into a purely masculine religion which does not know of any symbolic heavenly representation of wo/men.[21] Such religious kyriocentrism has produced not only the emotional poverty of Reformation spirituality but also determined the religious experience and questions of many Christian feminists.[22]

This Protestant approach is also inspired by biblical scholarship. Since the beginning of this century, Roman Catholic biblical scholarship has pointed out

---

19. See the contributions in Amy-Jill Levine with Maria Mayo Robbins, eds, *A Feminist Companion to Mariology* (Cleveland: Pilgrim, 2005).

20. See G. Heintze, "Maria im Urteil Luthers und in evangelischen Äusserungen der Gegenwart," in *Maria—Eine ökumenische Herausforderung*, ed. W. Beinert (Regensburg: Pustet, 1984), 57-74, and G. Maron, "Die Protestanten und Maria," in *Was geht uns Maria an? Beiträge zur Auseinandersetzung in Theologie, Kirche, und Frömmigkeit*, ed. Hans Küng, Elisabeth Moltmann-Wendel, and Jürgen Moltmann (Gütersloh: Mohn, 1988), 60-71.

21. See the collection of essays by Beverly Roberts Gaventa and Cynthia L. Rigby, eds., *Blessed One: Protestant Perspectives on Mary* (Louisville: WJK, 2002).

22. As representative for this discussion, see Nelle Morton, *The Journey Is Home* (Boston: Beacon, 1985) and Ursula Krattinger, *Die permutterne Mönchin: Reise in eine weibliche Spiritualität* (Zürich: Kreuz, 1983).

that an almost unbridgeable chasm exists between the historical figure, Mary of Nazareth, and the Queen of Heaven and mother of G*d celebrated in the cult of Mary. Although school the*logy always has distinguished between the veneration of Mary and the adoration of G*d, the impression rightly exists that the catholic cult of Mary loves and worships Mary like a divine being. The cult of Mary, with its candles, flowers, hymns, feast days, and pilgrimages, has developed a much richer tapestry of devotion and emotional fund of values than the the*logy of the word or a catechetical dogmatics ever will be able to do.[23]

Accepting Protestant the*logical challenges to the cult of Mary, the Second Vatican Council attempted to cut back the excesses of Marian piety in order to connect Catholic Marian cult and piety more strongly with Scripture and to place christology once more into the center of the*logical reflection. In the decrees of the Council, the Protestant christocentric emphasis has also become essential for Catholic the*logy. For that reason, Vatican II did not confirm Mary as mediatrix of all grace and as co-redemptrix with Christ, but instead proclaimed her as the ideal representative and central symbol of a more human church oriented toward the world. In the the*logy of the Council Fathers, Mary became the symbol of "the new humanity" and hence a paradigm for wo/men as well as men.[24]

Like the Reformation, the Second Vatican Council did not problematize the marginal ecclesial position of wo/men and the kyriarchal church structures that undergird it. Hence, this new "Protestant"-inspired formulation of Mariology was not able to develop an impetus for ecclesial change. Rather, Vatican II ended up further masculinizing the*logy and church, because it pushed back and repressed the almost divine female symbol of Mary in Catholic life and piety.[25] Although Mary was proclaimed as archetype and mother of the church, wo/men continue to remain second-class citizens in the Roman Catholic church insofar as they are not permitted to represent Christ and the church as ordained officials because of their sex.

Admittedly, Vatican II attempted to correct kyriarchal-hierarchical church structures of domination. Nevertheless, it was not able to do so because, in its search for "brotherhood,"[26] it did not touch on the status of wo/men in the church. Hence, the "opening to the world" and the "democratization" of the church were bound to fail. The exclusion of wo/men from the ordained leadership of the church resulted in a new emphasis on Scriptural patriarchal-the*logical "bride-mysticism" in which Mary, as the bridal representative of church and world,

---

23. See H. Pissarek-Hudelist, "Maria—Schwester oder Mutter im Glauben? Chancen und Schwierigkeiten in Verkündigung und Katechese," in *Maria—Für alle Frauen oder über allen Frauen*, 146-67.

24. See Elizabeth A. Johnson, "Saints and Mary," in *Systematic Theology: Roman Catholic Perspectives*, vol. 2, ed. Francis Schüssler Fiorenza and John Galvin (Minneapolis: Fortress Press, 1991), 155-63.

25. For this evaluation see also Anne Carr, "Mary in the Mystery of the Church: Vatican Council II," in *Mary according to Women*, ed. Carol Frances Jegen (Kansas City: Leaven, 1985), 5-32.

26. See the book by Joseph Ratzinger, *Die christliche Brüderlichkeit* (München: Kösel, 1960), whose the*logical outlook has influenced the Council's the*logy.

remains subordinated to Christ, her head, just as wives are subordinated to their husbands (cf. Eph 5:21-33). Whereas the hierarchy represents Christ's masculinity and God's Father power, all the so-called lay Christians, men and wo/men, are exhorted to imitate Mary, who perfectly represents the feminine qualities of receptivity, subordination, humility, expectation, openness, malleability, obedience, and passivity.

Feminist proposals that adopt this Reformation approach also turn to the Bible for developing a liberatory Mariology from below. The "Summary Statement on Mariology" of the Consultation of Asian the*logy from the perspective of wo/men, which took place in 1987 in Singapore, defines the task of feminist the*logy in a double manner: First, Asian wo/men must name the destructive formulations of two thousand-year-old malestream interpretations of Mary in order to become free of them. In a second step, wo/men must read Scripture *as wo/men* within their own cultural contexts in order to rediscover the liberated and liberating woman Mary.[27]

Like Asian wo/men, other feminist liberation the*logians picture Mary as the exemplary disciple, the poor wo/man of the people, the prophetic proclaimer of justice, the motherly sister, or the sorrowful mother. Wo/men, they argue, have no difficulty identifying with Mary as a historical being. Wo/men understand a Mary who had problems with her difficult son associating with disreputable people.[28] They sympathize with Mary, who is said to have cut the shirt of her child so big that it could be lengthened again and again (Mechthild von Magdeburg).[29] They admire a Mary who stood by her arrested and tortured child and mourned her executed son. With reference to Scripture,[30] and especially the Lukan infancy stories, Christian liberation the*logians picture Mary as the poor village girl from Nazareth who made salvation possible in and through her freely given consent. They see her as the perfect disciple who fulfilled G*d's liberating intention. They portray her as the spirit-filled mother or sister[31] who was the gathering agent of the new community.[32]

---

27. See Chung Hyun Kyung, *Struggle to Be the Sun Again: Introducing Asian Women's Theology* (Maryknoll: Orbis, 1990), 76.

28. Cf. Els Maeckelberghe, "'Mary': Maternal Friend or Virgin Mother?" in *Motherhood: Experience, Institution, Theology*, ed. Ann Carr and Elisabeth Schüssler Fiorenza (Edinburgh: T and T Clark, 1989), 120, 127.

29. However, Mechthild can also say about Mary: "Her son is God and she is Goddess."

30. For a historical discussion, see *Mary in the New Testament*, ed. R. E. Brown, K. Donfried, and J. A. Fitzmyer (Philadelphia: Fortress Press, 1978); F. Mussner, "Die Mutter Jesu im Neuen Testament," in *Maria—Eine ökumenische Herausforderung*, ed. W. Beinert (Regensburg: Pustet, 1984), 9-30; and Otto Knoch, "Maria in der Heiligen Schrift," in *Handbuch der Marienkunde*, ed. Wolfgang Beinert and Heinrich Petri (Regensburg: Friedrich Pustet, 1984), 15-92.

31. See Elizabeth A. Johnson, *Truly Our Sister: A Theology of Mary in the Communion of Saints* (New York: Continuum, 2006).

32. For an excellent discussion, see Maria Pilar Aquino, *Our Cry for Life: Feminist Theology from Latin America*, trans. Dinah Livingstone (Maryknoll: Orbis, 1993).

Since, however, the biblical references to Mary[33] are more than spotty, the "historical Mary" remains even more elusive than the "historical Jesus." This results in the pressure to fill in features of the historical Mary in an idealistic fashion; idealistic elaboration, however, not only resorts to cultural feminine patterns of the preconstructed sex-gender system. The attempt to see Mary positively as an exceptional Jewish woman also tends to re-inscribe the Christian-the*logical anti-Judaism that it seeks to avoid.[34] Since biblical texts on Mary contradict each other, a historicizing feminist Mariology for the most part has privileged the idealizing texts of the Gospels of Luke and John, without critically scrutinizing their dualistic anti-Jewish frame of meaning. It continues to do so, although in the meantime feminist biblical scholarship has challenged on exegetical grounds whether the Lukan work is a positive text for wo/men readers.[35]

Moreover, such historicizing and idealizing readings of biblical texts almost never transgress the boundaries set by church doctrine in their interpretation of Mary. For instance, I do not know of any feminist mariological reflection that would the*logically connect and develop the "free choice" of Mary with a woman's "right to choose" or sexual self-determination. Equally, the research-hypothesis of biblical scholars such as Jane Schaberg that Mary was raped[36] has not inspired systematic feminist elaboration. In my opinion a recourse to the historical Mary can only be set free to develop feminist-liberationist possibilities if it is combined with a critical feminist hermeneutics[37]—a hermeneutics that is able to embed the story of Mary of Nazareth in a critical reconstruction of a feminist liberationist and emancipatory history that articulates the solidarity of the *basileia movement as a discipleship of equals*.

It seems that even feminist liberation the*logical attempts at mariological reflection remain within the sex-gender framework. True, they attempt to place Mary, the historical woman of Nazareth, at the center of attention. Nevertheless, they tend to universalize her as the ideal type of woman and the paradigmatic model of submission in faith.[38] Rosemary Radford Ruether was among the first who articulated such an ideal-typical understanding of liberation Mariology.

---

33. See the collection of essays by the Jewish scholar Amy Jill Levine and Maria Mayo Robins, eds., *A Feminist Companion to Mariology* (Cleveland: Pilgrim, 2005).

34. See the work of Gebara and Bingemer on the one hand and of Christa Mulack on the other.

35. See the discussion and bibliography in my book *But She Said*, especially 51-78 and 195-219. See also Brigitte Kahl, *Armenevangelium und Heidenevangelium* (Berlin: Evangelische, 1987), 86-149, and Itumeleng J. Mosala, *Biblical Hermeneutics and Black Theology in South Africa* (Grand Rapids: Eerdmans, 1989), 137-89.

36. Jane Schaberg, *The Illegitimacy of Jesus* (San Francisco: Harper and Row, 1987) and "Die Stammütter und die Mutter Jesu," *Concilium* 25 (1989) 528-33.

37. For such an articulation of a critical feminist hermeneutics of liberation, see my books *Bread Not Stone*; *But She Said*; *Wisdom Ways*; and *Discipleship of Equals*.

38. See Anne Carr, "Mary: Model of Faith," in *Mary, Woman of Nazareth: Biblical and Theological Perspectives*, ed. Doris Donnelly (New York: Paulist, 1989), 7-24.

According to her book which appeared in 1977, Mary, the feminine face of the church, mirrors liberated humanity.[39]

In her later book *Sexism and God-Talk*, Ruether develops this approach even further. According to her, the figure of the church, which is portrayed as feminine, is represented in Mary. She asks whether an alternative Mariology that is not the reinscription of masculine/feminine relations is at all possible, and answers in the affirmative by the*logically elaborating on Luke's infancy account. Mary, female personification of the church, in her view represents liberated humanity redeemed from sexism and hence also the liberation of wo/men.[40]

Ruether joins other feminist liberation the*logians when she insists that the liberation of wo/men as the poorest of the poor "can become the model of faith." She joins me in insisting that the liberation of wo/men becomes a special the*logical "locus." But whereas I have argued that the struggle of wo/men on the bottom of the kyriarchal pyramid for survival and liberation is the "locus" of revelation, she sees as such a "locus" the "believing and liberated community."[41] Mary becomes a symbol of the church, Ruether argues, because according to Luke her free act of faith, her co-creatorship, and her responsiveness in faith have made it possible for G*d to enter history in the person of Christ in order "to effect a liberating revolution in human relationships. Mary is exalted because, through her, God will work this revolution in history."[42] In Luke's "liberation language," which is expressly economic and political, Mary is simultaneously portrayed both as a subject and object. She makes possible G*d's liberating action, and G*d's redemptive action liberates her.

Consequently, in this view Mary embodies and personifies those oppressed people who are being liberated: the hungry, who are being fed; the lowly, who have been lifted up; the weeping and mourning who receive consolation. In a similar manner, Ivone Gebara and Clara Maria Bingemer understand Mary as the "image of the people made fruitful by the Spirit of God, from whom is born the new humankind, which will be woven out of all the nations of the earth. Mary is symbol of the people that she begets from God, and Jesus is symbol of the new people begotten of God."[43]

In Latin America, Mary as the representative figure of the church always represents the church of the poor "of which the base communities are a new and outstanding embodiment."[44] As "Our Lady of Latin America" she is invoked

---

39. Rosemary Radford Ruether, *Mary: The Feminine Face of the Church*, 86.

40. Rosemary Radford Ruether, *Sexism and God-Talk: Toward a Feminist Theology* (Boston: Beacon, 1983), 152.

41. Ibid., 157.

42. Ibid., 155.

43. Ivone Gebara and Clara Maria Bingemer, *Mary—Mother of God, Mother of the Poor*, 43. However, it must not be overlooked that their chapter on Mary in Scripture is riddled with anti-Jewish, supercessionist statements.

44. Ibid., 163.

as "Mother of the Oppressed" and "Mother of the Forgotten." However, this ideal typical approach of feminist liberation Mariology, I suggest, is not able to overcome the kyriarchal-the*logical dynamics of the cultural preconstructed sex-gender system and symbolic frame of meaning. In conceptualizing Mary as the symbolic representative of the church, even of the church of the poor, or of the "new humanity," this approach does one of two things. It either re-inscribes the secondary status of wo/men and the feminine insofar as Mary as the representative of the church or of the new humanity clearly remains subordinated to G*d, who is conceived in male/masculine terms, or it submerges the poor woman Mary of Nazareth and hence sublates the mariological female symbol into the notion of the poor and subjugated people. Moreover, its stress on the church as the "new people" of G*d unwittingly reproduces the anti-Jewish tendencies associated with this expression since the beginnings of Christianity.

Deconstructing the Mariological Sex-Gender System: Rediscovering Mary of Nazareth

In order to break through the cultural-religious mindset of the mariological sex-gender system, I argue, it is necessary to unravel it. This can be done by deconstructing the dualism of good woman/bad woman as well as the *male divine/female human* dualism that it engenders. Such a deconstruction of dualisms needs to go hand in hand with rediscovering the struggle of the historical Mary as well as with a re-visioning of the divine.

Throughout the centuries, the tellers of the so-called infancy stories have articulated that the mighty, be it Herod, Pilate, or the generals of Haiti, will attempt to kill those who carry the vision of a different "world order"—*basileia*—of justice and well-being. Today, those who carry on this vision of justice and well-being still experience daily the violence evoked by it. The infancy stories in Matthew and Luke provide the imaginative the*logical site for feminist dialogue on how to realize the discipleship community of equals. The center of attention is the embrace of Miryam of Nazareth and Elizabeth of Ain Karim (Lk 1:39ff). Miryam, the young frightened girl who undertakes the arduous journey through the hill country in order to seek support from another wo/man, must become the center of feminist attention. The infancy stories of the Gospels might very well have been wo/men's stories that could have been retold again and again before they received their written form in Matthew's and Luke's Gospels,[45] although written down they have never been brought to closure. They

---

45. For literature and exegetical discussion of these texts, see Raymond E. Brown, *Birth of the Messiah: A Commentary of the Infancy Narratives in Matthew and Luke* (Garden City: Doubleday, 1977) and Richard A. Horsley, *The Liberation of Christmas: The Infancy Narratives in Social Context* (New York: Crossroad, 1989).

have been repeated, amplified, and totally changed in countless ways. They have been told throughout the centuries and still are told today.

Biblical scholarship points out, however, that already the infancy narratives of the canonical Gospels of Matthew and Luke began to turn the story about the pregnant Miryam into a fairy tale—or, as scholars say, into mythical or miraculous accounts that are historically suspect. Critical exegesis has sought to trace the literary development of the two quite different versions of the canonical Gospels and to contextualize them in the religious cultural ambiance of the first century. In contrast to biblical literalists who insist on the historical facticity of the infancy narratives, critical scholars stress their religious-symbolic meaning and spiritualized reality. Thus both approaches, the literalist and the scholarly, sustain the cultural fairy tale mentality.

In line with biblical studies, feminist scholars have suggested that despite their differences, the Gospels agree that Jesus is the child of Miryam. Against all patriarchal custom Jesus is called in Mark 6:3 "the son of Mary," which the Gospel of Matthew modified with the designation "the carpenter's son" (Mt. 13:55) and Luke corrected with "son of Joseph" (4:22). In addition, the infancy narratives of the Gospels of Matthew and Luke also concur that Mary became pregnant in the period between betrothal and completed marriage. And finally, the Matthean and Lukan Gospels also know that Joseph was not the biological father of Jesus. This information has lent itself to two different feminist the*logical interpretations.[46]

Those feminist the*logians who accept the Gospels' statement that Mary "was found to be with child of a holy spirit" (Mt. 1:18.20; Lk 1:34) interpret this text as positive. They stress Mary's independence from a man as well as her free choice and active self-determination in consenting to her unexpected pregnancy. Sojourner Truth already espoused this line of reasoning in the nineteenth century. Answering a clergyman who had objected to equal rights for wo/men on the grounds that Jesus was a man and not a woman, Sojourner Truth asserted: "Where did your Christ come from? From God and a Woman. Man had nothing to do with him."

Those feminist scholars in religion who hold that divine agency does not miraculously replace male agency in conception either believe that Miryam was seduced by Joseph or someone else during the time of their betrothal, or they point to the persistent rumor found in Jewish and Christian ancient literatures that Miryam was raped by a Roman soldier.[47] In the latter case she joins

---

46. For two quite different feminist biblical interpretations, see Luise Schottroff, *Let the Oppressed Go Free: Feminist Perspectives on the New Testament* (Louisville: WJK, 1993), 158-67, and Janice Capel Anderson, "Mary's Difference: Gender and Patriarchy in the Birth Narratives," *The Journal of Religion* 67/2 (1987): 183-202.

47. See Jane Schaberg, "Feminist Interpretations of the Infancy Narrative of Matthew," *Journal of Feminist Studies in Religion* 13 (1997): 35-62.

the countless wo/men ravished by soldiers in war and occupation. The raped wo/men of Sudan, Bangladesh, Kuwait, Sarajevo, Afghanistan, or Iraq interrupt the mythology of the perpetual virgin and Queen of Heaven.

In Luke's account, Mary does not remain alone with her anxieties but seeks support from another woman, Elizabeth. Filled with the Holy Spirit who exalts the violated and makes the fruit of illegitimacy holy, the two wo/men rejoice in G*d's liberating action. In the Magnificat, the pregnant Mary annunciates G*d's salvation and well-being to the humiliated and downtrodden. The future of G*d's well-being for all without exception is not to be awaited passively. It is being born among us today, from our flesh and blood, from the commitments and struggles of the discipleship community of equals for the justice and well-being of the *basileia*, G*d's alternative world. It is born as the hope for those who are without hope.

To place the agency of Miryam, the "single" mother, into the center of our attention, I suggest, interrupts the kyriocentric celebration of the eternal feminine. Such a feminist move is dangerous in the eyes of both ecclesiastical and political authorities. For instance, the German the*logian Dr. Sylvia Schroer was denied a distinguished professorship by the bishop of Tübingen just because she had written a popular article pointing out that the Gospel of Matthew pictures Mary in "bad company" by mentioning four biblical wo/men: Tamar, Rahab, Ruth, and Bathsheba of questionable fame. In the U.S., professor Jane Schaberg has been attacked and vilified by the Religious Right because of her book on the *Illegitimacy of Jesus*.

The "dangerous memory" of the young woman, and teenage mother, Miryam of Nazareth—probably not more than twelve or thirteen years old, pregnant, frightened, and single, who sought help from another wo/man—can subvert the tales of mariological fantasy and cultural femininity. In the center of the Christian story stands not the lovely "White Lady" of artistic and popular imagination, kneeling in adoration before her son. Rather it is the young pregnant wo/man, living in occupied territory and struggling against victimization and for survival and dignity. It is she who holds out the offer of untold possibilities for a different the*logy. As Katie G. Cannon has underscored, central for struggling communities such as the Black Church are three things: the notion of *imago dei*, justice and love, and last but not least solidarity in community.[48]

---

48. Katie Geneva Cannon, *Black Womanist Ethics* (Atlanta: Scholars, 1988).

Changing Mariology—Changing G*d-Language[49]

Instead of assuming that a "feminine" style of thinking or a mode of the*logizing from "the woman's perspective" promotes liberationist discourses in the interest of wo/men, I have argued here that one needs to explore critically how discourses on biblical wo/men can perpetrate kyriarchal mindsets. In addition, one has to inquire whether and to what degree the textualized wo/men characters of the Christian Testament communicate kyriarchal values and visions. One must also consider that wo/men, sometimes even more than men, have internalized cultural-religious feminine values and hence are in danger of reproducing the "preconstructed" kyriarchal politics of either womanly submission or of feminine glorification in their own speaking and writing. Hence, feminist the*logical discourses have to position themselves in such a way that they are "crossing" the "double cross" of the "preconstructed" sex-gender frame of meaning that is also determinative of Mariology.

Consequently, the category of *woman* must be problematized rather than presupposed or idealized as an authentic source of feminist insight. It must be shown for what it is, the "common sense" construct of the cultural-religious, sex-gender system that serves kyriarchal interests. Fortunately today, more and more diverse resistant discourses of emerging feminist movements around the world interrupt those discourses of middle-class academic gender or wo/men's studies that have conceptualized feminist inquiry in terms of reading or speaking *as a woman*. Feminist global discourses challenge universalistic kyriarchal claims that all wo/men have a feminine nature in common which defines them as "others" or as "subordinates" to men.

If the feminist discourse on Mary should displace the politics of meaning that is determined by the cultural kyriarchal sex-gender system, it can no longer articulate wo/men's identity in essentialist universalistic terms. Instead it must carefully analyze its own assumptions as well as those of malestream mariological discourses as to how much they take into account the diverse cultural-religious contexts, the historically shaped subjectivity, as well as the plurivocality of wo/men. By so doing, feminist the*logy is able to unravel the unitary exclusive conceptualizations of cultural-religious discourses that define wo/man as the "naturalized" or "revealed" Other of man, an Otherness which is in reality that of *elite woman to elite man*. The insights into the collusion of the*logical discourses with the kyriarchal structures of race, class, heteronormativity, and colonialist oppression compel us not to duplicate or proliferate those white-malestream mariological discourses which are drawn upon the "preconstructed" rock of the cultural sex-gender system.

---

49. See Mayra Rivera, *The Touch of Transcendence: A Postcolonial Theology of God* (Louisville: WJK, 2007).

Instead feminist the*logians are challenged to firmly situate their discourses within the emancipatory movements of wo/men around the globe. The biblical wo/men's liberation movements have their historical roots in the liberation from slavery and oppression announced by Mary, in the repentance preached by John, and in the *basileia* vision of the movement named after Jesus of Nazareth. Those wo/men who have been engaged in such discipleship communities of equals have sought throughout the centuries again and again to realize the *basileia* of G*d not only as a power for abolishing kyriarchal domination and exploitation but also as a force for establishing the salvation and well-being of all, which Mary proclaimed in the Magnificat. At the same time this Christian vision of the discipleship praxis of equals realizes that the *basileia* that is G*d's alternative world of well-being and love is not yet here, not yet an accomplished reality. Wo/men still have to struggle and hope for the liberation and well-being of all, a vision still to be realized by G*d in the future. Nevertheless, like Miryam of Nazareth, feminist liberation the*logians proclaim that the *basileia*—G*d's different world and renewed creation, symbolized by the abundant table set by divine Wisdom— is promised especially to those wo/men suffering from multiple oppressions and struggling for survival, dignity and well-being.

Finally, in order to see Mary as a wo/man struggling against domination, we need to deconstruct the divine masculine/divine feminine dualism. Feminist the*logy has sought to address this problem by introducing female/feminine images into Christian G*d language.[50] It has done so either by re-valorizing the traces of feminine imagery in the Bible, such as those of divine Wisdom, or by recovering lost Goddess traditions.[51] Jewish feminists in turn have reclaimed the female figure of the Shekinah, particularly as She was elaborated in Kabbalah, whereas Christian theologians have focused on rearticulating the Trinity in terms of relationality[52] and female imagery. Feminists of various persuasions have begun to celebrate the female divine in liturgy and art. They have sought to rearticulate traditional formulas and rituals not just in inclusive terms but in terms of wo/men's experience.

To that end, Neopagan and post-biblical thealogians have revived Goddess cult and Goddess traditions.[53] They have postulated that patriarchal warrior

50. See the overview by Linda A. Moody, *Women Encounter God: Theology across the Boundaries of Difference* (Maryknoll: Orbis, 1996).

51. Silvia Schroer, "Die göttliche Weisheit und der nachexilische Monotheismus," in *Der eine Gott und die Göttin: Gottesvorstellung des biblischen Israel im Horizont feministischer Theologie*, ed. Marie-Theres Wacker und Erich Zenger (Freiburg: Herder, 1991), 151-83.

52. See Catherine Mowry LaCugna, "God in Communion with Us," in *Freeing Theology: The Essentials of Theology in Feminist Perspective*, ed. Catherine Mowry LaCugna (San Francisco: HarperSanFrancisco, 1993), 83-114, and Elizabeth A. Johnson, *She Who Is: The Mystery of God in Feminist Theological Discourse* (New York: Crossroad, 1992).

53. See Carol Christ, *The Rebirth of the Goddess: Finding Meaning in Feminist Spirituality* (Reading: Addison-Wesley, 1998) and her very important book *She Who Changes: Re-Imagining the Divine in the World* (New York: Palgrave, 2003).

societies were preceded by peaceful matrilineal societies in which the Goddess was worshipped. They have rediscovered not only so-called prehistoric Goddesses but also sought to free those of classic Rome, Greece, or Egypt from their embeddedness in patriarchal myth. Feminists working in the area of comparative religion have made known to Western audiences the Goddesses of Asia, the Americas, Africa, and indigenous peoples around the world. In her now classic essay "Why Wo/men need the Goddess," Carol Christ has summed up this quest for the Goddess as a quest for spiritual female power.[54]

My own work has introduced and elaborated the *Wisdom-Sophia* tradition of the discipleship of equals as one but *not as the sole* early Christian discourse that might open up yet unfulfilled possibilities for feminist the*logical reflection.[55] Jewish sophialogy that is funded by the interactive meaning-making of apocalyptic, prophetic, and wisdom traditions valorizes life, creativity, and well-being in the midst of injustice and struggle. The elements of the biblical Wisdom traditions—open-endedness, inclusivity, and cosmopolitan emphasis on creation spirituality as well as practical insight—have been especially attractive not only to feminists but also to Asian liberation theological reflections, as I will show in the last section of this chapter.

Yet, it also must be pointed out that feminist G*d-talk is always in danger of succumbing to a "romantic" cultural notion of femininity,[56] or what I have called the ideology of the (White) Lady. Thereby it is in danger of re-inscribing the Western, androcentric gender binary of Mariology that either devalues women and femininity or idealizes femininity as representing superior transcendent and salvific qualities. In extolling the femininity of Wisdom or of the Goddess, such a feminist binary-gender approach cannot but re-inscribe Western cultural systems of domination in theological terms, insofar as it divinizes the hegemonic gender ideology of cultural femininity that is shaped after the image and likeness of the White Lady. Whenever the*logy is positioned within a framework of essential gender dualism, it cannot but reproduce this ideological frame.[57]

In order to avoid this pitfall, I have argued,[58] one must explicitly read against the grain of the cultural framework of the feminine and shift the discussion of a divine female figure from the ontological-metaphysical level to a linguistic

---

54. Carol Christ, "Why Women Need the Goddess: Phenomenological, Psychological, and Political Reflections," in *Women Spirit Rising: A Feminist Reader in Religion*, ed. Carol Christ and Judith Plaskow (San Francisco: Harper and Row, 1979), 273-87.

55. See my books *In Memory of Her*; *Jesus: Miriam's Child and Sophia's Prophet*, 131-63, and *Sharing Her Word: Feminist Biblical Interpretation in Context*, 137-60. Elizabeth A. Johnson, *She Who Is*, builds on this work and develops it in systematic the*logical terms.

56. See the roundtable discussion Catherine Madsen et al., "If God Is God, She Is Not Nice," *Journal of Feminist Studies in Religion* 5/1 (1989): 103-18.

57. As a case in point, see Christa Mulack, *Jesus der Gesalbte der Frauen* (Stuttgart: Kreuz, 1987).

58. See my book *The Power of the Word: Scripture and the Rhetoric of Empire* (Minneapolis: Fortress Press, 2007).

symbolic rhetorical level of reflection. Such a shift is justified insofar as divine female/mother as well as divine male/father language are not unified theological discourses about the essence and true being of G*d, but rather discourses embodying a variegated "reflective mythology."[59] The grammatically masculine language that determines ancient Wisdom discourses and modern biblical interpretation, the*logy as well as thealogy, has a difficult time speaking adequately of the G*ddess or divine Wisdom in the kyriocentric framework of Western language systems. Insofar as, for instance, biblical language about divine Wisdom struggles to avoid turning Her into a second feminine deity who is subordinate to the masculine deity, it also struggles against the the*logical reification of monotheism in terms of western cultural elite male hegemony.

When speaking about the biblical G*d, Christian the*logies have often succumbed to this danger insofar as they have used predominantly masculine language, metaphors and images to speak of the divine, although the*logy has always known that human language is not able to express the divine adequately. Mariology re-inscribes such kyriocentric G*d language as given or revealed when it understands female images for G*d in metaphorical terms but understands malestream language about G*d, the Father, King, and Lord, as descriptive theological language that adequately expresses G*d's nature and being.

In short, it is neither patriarchal God nor matriarchal Goddess, neither the Masculine nor the Feminine, neither divine Fatherhood nor complementary Motherhood that sustains the discipleship of equals. Rather all kyriocentric symbols—masculinity and femininity, pale and dark skin, domination and subordination, wealth and exploitation, nationalism and colonialism—are to be carefully tested out in an ongoing feminist critique of ideology. Such a feminist ideological critique may take its cues neither from established dogmatics nor from cultural systems of domination. Instead it must attempt to name the negative as well as the positive G*d experiences of wo/men under imperial conditions and critically reflect on them. To do so, it needs not only to sustain a permanent critical self-reflexivity which is able to reject male language about G*d that inculcates dominant masculinity or the ideal feminine; it also must be critical of the language of imperial domination that projects not only the western cultural sex-gender system but also the mentality and imagination of empire into heaven when it celebrates Mary as the Queen of Heaven. Instead, I have argued, we need to reimagine Mary as partaking in the *Wisdom-Sophia* discipleship of equals.

---

59. For this expression see my article, "Wisdom Mythology and the Christological Hymns of the New Testament" in *Aspects of Wisdom in Judaism and Early Christianity*, ed. Robert L. Wilken (Notre Dame: Notre Dame, 1975), 17-42. I became fascinated with the Wisdom tradition in the Christian Testament in the context of the 1973 Rosenstil seminar on Wisdom in Early Judaism and Christianity sponsored by the Department of Theology at University of Notre Dame.

11

Monotheism and Kyriarchy

A Critical Feminist Inquiry

In the last two decades there has been much discussion within the*logical schol-arship, especially German scholarship, about monotheism and its consequenc-es.[1] The fronts are clearly drawn: either one is for monotheism or against it. Feminist the*logy, too, has hotly debated the topic of "patriarchal monotheism," particularly in the 1980s and 1990s. It has critically questioned the masculinity and domination of the monotheistic Father-God and made the Goddess again present as a life-giving power. But this feminist discussion has been scarcely acknowledged in dominant the*logical scholarship or it is brushed aside as mar-ginal, although in my opinion it can throw some important light on the problem of monotheism and contribute to the question as to how Christian the*logy should deal with it.[2]

After sketching the discussion of monotheism I will deconstruct the theoretical-dualist scheme "monotheism-polytheism" in order to understand the problem of monotheism not as onto-the*logy but as rhetoric. The standpoint from which I address this topic is that of a critical, feminist, Christian the*logy and hermeneutics of liberation. A critical feminist rhetorical analysis can show, I argue, that the debate on monotheism is not so much a debate about the*logy,

1. First published as "Monotheismus und Herr-schaft. Eine kritisch-feministische Anfrage," *Theologische Zeitschrift* 62/4 (2007): 487-502. I wish to thank Professor Stegemann and the theo-logical faculty of Basel for their invitation to the faculty conference. My gratitude goes also and especially to Dr. Gabriella Gelardini for her outstanding preparation of this essay and to Linda Maloney for her initial translation of it.

2. See also my book *The Power of the Word*, 213-20.

that is, about the discourse about G*d in the proper sense of the word, but rather about the problem of a biblical-Christian legitimation of kyriarchy and violence. Therefore it is important to articulate the problem anew as to how to speak about G*d the*logically. In a concluding argument, I will then introduce the four ways (the *via negativa, positiva, eminentiae,* and *practica*) of traditional the*logy as a rhetorical method.

Accordingly, I will approach the problem in *four* analytical steps: *first*, I will briefly sketch the critique of monotheism; *second*, I will present my own theoretical approach; *third*, I will problematize the dualistic thought pattern monotheism-polytheism; *fourth*, and finally, I will present the four methods of traditional the*logy as a rhetorical possibility for overcoming this dualism in favor of an inclusive formation of identity.

It seems to me important to bring established and feminist biblical-the*logical discourses on the topic of "monotheism and domination" into a critical conversation. While feminist discourse concentrates on a critique of male G*d language and the problem of divine Father-God and divine Mother-Goddess, the established discourse focuses on the violence and exclusivity of monotheism and places monotheism in an antagonistic relationship to polytheism, pantheism, or cosmotheism. Therefore it is important not only to keep monotheism and kyriarchy in view, but also to see how the idea of a violent monotheism is rhetorically constructed by the counter-image of a nonviolent and all-encompassing polytheism/cosmotheism.

The Debate on Monotheism

In 1997 two important books appeared in English that have significantly affected biblical scholarship and the*logy in the last decade.[3] One well-known and controversial book was Jan Assmann's *Moses der Ägypter*;[4] the other was Regina M.

---

3. On this scholarship see Manfred Oeming and Konrad Schmid, eds., *Der eine Gott und die Götter: Polytheismus und Monotheismus im antiken Israel* (Zürich: Theologischer, 2003); Markus Witte, ed., *Der eine Gott und die Welt der Religionen: Beiträge zu einer Theologie der Religionen und zum interreligiösen Dialog* (Würzburg: Religion and Kultur, 2003); Magnus Striet, ed., *Monotheismus Israels und christlicher Trinitätsglaube* (Freiburg: Herder, 2004); Hermann Düringer, ed., *Monotheismus—Eine Quelle der Gewalt?* (Frankfurt: Haag und Herchen, 2004); Mark S. Smith, *The Memoirs of God: History, Memory, and the Experience of the Divine in Ancient Israel* (Minneapolis: Fortress Press, 2004); Wiard Popkes and Ralph Brucker, eds., *Ein Gott und ein Herr: Zum Kontext des Monotheismus im Neuen Testament* (Neukirchen-Vluyn: Neukirchener, 2004); and Reinhard Gregor Kratz and Hermann Spieckermann, eds., *Götterbilder, Gottesbilder, Weltbilder: Polytheismus und Monotheismus in der Welt der Antike* (Tübingen: Mohr Siebeck, 2006).

4. ET Jan Assmann, *Moses the Egyptian: The Memory of Egypt in Western Monotheism* (Cambridge: Harvard University Press, 1997); see also Assmann, *Herrschaft und Heil: Politische Theologie in Altägypten, Israel, und Europa* (Munich: Carl Hanser, 2000); Assmann, *Religion und kulturelles Gedächtnis* (Munich: Beck, 2000; ET *Religion and Cultural Memory: Ten Studies*, trans. Robert Livingstone [Stanford: Stanford University Press, 2006]); Assmann, *Die Mosaische Unter-*

Schwartz's *The Curse of Cain. The Violent Legacy of Monotheism*,[5] which however was little noticed in the German-language discussion of monotheism. Both books refer to the Hebrew Bible or the Old Testament. Whereas according to Assmann the "either-or" of monotheism (something is either true or not) engenders practices of domination, according to Schwartz, it is the principle of scarcity as the principle of the one (one G*d, one country, one nation) which engenders violence and competition by dividing people into Israelites and non-Israelites, insiders and outsiders, and thereby defines religious identity as exclusive. Monotheism and its the*logy, that is, the speaking about the divine must therefore be problematized in domination-critical terms.

However, this debate on biblical monotheism is much older than one or two decades. As early as 178 C.E., Celsus criticized Christian monotheism in his polemic against Christianity. Celsus called the Christian refusal to worship any gods besides their own "the cry of sedition of people who separate themselves and stand aloof from all human society" (Origen, *Contra Celsum* 8.2). In presenting monotheism as a threat to the order of the Roman Empire, Celsus associates Christian monotheism and its the*logy—that is, its way of speaking about G*d—with violence and contempt for humanity.

According to Marie-Theres Wacker, who in a number of works has surveyed feminist and malestream scholarly discussions of monotheism in the First, or Old, Testament and sought to bring them into conversation with each other, the critique of monotheism crystallizes itself in three contradictory dichotomies: *first*, a totalitarian idea of unity versus a sharing of power and pluralism; *second*, a dualistic worldview versus divinization of the cosmos; *third* and finally, violence versus tolerance.[6] She also points to "continually recurring anti-Jewish expressions in the malestream and feminist critiques of monotheism."[7] Important for the feminist quest for the Goddess is the religious-historical awareness that "Israel's pre-exilic belief in God cannot yet be called monotheistic, inasmuch as the power of other gods and the fascination they exercised over Israel" are considered to have been "very influential."[8] Wacker asks further whether the figure of divine Wisdom can disrupt the rigid pattern of "postexilic monotheism" and how with reference to divine Wisdom an inclusive monotheism can be articulated.

As a result of her discussion she draws this conclusion:

---

scheidung oder der Preis des Monotheismus (Munich: Carl Hanser, 2003; ET *The Price of Monotheism*, trans. Robert Savage [Stanford: Stanford University Press, 2010]).

5. Regina M. Schwartz, *The Curse of Cain: The Violent Legacy of Monotheism* (Chicago: University of Chicago Press, 1997).

6. Marie-Theres Wacker, *Von Göttinnen, Göttern, und dem einzigen Gott: Studien zum biblischen Monotheismus aus feministisch-theologischer Sicht* (Münster: LIT, 2004), 80-87.

7. Ibid., 87.

8. Ibid., 91.

The alternative of a women-friendly Goddess religion must be kept in mind whenever the biblical tradition of monotheism is claimed in the interests of those dominant at the time, perhaps as Euro-centrism in politics and economics, as racism, as androcentrism. . . . However, if the demand for universal justice is permanently connected with the God of the Hebrew Bible, then we must speak of this God today and witness actively to his name in such a way that it becomes apparent that his justice also pertains to women.[9]

Such a domination-critical moment is also necessary with regard to the New, or better, the Christian, Testament and the history of early Christianity, since they were articulated in the context of the Roman *imperium*. Erik Peterson's tractate, "Der Monotheismus als politisches Problem," had already appeared in 1935, but in the late 1960s it gave a new impulse to discussions of political the*logy.[10] According to Peterson, Philo merged the philosophical principle of *monarchia*, first attested by Aristotle, with the G*d of the Jews and then came into contact with a pagan political the*logy according to which, in analogy to the Roman *imperium*, the divine monarchy had to rule just as the national Gods of Rome had to govern. The *Pax Augusta* could thus be understood by Christians as the fulfillment of the Old Testament prophecies.

Erik Peterson thus recognized the intertwining of monarchical monotheism and the political imperial rhetoric that legitimated the Roman empire. However, he plays down this insight by asserting at the same time that, on the one hand, the doctrine of the divine monarchy had to fail in the face of the trinitarian dogma and, on the other hand, the interpretation of the *Pax Augusta* had to fail in the face of Christian eschatology. Jürgen Moltmann argues similarly, by adopting Peterson's theses in a positive sense and expanding them in a critique of patriarchy.[11] But this the*logical apologetics fails to provide an answer to the question of why Christianity, despite the achievement of its trinitarian monotheism, exercised imperial domination and violence, especially in times when it had direct access to political power. Defenders of Christian-trinitarian monotheism do not ask this question on the one hand, and on the other in the face of the postmodern challenge to monotheism, formulate apologetic arguments according to which Christian monotheism is to be preferred to Jewish and Islamic monotheism because it is less violent. However, there is no doubt historically, that Christianity has exercised imperial domination in the name of the triune G*d and today continues to legitimate kyriarchy either biblically or the*logically wherever the exercise of its power is at stake.

---

9. Ibid., 102-3.

10. Erik Peterson, *Theologische Traktate*, 1st ed. (Munich: Kösel, 1951), 23-82; See also Alfred Schindler, ed., *Monotheismus als politisches Problem? Erik Peterson und die Kritik der politischen Theologie* (Gütersloh: Gütersloher, 1978).

11. Jürgen Moltmann, "Kein Monotheismus gleicht dem anderen: Destruktion eines untauglichen Begriffs," *Evangelische Theologie* 62/2 (2002): 112-22.

The scholarly discussion of monotheism in the last decades, however, has not concerned itself so much with the rhetoric of Christian monotheism shaped by imperial kyriarchy, as it has instead concentrated primarily on the monotheism of the Hebrew Bible. But while Jan Assmann's thesis of the "Mosaic Difference" was broadly accepted and critically evaluated, Regina Schwartz's book has been scarcely noticed. Both argue that biblical monotheism, with its commandment: "you shall have no other gods beside me," goes hand in hand with violence and exclusion.[12]

Regina Schwartz, a literary critic, emphasizes that her book was inspired by a college student's question. After a lecture on the Bible in which Schwartz had stressed that Israel's G*d was a G*d of justice and liberation, a student asked: "What about the Canaanites? Did that apply to the Canaanites too?" Yes, she thought, how about the Canaanites, the Amorites, the Moabites, the Hittites, and all the other peoples whom the biblical G*d confronted with violence? It is this question of violence toward the Other and the formation of identity created by it that inspires her book.

Although Schwartz long before had realized that the Bible often served to fan the flames of hatred against Blacks, Jews, gays, wo/men, and the poor, it was only at this point that she began to understand the Bible's complicity in these prejudices, "for over and over the Bible tells the story of a people who inherit at someone else's expense."[13] Hence, she began to do research on monotheism and collective identity. She was concerned not only to analyze the biblical narratives in which liberation and justice are associated with the extirpation of the Canaanites, but also to understand how knowledge of the Bible negatively has shaped Western culture and has defined ethnic, religious, and national identity as standing in violent opposition to the Others. The question of "monotheism and collective identity" is for Schwartz not so much a matter of one G*d as distinct from many Gods, but a question of the price to be paid when collective identity becomes a demand for allegiance to a single principle, whether it is G*d or nationalism, that engenders violence against others. As noted above, she argues it is scarcity as the principle of the One (one G*d, one people, one nation) that evokes violence by separating people into Israelites and non-Israelites, Insiders and Outsiders, and by determining religious identity as exclusive.

As a Jewish scholar, Regina Schwartz is very conscious that her interpretations can be construed as anti-Jewish. Therefore she repeatedly emphasizes that these biblical texts of violence are not historical descriptions but were written

---

12. In his most recent book, *Monotheismus und die Sprache der Gewalt* (Vienna: Picus, 2006), Assmann emphasizes "that violence is not inscribed in monotheism as its necessary consequence" (56). He sees the problem as much more in that "the language of violence is inscribed in the sacred scriptures of the Jews, Christians, Muslims, and many other religions founded on an exclusive concept of truth" (20), a problem that has been extensively treated in feminist and postcolonial hermeneutics.

13. Schwartz, *The Curse of Cain*, x.

many centuries later, after the exile, when Israel was powerless. The conquest of the Canaanites was the fantasy of a people in exile and could only produce social-political violence when it was adopted by groups that held ruling power in Christianity. Jan Assmann is equally careful not to make the Jews responsible for the gruesome deeds of monotheism. While according to him Judaism "excluded" itself, Christianity and Islam have excluded others with the help of state power. Such violence has directed itself inward in the condemnation of heretics and outward in the violent missionizing of peoples.

However, Schwartz stresses repeatedly that inscribed in the Bible are also glimpses of monotheistic abundance and of G*d's unending gift of well-being for all. However, these moments of abundance did not have the same cultural-religious impact on politics, culture, and religion as those of the scarcity conditioned by monotheism. The violence inscribed in the Bible can thus be treated in two different ways: it can be validated by being preached as G*d's revelation, or it can be deconstructed again and again through a hermeneutics of suspicion and evaluation in order to bring to critical attention the biblical-Christian identity that stands in violent opposition to the Other in order to replace it with an inclusive biblical discovery of identity.

Theoretical Approach

At this point it is necessary that I briefly describe my own methodical approach and hermeneutical lens with which I view the problem. No one will probably be surprised to learn that I approach the problem of "monotheism versus polytheism" with a critical feminist lens. Yet, feminism is still for many a negative concept that is regarded in the academy as "ideological" and not "scientific" or "scholarly." Hence, it is not surprising that the broad feminist discussion on the question of G*d is almost never mentioned in malestream debates on monotheism. It is also rarely recognized that feminist the*logy and religious studies consist of many different theories and voices, depending on their central category of analysis: *woman, the feminine, gender, patriarchy* or *kyriarchy*.

In my understanding, feminism is a theory and a movement that critically places at the center of its scholarly and practical attention structures of domination and subordination that marginalize wo/men and other peripheral people, exploit them and make them second-class citizens. Feminist the*logy and religious studies attempt to uncover and analyze such religious structures of kyriarchy. They insist the*logically that women as well as men are made in G*d's image.[14] Hence they make the divine present here and now.

---

14. See Helen Schüngel-Straumann, Chana Safrai, Elisabeth Gössmann, and Irene Willig, "Gottebenbildlichkeit," in *Wörterbuch der feministischen Theologie*, ed. Elisabeth Gössmann et al. (Gütersloh: Gütersloher, 2002), 257-65.

The hermeneutical lens and method with which I approach the topic are those of a Christian feminist hermeneutics of liberation and critical rhetorical analysis. With liberation the*ology, I am convinced that the central the*logical question today is not the modern question as to whether G*d exists—that is, whether there is one G*d or many—but the rhetorical question of how we speak about G*d the*logically and what kind of G*d we proclaim. Is it a G*d of domination, violence, and subordination or is it a G*d who engenders the well-being of all without exception and out of whose abundance community, peace, and happiness are made possible in our global world? If the slogan "my G*d is the true one, and not your Goddess" is ontologically reified, biblical texts of violence and exclusion will again and again contribute to a violent religious identity formation. Hence, I argue, the problem of "monotheism versus polytheism" must not be approached as an ontological one, but must be analyzed as a dualistic rhetoric and reformulated in terms of the*logy critique.

A critical feminist rhetorical analysis can show that what is at stake in the monotheism debate is not so much the*logy in the proper sense of the word, but rather the problem of exclusion, domination, and power, which are either continued and advanced or called into question by biblical the*logy. Intertwined with this problem is the question of how the symbol "G*d" strengthens or undermines ideological power relationships. It is therefore important to analyze rhetorically how the problem of "monotheism" is discussed, in order to be able to find the*logically a different way of imagining and articulating the divine.

Language, and hence also biblical language about G*d, is always already rhetorical and communicative. It is shaped and formed by its social, political, and religious contexts. Therefore the*ology must not only attempt to investigate what is said about the biblical G*d, but also ask why monotheism is so hotly contested. Its first aim is not to determine ontologically what monotheism is, but to investigate how monotheism is rhetorically constructed in particular social-political contexts.

While the concern of hermeneutics is ontology, the discovery of meaning, the surplus of meaning and cultural memory, of text as "being that can be remembered,"[15] a critical-rhetorical analysis focuses on the lack and the deformation of meaning contexts and scholarly methods that are caused by oppressive power relationships, that is relationships of kyriarchy. Cultural, religious, and social speech acts and traditions are constituted within relationships of unequal power and must therefore be critically investigated. This applies also to monotheism and the language about G*d.

Kyriocentric language and knowledge about the divine are rhetorical, that is, they are articulated by particular people for a particular group of readers or

---

15. Jan Assmann, *Religion and Cultural Memory* (2006), ix.

hearers, and work with particular articulated or suppressed interests and goals. If all the texts of sacred Scripture and all knowledge about the divine and the world are both rhetorical and political, it is possible to critically question the cultural relationships, religious theoretical frameworks and ideological constructs that are continually re-inscribed by such texts and traditions, in order to change them.

Just like critical theory, so also a feminist critical rhetorical analysis focuses on the corruption and ideological alienation of speech acts. Its fundamental methodical insight is the recognition of the androcentric or, better, kyriocentric function of language.[16] It emphasizes the rhetorical nature of language: grammatically andro-kyriocentric language pretends to be generic-inclusive language that, on the one hand, subsumes wo/men under grammatically masculine expressions such as monotheists, Christians, Americans, slaves, disciples, or Gods,[17] and on the other hand excludes us from full humanity and the divine because both are masculine-defined.

Thus grammatically andro-kyriocentric language does not describe and reflect the reality and being of G*d; it only regulates and constructs it.[18] Kyriocentric language is not reflective, but active-performative. It both creates and shapes the symbolic worlds it claims only to represent. Insofar as God is unreflectively called *he* and *him*, kyriocentric language creates again and again an elite, male-determined world and identity of the divine.

But language is not only active-performative; it is also always already political and normative. Kyriocentric language shapes and at the same time is shaped by existing ideas of reality and relationships of kyriarchy. Kyriocentric language

---

16. See Elisabeth Schüssler Fiorenza, *In Memory of Her: A Feminist Reconstruction of Christian Origins* (New York: Crossroad 1983); Dennis Baron, *Grammar and Gender* (New Haven: Yale University Press, 1986); Robert H. Robins, *A Short History of Linguistics* (London: Longmans, 1979); Casey Miller and Kate Swift, *Words and Women: New Language in New Times* (Garden City: Doubleday, 1977); Gloria A. Marshall, "Racial Classifications: Popular and Scientific," in *The "Racial" Economy of Science*, ed. Sandra Harding (Bloomington: Indiana University Press, 1993), 116-27. For a comparison of sexist and racist language, see the essays in Mary Vetterling-Braggin, ed., *Sexist Language: A Modern Philosophical Analysis* (Littlefield: Adams, 1981).

17. See Luise F. Pusch, *Das Deutsche als Männersprache* (Frankfurt: Suhrkamp, 1984); Marilouise Janssen-Jurreit, *Sexism: The Male Monopoly on History and Thought* (New York: Farrar, Strauss, and Giroux, 1982), 291-92.

18. This has far-reaching consequences for the writing of history. Not only are wo/men marginalized historically by androcentric texts or written entirely out of historical sources; they are doubly marginalized and historically eliminated by andro-kyriocentric models of reconstruction. For example, Alföldy's social reconstruction model, much used in biblical scholarship, makes no explicit mention of wo/men. This is rightly recognized by Ekkehard W. and Wolfgang Stegemann, *The Jesus Movement: A Social History of its First Century*, trans. O. C. Dean Jr. (Minneapolis: Fortress Press, 1999), 65-67, but it is not mitigated by the addition of a fourth section on "social roles and situations of women." Instead, it is intensified, since the rest of the book then speaks about the social history of early Christian communities without specifying that this refers only to men.

about G*d such as Lord, King, Almighty serves kyriarchal interests and, in turn, kyriarchal interests determine the content of kyriocentric language about the divine. Hence, an intra- and intertextual analysis of language and text are insufficient. They must be laid open by a critical systematic analysis of religio-political structures of kyriarchy that practice violence and exclusion in order to be revealed as legitimating domination or critically questioning it.[19]

It is relationships of domination and power over others that evoke these distorted forms of communication and legitimate the interests, needs, and perceptions of the social and religious world as "common sense." Hence, the feminist critique of ideology understands language as a way to inscribe forms of power into meaning contexts. It asks why monotheism is so hotly disputed today. It does not seek in the first place to confine monotheism by defining it, but tries instead to understand how monotheism is rhetorically the*logically constructed by scholarship.

Studying ideologies means not only to nail down a particular discourse, but also to investigate ways of interpretation and of meaning making rhetoric, that either serve to strengthen the violence of kyriarchy or to undermine it. A critique of ideology, however, also demands that the theoretical frameworks and patterns that organize and shape biblical knowledge and interpretations must be critically analyzed.

The Dualistic Thought-Pattern: Monotheism-Polytheism

The discussion of biblical monotheism is firmly embedded in the religious-philosophical dualism of *monotheism-polytheism* or the pattern *monotheism-cosmotheism-pantheism*. Therefore it is necessary to contextualize and deconstruct this theoretical-dualistic religious-philosophical pattern, "monotheism-polytheism," in order to be able to understand "monotheism" not as onto-the*logy, but as rhetoric.

It is generally acknowledged that the concept of monotheism is not a biblical-the*logical, but a modern concept. The monotheism-polytheism dualism was introduced as a religious-philosophical method for classifying religions in terms of their ideas about G*d. The concept of *polytheism* goes back to Philo and was rediscovered by Jean Bodin in 1580. It was then introduced by Henry Moore in 1660 as a *contrasting concept* over against *polytheism*. Monotheism is thus a dualistic concept that cannot survive without its opposite. This contrast was then used by Christian the*logians to assert the superiority of Christianity as *"vera*

---

19. Although such feminist models of social reconstruction exist, they are often simply not acknowledged, let alone discussed. See Hannelore Schröder, "Feministische Gesellschaftstheorie," in *Feminismus: Inspektion der Herrenkultur—Ein Handbuch*, ed. Luise F. Pusch (Frankfurt: Suhrkamp, 1983), 449-76, or my work on kyriarchy.

religio," the only true religion, and to disqualify polytheistic religions as paganism.[20] This religious-philosophical dualistic pattern of "monotheism-polytheism" articulated demeaning, excluding structures for non-monotheistic religions, while arguing that monotheism is a positive category originating in Christian religion and asserting the superiority of the Christian notion of G*d.[21]

And yet, since the nineteenth century voices to the contrary have also been raised who point out that, with its insistence on the one, other-worldly G*d alone, monotheism leads not only to the impoverishment of religion and to "the suppression of the development of the vital spirit of humanity" but also to the authorizing and sanctioning "of all kinds of freedom and maturity."[22] At the beginning of the twenty-first century, monotheism—with its denial of all other Gods—is no longer a matter of "common sense" in a pluralistic society in which many religions coexist. The logic of monotheism struggles against the principle of pluralistic Western societies that insist on respect for human dignity and freedom of religion to the extent that the ultimate conclusion of its logic is a denial of the truth of other religions.[23]

The contrasting dualism of "monotheism-polytheism" is given different accents and applications within this debate. Christian the*logians seek to defend monotheism in a positive way against its cultural critics. They often do this in order to assert their own particular monotheism as "better" over against the representatives of other monotheisms.

This discussion of monotheism and polytheism moves largely on the philosophical-ontological level and does not question the dualistic rhetoric that constructs monotheism and polytheism antagonistically. This dualistic religious-philosophical pattern, as Grace Jantzen has shown, cannot avoid continuing and newly inscribing the series of oppositional principles of unity and multiplicity, any more than the ancient Neoplatonic-Pythagorean dualism could do so.[24] Grace Jantzen refers to Aristotle for the construction of such dualisms.

In his *Metaphysics* (986a), Aristotle in turn attributes the following table to Pythagoras:

---

20. Gregor Ahn, "Monotheismus und Polytheismus als religionswissenschaftliche Kategorien?" in *Der eine Gott und die Götter*, ed. Oeming and Schmidt (Zürich: Theologischer, 2003), 1-10.

21. See the overview of the use of the concept of monotheism in the modern history of the*logy by Christoph Schwöbel, "Monotheismus IV," *TRE* 23 (1994): 256-62.

22. Friedrich Nietzsche, "Der Antichrist," in *Sämtliche Werke: Kritische Studienausgabe in 15 Bänden*, ed., Giorgio Colli and Mazzino Montinari (Berlin: de Gruyter, 1999), 6:185.

23. Wolf Krötke, "Der Glaube an den einen Gott. Zur christlichen Prägung des 'Monotheismus,'" *Berliner Theologische Zeitschrift* 22 (2005): 74.

24. Grace M. Jantzen, *Becoming Divine: Toward a Feminist Philosophy of Religion* (Bloomington: Indiana University Press, 1999), 265-75.

Monas (unity: positive series)	*Dyas* (multiplicity: negative series)
limit	limitlessness
even numbered	odd numbered
unity	multiplicity
right	left
male	female
at rest	in motion
straight	crooked
light	darkness
good	evil
simultaneous	non-simultaneous

The first century C.E. Jewish writer Philo presupposes this form of onto-the*logy. According to Erik Peterson, Philo associated this onto-the*logy with the concept of *monarchia*. Roman legal philosophy took up the opposition of unity (monarchy, peace, empire) and multiplicity (chaos, war, violence). The One is the symbol of the *Pax Romana*, the Two that of *discordia*. This ontological thought-pattern of unity and multiplicity shaped the ideological consciousness of the Hellenistic period and of early Judaism and Christianity.

Feminist analysis has further shown that such dualisms are not logical pairs, but constitute ideological dual-ness in which are inscribed unequal power-relationships that must be examined. The positive left side of the table is orderly, good, and male, while the right side is chaotic, bad, and female. In Platonic philosophy the left side was associated with spirit and reason and the right side with body and matter. Wo/men and world were thus conceptually equated with earth, matter, chaos, and evil, while men were seen as linked to G*d, goodness, spirit, and truth. In Western symbolism the divine One was thought of as pure spirit, pure goodness, and male, as the Wholly Other in contrast to the material world, chaos, and the female. This polarizing dualism was understood kyriocentrically, so that the subordinate term represents solely denial or negation, absence and deprivation of the primary concept. The primary term is self-defining in that it excludes its Other.

Ontological dualisms that serve definitional ends thus simultaneously conceal the relationships of domination that they seek rhetorically-ideologically to legitimate. Such relations of domination are usually labeled "hierarchical" in scholarly discourse. But this label applies only to sacral relations of kyriarchy and thus conceals the lord-*kyrios*-determined social and political pyramid of dominance and ideology. Hence, hierarchy is best understood as kyriarchy, and its ideology as kyriocentrism.

While kyriarchy theoretically names the imperial-master intertwined power structures of the ancient and modern male-determined pyramid of domination, kyriocentrism is its ideological legitimation, necessary wherever the radical democratic ethos of "the equal power of the many" (Hannah Arendt) challenges kyriarchy fundamentally. Since democracy claims equal power and dignity for the many, but historically has been largely limited to a male elite, that is, to propertied, educated gentlemen (Greek *kyrioi*), the ideological and the*logical legitimation of kyriarchy became again and again necessary.

The critique of monotheism, then, is not really so much about the question of how one can conceive of and express *divine being* but more about the problem of the exclusivist claim to truth, the exclusivist formation of identity, and the exclusion of the female—problems that unavoidably indicate the presence of kyriarchy and violence. But violence and domination are not only a problem of monotheistic religions; they are also a problem of polytheistic, pantheistic, or cosmo-theistic religions. It is not monotheism but access to dominant power that produces violence, as the example of the Roman Empire richly documents.

The problem of domination and the question of violence require that we critically question the opposition between monotheism and polytheism as well as their underlying onto-the*logy, if we are to overcome the rhetoric of kyriarchy that is inscribed in this binary opposite. This cannot be done, as we have seen, on the religious-philosophical, ontological level, since the dualism that excludes and negatively describes the Other is essentially inscribed in the monotheism-polytheism schema.

Speaking about the Divine

It is necessary to rhetorically deconstruct the pattern "monotheism-polytheism" and its dualistic conceptions in order to reflect anew on *the*legein*, that is on speaking about the divine, and to rhetorically overcome the ontological dualism of the One and the Many in order to make it the*logically fruitful. This is possible, I argue, when we take up the four methods of traditional Christian the*logy for speaking about G*d—the *viae affirmativa, negativa, eminentiae,* and *practica*—and combine them to correct one another. All four rhetorical-the*logical strategies must be engaged together and not in isolation, while at the same time remaining rooted in the *via practica*.

First, since G*d radically exceeds human experience, since She/He/It is the X beyond all of beyond-being, no human language, not even that of the Bible, is adequate for speaking about G*d.[25] Therefore the *via negativa* of classical the*logy underscores

---

25. See Frank Crüsemann, "Gott Abrahams, Gott Isaaks, Gott Jakobs: Notizen zur Frage eines Kriteriums eines theologischen Redens von Gott," in *Zugänge zur Wirklichkeit: Theologie und Philosophie im Dialog*, ed. Karl Holzmüller and Norbert Ihmig (Bielefeld: Luther, 1997), 163-69, quoting Martin Buber: "For the idea of God, the masterwork of the human, is nothing but the image of images, the most sublime of all images," thus emphasizing that the prohibition against

that we are not really able to say who G*d is but must repeatedly emphasize who G*d is *not*. S/he is not like a man, not like a sage, not like a father, not like a king, not like a ruler, not like a master. S/he is also not like a woman, not like a mother, not like a queen, not like a lady. Nor is It like fire, or like a mother's womb, or like a wind, or like an eagle, or like a burning bush. Such a critical rejection and deconstruction of kyriocentric maleness and femaleness, guidance and subjection, orthodoxy and heresy, monotheism and polytheism as determinants for speaking about G*d is one of the most important tasks of the*logy, not only of feminist the*logy.

Second, Christian talk about G*d begins with the conviction that the biblical G*d is not a G*d of oppression and violence, but of liberation, goodness, and well-being, and it attempts to express this conviction in varied ways. Therefore an affirmative the*logical strategy (*via affirmativa* or *analogica*) attributes to G*d in a positive way all utopian desires for justice and well-being of which countless peoples dream and for which they hope. Such an affirmative analogical discourse about G*d, however, dare not restrict itself to anthropological individualism; it must remain oriented toward the reality and vision of the fullness of creation.

If the*logy remains critically aware of the analogical character of its language about G*d and the apophatic[26] character of the divine it will also be able to introduce into Christian speaking about G*d the multifaceted images and names of the G*ddess, like those that are for example, in Catholicism traditionally kept alive in and through the cult of Mary.[27] As Judith Plaskow has demanded of Jewish the*logy, so also Christian feminists must insist that Christian the*logy overcome its "fear of the Goddess."[28] The danger of Jewish and Christian monotheism does not consist in the worship of the divine in fe/male form,[29] but in the fact that monotheism has served to legitimate kyriarchal domination.[30]

---

images is the criterion for every kind of the*logical speaking about God (165). However, he does not reflect that according to his title G*d is conceived only in terms of maleness and patriarchy.

26. Apophatic, or negative, the*logy asserts that the divine is ineffable and can be known to humans only in terms of what the divine is not (such as "G*d is unknowable").

27. Such a set of many-faceted, the*logical wisdom associations and imaginative expansions is visible, for example, in *Akathistos*, a Marian hymn of the Eastern church. We can see in it how biblical language can be adapted in feminist ways: "Hail, O Sea who drowned the symbolic Pharaoh; hail, O Rock who quenched those who thirst for Life; hail, O Pillar of Fire who guided those in darkness . . . Hail, O Land of the promised good; hail, O you who flows with milk and honey! Hail, O Bride and Maiden ever-pure." Cf. Gerhard G. Meersemann, ed., *Der Hymnos Akathistos im Abendland: Die älteste Andacht zur Gottesmutter* (Freiburg: Herder, 1958). For English see the Medieval Sourcebook: www.fordham.edu/halsall/source/akathis.html.

28. Judith Plaskow, *Standing Again at Sinai: Judaism from a Feminist Perspective* (New York: Harper and Row, 1990), 121-69.

29. For an extensive, annotated bibliography, see Anne Carson, *Goddesses and Wise Women: The Literature of Feminist Spirituality, 1980–1992* (New York: Freedom, 1992). For interreligious discussion, see Carl Olsen, ed., *The Book of the Goddess: Past and Present* (New York: Continuum, 1983). For a personal, the*logical accounting, see especially Carol P. Christ, *Laughter of Aphrodite: Reflections on a Journey to the Goddess* (San Francisco: Harper and Row, 1987).

30. For the connections between speaking about G*d and wo/men's self-esteem see Carroll Saussy, *God Images and Self Esteem: Empowering Women in a Patriarchal Society* (Louisville: WJK, 1991).

The *third* strategy of classic the*logical rhetoric, the *via eminentiae*, pre-supposes the first two strategies but emphasizes that both the rejection of male language about G*d and the way of speaking of G*d positively in fe/male terms as G*ddess are also inadequate. The divine is always greater and always more than human language and experience can express. This "surplus" of the divine makes necessary a conscious multiplication and expansion of images and symbols for G*d that are derived from both human life and nature, and cosmological realities. The *via eminentiae* is thus able to reclaim a rich treasure of biblical symbols and metaphors, together with the multifaceted images and traditions of the G*ddess, for the*logical discourse about the divine.

Fourth, the final traditional the*logical strategy, the *via practica*, is usually associated with liturgy and spirituality. However, a critical feminist the*logy[31] seeks to locate language about G*d especially in the praxis and solidarity of anti-kyriarchal social and ekklesial liberation movements. The creativity and emotionality of our speaking about the divine must remain rooted in such social movements so that it cannot be misused in a kyriarchal and reactionary fashion to inculcate cultural femininity or racist mentality. Thus the *via practica* must critically consider and determine all languages about G*d, especially those that shape our praxis.

Although G*d is "beyond" oppression, Her revelatory presence can be experienced in the midst of the struggles against dehumanization and injustice. Therefore the divine must be named ever anew in such experiences of struggles for justice and the transformation and reformation of oppressive structures and dehumanizing ideologies. G*d, as the active power of justice and well-being in our midst, is to be called upon in ever new and different ways. It is She/He/It who strengthens us in our struggles against injustice and for justice, just as She/He/It accompanied the Israelites on their way through the wilderness, from slavery to freedom.[32] Such a the*logical method makes it possible to perceive anew the all-encompassing divine Harmony and concord expressed in the domination-free pluralism of images and symbols that is at stake in the debates of monotheism, and to translate them into actions that transform kyriarchy.

---

31. See Ruth C. Duck, *Gender and the Name of God: The Trinitarian Baptismal Formula* (New York: Crossroad, 1991).

32. See Wisdom 10:1-21.

12

Toward a Feminist Wisdom Spirituality of Justice and Well-Being[1]

In the last decades spirituality has become a key topic not only in the*logy but also in commercialized forms of self-help groups and the New Age movements. Spirituality has become a big business. Leading companies everywhere are tuning into the power of spirituality as they look for conveying company goals and for inspiring their people to do their best in the global market place. In the process, spirituality has become a popular but also an enigmatic and vacillating term that means different things to different people. By focusing on wisdom/ Wisdom, human or divine, as the horizon of a feminist spirituality of struggle, I want to probe the possibilities for articulating a political Wisdom spirituality that sustains rather than mutes struggles for survival and liberation. Such a spirituality has to focus on wo/men's struggles to survive and transform relations of domination. At its heart is the discernment of Wisdom-Spirit working in different global contexts.

Wisdom

In the past two decades feminists have rediscovered and recreated the submerged traditions of divine Wisdom in all their splendor and possibilities. Feminist the*logians have discovered anew the creativity of Wisdom and have searched for Her presence in the blank spaces "in-between" the discernible letters. They have sought "to hear Wisdom into speech," to use an expression coined by Nelle

---

1. First published in Portuguese as "Rumo a uma Espiritualidade Sapiencial Feminista de Justica e Bem-estar," in *Teologias come sabor de Mangostao: Ensaios em homenagem a Lieve Troch*, ed. Isabel Aparecida Felix (Sao Bernardo do Campo: Nhanduti, 2009), 191-208.

Morton, one of the first feminist the*logians and teachers of wisdom/Wisdom, who recognized that "Wisdom is feminist and suggests an existence earlier than Word."[2]

In the Bible, "spirit" (*ruach*), "presence" (*shekhinah*), and "wisdom" (*chokmah*) are all three grammatically feminine terms. They refer to very similar female figurations in the Hebrew Bible[3] which express G*d's saving presence in the world. They signify that aspect of the divine that is involved in the affairs of humanity and creation:

> For within Her is a spirit intelligent, holy, unique, manifold, subtle,
> Active, incisive, unsullied, lucid, invulnerable, benevolent, sharp,
> Irresistible, beneficent, loving humans, steadfast, dependable, unperturbed
> Almighty, all-surveying, penetrating all intelligent, pure and most subtle
>   spirit.
> For Wisdom is quicker to move than any motion;
> She is so pure, she pervades and permeates all things.
> She is a breath of the power of G*d, pure emanation of divine glory
> Hence nothing impure can find a way into her. . . .
> Although alone, she can do all; herself unchanging, she makes all things
>   new.
> In each generation she passes into holy souls,
> She makes them friends of G*d and prophets;
> For G*d loves only the one who lives with Wisdom.
> She is indeed more splendid than the sun, she outshines all the
>   constellations;
> Compared with light, she takes first place, for light must yield to night,
> But over Wisdom evil can never triumph (Wisdom 7:22-25. 27-30).[4]

Traditional the*logy has focused on the Spirit, who is in Latin grammatically masculine (*spiritus*) and in Greek grammatically neuter (*to pneuma*), whereas feminist the*logy has rediscovered the divine in female Gestalt or form. Jewish feminists have rediscovered a spirituality of Shekhinah who plays a significant part in some Jewish traditions, and Christian, especially Catholic feminists have elaborated the female figure of divine Wisdom (which in Greek is called Sophia and in Latin Sapientia). Several books of the Bible speak about Her, some of which, however, are not found at all or only in an appendix in Protestant versions

---

2. Nelle Morton, *The Journey Is Home* (Boston: Beacon, 1985), 175. See also my book *Wisdom Ways: Introducing Feminist Biblical Interpretation* (Maryknoll: Orbis, 2001).

3. I use Hebrew Bible instead of Old Testament and Christian Testament instead of New Testament because Old and New Testament are Christian expressions that announce the superiority of Christianity over Judaism.

4. I am quoting from the text of the Revised Standard Version (RSV) of the Bible but have changed masculine language for G*d and humans.

of the Bible.[5] Divine *Wisdom-Sophia*-Sapientia plays a significant role in Orthodox the*logy but less so in modern western the*logy.

In biblical as well as in contemporary religious discourses the word *wisdom* has a double meaning: It can either refer to a quality of life and of a people and/or it can refer to a figuration of the divine. Wisdom in both senses of the word is not a prerogative of the biblical traditions but it is found in the imagination and writings of all known religions. It is trans-cultural, international and inter-religious. Wisdom is practical knowledge gained through experience and daily living as well as through the study of creation and human nature. Both word meanings, that of capability (wisdom) and that of female personification (Wisdom), are crucial for articulating a feminist biblical spirituality that seeks to fashion biblical readers as critical subjects of interpretation.

Wisdom is a state of the human mind and spirit characterized by deep understanding and profound insight. It is elaborated as a quality possessed by the sages but also treasured as folk wisdom and wit. Wisdom is the power of discernment, deeper understanding, and creativity; it is the ability to move and to dance, to make the connections, to savor life and to learn from experience. Its root meaning comes to the fore in its Latin form *sapientia,* which is derived from the verb *sapere* = to taste and to savor something. Wisdom is intelligence shaped by experience and sharpened by critical analysis. It is the ability to make sound choices and incisive decisions.

Wisdom, unlike intelligence, is not something with which a person is born. It only comes from living, from making mistakes and trying again and from listening to others who have made mistakes and trying to learn from them. It is a perception of wholeness that does not lose sight of particularity, relativity and the intricacies of relationships. Wisdom understands complexity and seeks integrity in relationships. It is usually seen as integrating the left and right brain in a union of logic and poetry, as bringing together self-awareness and self-esteem with the awareness and appreciation of the world and the other. Wisdom is neither a specialized discipline nor a discrete field of study. It is a radical democratic concept insofar as it does not require extensive schooling and formal education. Unschooled people can acquire wisdom and highly educated people might lack it.

Wisdom, however, is most fascinating to feminists as a representation of the divine in female form and "Gestalt." She is a divine female figure who in extra-biblical traditions is represented by a variety of Goddesses and Goddess traditions.

---

5. The following books that are called by Protestants "apocryphal" or "deuterocanonical" are usually printed in Protestant Bible editions in an appendix placed after the Christian Testament. They are found in the Roman Catholic, Greek, and Slavonic canon: Tobit, Judith, Wisdom of Solomon, Ecclesiasticus (also called the Wisdom of Jesu Ben Sirach), Baruch, 1 and 2 Maccabees, 3 Maccabees (only in Greek and Slavonic Bibles), 4 Maccabees (only in an Appendix to Greek Bible), 1 Esdras (in Greek Bible; 2 Esdras in the Slavonic Bible), Prayer of Manasseh (in Greek and Slavonic bibles; as appendix in the Vulgate), Psalm 151 (following Psalm 150 in Greek Bible), and additions to the books of Daniel and Esther.

The biblical texts about divine *Wisdom-Chokmah-Sophia-Sapientia* retain the subjugated knowledges and the submerged language of the Goddess within Christian tradition just as the divine *Shekhinah*-Presence does within Judaism. Although the Christian feminist scholarly search for the footprints of *Wisdom-Sophia* in biblical writings encounters a host of historical-the*logical problems, it is nevertheless commonly accepted that the biblical image of *Wisdom-Chokmah-Sophia-Sapientia* has integrated Goddess language and traditions.

Whereas the biblical Wisdom literature generally has been seen as kyriocentric literature written by and for elite educated men, more recent feminist studies have argued that post-exilic wo/men in Israel and Hellenistic Jewish wo/men in Egypt have conceived of divine Wisdom as prefigured in the language and image of Egyptian (Maat, Isis) or Greek (Athena or Dikē) Goddesses. According to a very well known-prayer, all the different nations and peoples use divine titles derived from their own local mythologies when they call on the Goddess, Isis. They do so in the full knowledge that Isis is one, but encompasses all.

In the same way as the widespread Isis cult and mythology, so also the variegated Wisdom discourses of post-exilic Palestinian sages elaborate the image and figure of divine *Chokmah-Wisdom* as the "other name" of G*d. Her ways are ways of justice and well-being. In the figure of *Chokmah-Sophia-Wisdom*, ancient Jewish scriptures seek to hold together belief in the "one" G*d of Israel and the language and metaphors of a female divine being. Hence the texts struggle to subordinate Wisdom to YHWH:

> From everlasting I was firmly set,
> From the beginning before earth came into being.
> The deep was not, when I came into existence,
> There were no springs to gush with water. . . .
> When G*d fixed the heavens firm, I was there . . .
> When G*d assigned the sea its boundaries
> —and the waters will not invade the shore—
> When G*d laid down the foundations of the earth,
> I was by G*d's side, a master craftswoman, delighting G*d day after day,
> Ever at play in G*d's presence, at play everywhere in the world,
> Delighting to be with the children of humanity. (Proverbs 8:23-24, 27, 29-31)

Scholarship and texts about divine *Wisdom-Chokmah-Sophia* have received intensive feminist attention because of the grammatically female gender of *Chokmah-Sophia-Wisdom*. Feminists in the churches have translated the results of biblical scholarship on early Jewish and Christian Wisdom discourses into the idiom of song, poem, story, art and ritual. This practical and creative feminist attention to the divine female figure of Wisdom has brought the results of scholarship on biblical wisdom literature to public attention and has generated vociferous public objections.

For instance, in 1993 Protestant feminists sponsored a conference in Minneapolis that not only featured lectures on divine *Sophia* but also invoked and celebrated her in prayer and liturgy. This Re-Imagining Conference was allegedly the most controversial ecumenical event in decades. Conservatives claimed that it challenged the very foundations of mainline Protestantism in the United States. The reaction of the Christian Right to this conference was so violent that one high-ranking woman lost her church job and others have run into grave difficulties.[6] This struggle indicates the significance and challenge of the divine female figure *Chokhmah-Sophia-Wisdom* for contemporary Christian self-understanding.

Some European feminist the*logians have raised serious historical and the*logical objections against attempts at recovering the earliest Sophia discourses in order to valorize "Lady Wisdom." They have argued that one must reject the figure of divine "Lady Wisdom" as an elite male creation that serves both misogynist and elitist interests. The fascination of feminist the*logy with the figure of *Wisdom-Sophia* is misplaced, they maintain. Wisdom speculation is at home in Israel's elite male circles and bespeaks their interests. They also point to the possible the*logical dangers inherent in such biblical language and imagination.

Shekhinah

A similar debate is taking place among Jewish feminists with respect to the Shekhinah, a biblical figure akin to *Chokmah-Sophia-Sapientia-Wisdom*. The Bible contains only a few references to "the glory of the *Shekhinah*" and to "the wings of the *Shekhinah*." While the meaning of these verses is not at all obvious, the rabbinic sages of the Talmud and Midrash interpreted them as having to do with situations in which the manifestation of G*d and G*d's nearness to humankind or to specific individuals is spoken of.

In the course of gradual the*logical developments that came to fruition in the Kabbalah, the (mystical) literature of the High Middle Ages, the designation *Shekhinah* came to be understood not only as feminine but also as the personification of God's immanent presence in the world. Kabbalistic texts, written by men and prone to extreme objectification of wo/men and femininity,[7] depict a highly esoteric view of creation as a process in which G*d manifests G*d-self in a series of emanations. In the terminology of the Kabbalah, G*d is referred to as *Eyn Sof* (Without End), and is never pictured in human form. In order to create the universe, *Eyn Sof* created ten *Sefirot* (emanations) each corresponding to a

---

6. See Nancy J. Berneking and Pamela Carter Joern, eds., *Re-Membering and Re-Imagining* (Cleveland: Pilgrim, 1995).

7. For a detailed analysis of gender in Kabbalistic literature, see Elliot R. Wolfson, *Circle in the Square* (Albany: SUNY Press, 1995).

different element of his/her divinity. Half of these emanations are portrayed as masculine, half as feminine. The "lowest" of the emanations, *Shekhinah*, is the aspect of God closest to this world. The *Shekhinah*, a feminine hypostasis of G*d in Kabbalistic thought, must be re-united with the male Holy One Blessed Be He, in order for *tikkun* (cosmic reparation) to take place.

With the rise of Jewish feminism in the 1970s, the *Shekhinah* took on new life. Eager to find non-masculine ways to think about G*d, some Jewish feminists embraced the *Shekhinah* in much the same way that non-Jewish feminists embraced a variety of pre-Christian Goddesses and Christian feminists embraced *Wisdom-Sophia*. The *Shekhinah*-songs and rituals of Jewish feminists have tended to crystallize around two interlinked themes: healing of wo/men's ills and creating of wo/men's communities. In all-wo/men groups, Jewish feminists have forged communities of spiritual sisterhoods, have explored Jewish sources for hints about the lives of our foremothers, have created novel biblical exegesis, and have searched for spiritual responses to the transitions, triumphs, and life crises that members have faced over the years. *Shekhinah*-prayers seem to have gathered the most momentum among groups of Jewish wo/men throughout the United States, and more recently around the world, who have been gathering to help one another find spiritual healing in the aftermath of rape, hysterectomy, miscarriage, and other losses.

For instance, Nancy Helman Schneiderman describes a wo/men's healing ritual that she organized after she had a hysterectomy. I quote here the part of the ceremony that is most explicitly related to the *Shekhinah*:[8]

> Two holes, about a foot deep, have been dug in the garden before the ceremony. I stand between them holding my womb in a hard pottery bowl to have it blessed and purified by the pouring of water from a pottery pitcher. *I now join both parts of my life together by the planting of my womb. We draw from our depths the essentials of our sustenance. Our spiritual thirst has caused us to look for new ways of cleansing our bodies and souls.*
>
> All say: (While a friend pours water over the womb)
>
> *Women are like water.*
> *We flow and flow and flow.*
> *Shekhinah is like water.*
> *She bubbles from below.*
>
> Nancy: (Transfers womb to greenware bowl for planting.)
>
> *I offer my womb as a covenant, returning it to the earth, honoring the Source of all life. As I plant it in the ground, my mourning is complete and I am released*

---

8. "Midlife Covenant: Healing Ritual after Hysterectomy," in *A Ceremonies Sampler: New Rites, Celebrations, and Observances of Jewish Women*, ed. Elizabeth Resnick Levine (La Jolla: Women's Institute for Continuing Jewish Education, 1991), 55-60.

from this part of my life (We planted two pear tree saplings, one over the womb and the other in the empty hole).

The image that emerges in Jewish feminist ritual is the image of the Shekhinah understood as female who is associated with such "feminine" elements as the moon. Another image of Her is as a bringer of comfort—particularly, although not exclusively, to wo/men. Talmudic understandings of the Shekhinah's immanence, and Kabbalistic understandings of the Shekhinah, being that part of G*d that is closest to humans, is given new the*logical dimensions: The Shekhinah is "deep within us" and always accessible to us. Hence, we simply need to learn how to look and listen.

However, critical Jewish feminists have pointed to the dangers of such a revival of the *Shekhinah*. Marcia Falk, whose *Book of Blessings* has become a liturgical classic among Jewish feminists, for instance, has rejected *Shekhinah* as a suitable term for Divinity:

> The Shekhinah was not originally a female image; it did not become so until Kabbalistic times. And when it became explicitly associated with the female, it did not empower women, especially not in Kabbalistic thought, where male and female were hierarchically polarized. . . . In Jewish tradition, the Shekhinah has never been on equal footing with the mighty *Kadosh Baruch Hu*, the Holy One Blessed Be He, her creator, her master, her groom, the ultimate reality of which she was only an emanation.[9]

Susan Sered also points to the critical problems that the *Shekhinah* poses for Jewish feminists. The Shekhinah is part of a culture that genders not only aspects of G*d, but also time (the Sabbath is gendered feminine in Jewish culture), space (Jerusalem is gendered feminine in Jewish culture), and the visible "heavenly bodies" (the moon is gendered feminine in Jewish culture). The attribution of gender to G*d, time, and space presents gender as immutably built into the geography of the cosmos. Eternally infused with gender, the universe is understood to be "naturally" gendered. Human resistance to gender roles, in that case, is both aberrant and futile—the universe itself is imbued with gender.

The problem of the *Shekhinah-Presence as well as of Chockmah-Wisdom* raises extremely difficult questions that have to do with the possibility of feminist reclamation of any sort of gendered religious symbol. Can it ever be to wo/men's benefit, Sered asks, to choose to align themselves with feminine symbols and symbolic objects that are at best objectifications of gender difference, and at worst sacred prescriptions for a kyriarchal social order? "Isn't it likely to be the case that the reclamation of gendered religious symbols will simply re-animate and re-energize notions of the perpetual gendering of the universe—notions that

---

9. "Notes on Composing New Blessings," in *Weaving the Visions: Patterns in Feminist Spirituality*, ed. Judith Plaskow and Carol P. Christ (San Francisco: Harper and Row, 1989), 129-30.

serve to constrain the possible life paths open to all individuals by making it seem as if socially constructed gender roles are mirrored in—or mirrors of—divine and cosmic attributes?"[10]

Similar questions can be raised with regard to *Chokmah-Sophia-Sapientia-Wisdom*. The spirituality of the divine feminine that extols the ideal of the *Lady* has a long ideological tradition in biblical religions and is even still pervasive in feminist spirituality. The True Womanhood, or the cult of Eternal Feminine, that I have dubbed the discourse of the "White Lady" was developed in tandem with Western colonization and romanticism that celebrated Christian white elite European wo/men/ladies as paradigms of civilized and cultured womanhood. This ideology legitimated both the exclusion of elite wo/men from positions of power in society and church and at the same time made them colonial representatives who mediated European culture and civilization to the so-called savages.

The philosophy and image of the Eternal Feminine and the cult of the Lady is a projection of elite, western, educated gentlemen and clerics who stress the complementary nature of wo/men to that of men in order to maintain a special sphere for upper class white wo/men. This construct does not have the liberation of every wo/man as its goal but seeks to release the repressed feminine in order to make men whole. Associated with this cult of the "White Lady" was and is a spirituality of self-alienation, submission, service, self-abnegation, dependence, manipulating power, backbiting, powerlessness, beauty and body regimen, duplicity and helplessness—"feminine" behaviors which are inculcated in and through cultural socialization, spiritual direction, and ascetic disciplines such as dieting and cosmetic surgery.

In and through traditional biblical spirituality wo/men either internalize that they are not made in the divine image because G*d is not She but He, Lord/Slave-master/Father/Male, or they are told that if they fulfill their religious and cultural calling to supplement and complement the divine other, they will embody the divine feminine. In both cases cultural and religious structures of self-alienation and domination are kept in place in and through biblical Wisdom spirituality and the the*logical articulation of the divine as Lord.

Feminist objections against the valorization of the biblical Wisdom tradition also point out that this tradition is permanently suspect not only as an elite male tradition but also as one that, in a dualistic fashion, plays out the "good" woman against the "evil" woman.[11] Such a misogynist tradition cannot be concerned with justice at all. However, other scholars specializing in Wisdom literature have rightly objected to such a totally negative evaluation of the Wisdom traditions.

---

10. Susan Sered, "Jewish Wo/men and the Shekhinah," in *In the Power of Wisdom: Feminist Spiritualities of Struggle* ed. Elisabeth Schüssler Fiorenza and Maria Pilar Aquino (London: SCM, 2000), 78-90.

11. However, in fairness to the Wisdom traditions, it must be pointed out that the prophetic or apocalyptic traditions are equally suspect because they are also permeated by kyriocentric bias.

They have pointed out not only that Wisdom discourses are permeated with the teachings of justice,[12] but they also agree that in the first century, prophetic-apocalyptic and sapiential (Wisdom) traditions were intertwined, integrated and changed. These traditions espouse a cosmopolitan ethos that can respect local particularities without giving up claims to universality.

In addition, the advocates of Wisdom argue that the wisdom traditions had long been democratized and that much of the sapiential traditions of the Gospels reflect folk wisdom that very well could have been articulated by and for wo/men. Finally, they point out that feminist exegetical-historical objections against the feminist regeneration of divine *Chokmah-Sophia-Wisdom* may also be due to different confessional locations and indebtedness to Neo-orthodox the*logy.

Moreover, a closer look at the biblical Wisdom traditions reveals that these traditions do not portray divine Wisdom in terms of the Lady. Divine Wisdom is a cosmic figure delighting in the dance of creation, a "master" craftswo/man and teacher of justice. She is a leader of her people and accompanies them on their way through history. Very unladylike she raises her voice in public places and calls everyone who would hear her. She transgresses boundaries, celebrates life, and nourishes those who will become her friends. Her cosmic house is without walls and her table is set for all.

Hence, I suggest biblical discourses on divine Wisdom are still significant today not only because they are a rich resource of female language for G*d but also and more importantly because they provide a framework for developing a feminist ecological the*logy of creation and a biblical spirituality of nourishment and struggle. Moreover, they embody a religious ethos that is not exclusive of other religious visions but can be understood as a part of them, since Wisdom is celebrated in all of them. The earliest Sophia-traditions that still can be traced in the margins of early Christian works intimate a perspective that combines Jewish prophetic, Wisdom and *basileia* (which means "the political realm of G*d" or "G*d's vision of a transformed creation and world") traditions as central to a political, open-ended and cosmopolitan religious vision of struggle and well-being for everyone. In short, biblical Wisdom spirituality is a spirituality of roads and journeys, public places and open borders, nourishment and celebration. It seeks for sustenance in the struggles for justice and cultivates creation and life in fullness.

The goal of wisdom/Wisdom teaching is to enable one to cope with life and to impose a kind of order on the myriad experiences that determine a person. Wisdom teaching is an orientation to proper action, to knowing when to do what. It means to engage in value judgments that urge a certain course of action. Truthfulness, fidelity, kindness, honesty, independence, self-control;

---

12. See also Claudia V. Camp, *Wisdom and the Feminine in the Book of Proverbs* (Sheffield: Almond, 1985).

doing justice means to walk in the way of wisdom/Wisdom. In short, wisdom/ Wisdom holds out as a promise the fullness and possibility of the "good life"; it is a search for justice and order in the world that can be discerned by experience. Wisdom teaching does not separate faith and knowledge, it does not divide the world into religious and secular, but provides a model for living a "mysticism of everyday things."

The Radical Democratic Space of Wisdom

In distinction to traditional spirituality, which is individualistic and privatized, the practice and space of Wisdom spirituality is public. Wisdom's spiraling presence (*Shekhinah*) is global, embracing all of creation; Her voice is a public, radical democratic voice rather than a "feminine" privatized one. To become one of Her justice-seeking friends, one needs to re-imagine a feminist spirituality of justice as the spiraling circle dance of Wisdom. It means to re-imagine feminism as a Spirit/spiritual movement in the open space of Wisdom who calls us out of isolation and invites us to join Her justice movements around the world. She invites us to re-invigorate a feminist movement for change and transformation that is inspired by a vision of justice and human flourishing or well-being. Such a movement is best envisioned in the radical democratic space of wisdom/Wisdom, as the *ekklēsia of wo/men.*

A *radical,* that is *grassroots* (from Latin *radix,* "roots"), democratic Wisdom space is carved out today by social movements for change. Wo/men's grassroots movements around the globe have initiated processes of democratization that allow wo/men to determine their lives, participate in decision making and contribute to the creation of a just civil society and religious community. When I use the word *democracy* I do not mean representative formal democracy, however.

Three broad understandings of democracy and democratization can be distinguished: liberal democracy, Marxist/socialist democracy and direct participatory democracy. *Liberal democracy* entails a shift from the direct rule of the people to representative government that protects individual rights, equal opportunity, constitutional government and separation of powers. *Marxist/socialist democracy* argues that class and other inequalities prevent effective participation of citizens in the political process. Human emancipation is only possible with the overthrow of the global capitalist system. However, socialist democrats increasingly seek to incorporate pluralism and multiculturalism into the theory of democratization.

Participatory radical democracy insists on the literal understanding of democracy as "rule of and by the people." It distinguishes itself from other forms of democracy by the conviction that such "people democracy" is actually realizable. It entails equal opportunities for all to take part in decision making in matters affecting not only the political realm but also the workplace, the community, the church, and interpersonal relations. It encourages wo/men to take control over the course of their lives and supports structural arrangements that encourage us to exercise self-determination, respect the rights of others, to take part in debates about the "common good," and to create new institutions that are truly participatory and egalitarian. Participatory democracy recognizes that "Democracy needs to continue to undergo a process of re-creation and that a more active and substantial participation can only take place as a result of experimentation with new and different ways that seek to enhance citizen involvement and discussion. In a sense, democracy can never be achieved in any final form—it has to be continually re-created and renegotiated."[13]

Grassroots movements are the embodiment of such ongoing democratizing processes. They are community-based initiatives, base groups, or peoples organizations that address practical everyday problems, are committed to improve living conditions in a particular location, and promote values associated with local, decentralized democracy. They redefine the form and content of politics by seeking to create and to expand spaces for democratic decision making, consciousness raising, individual self-development, group solidarity, and more effective public participation. Wo/men are and have been at the forefront in creating and shaping such global processes of democratization.

In modernity most of the social movements for change have been inspired by the dream of radical democratic equality and equal human rights. Since the Western democratic ideal has promised equal participation and equal rights to all but in actuality has restricted power and rights to a small group of elite gentlemen, those who have been deprived of their human rights and dignity have struggled to transform their situations of oppression and exclusion. However, such radical grassroots democratic struggles are not just a product of modernity, nor is their ethos and vision of radical democracy a product restricted to the West. Rather, their ethos and vision is inspired by a radical democratic Wisdom spirituality that empowers people for changing structures of domination.

Just as traditional Christian spirituality, so also a feminist Wisdom spirituality seeks to name dehumanizing and life-destroying evil and deception as well as to identify sources of well-being. Such practices of critical reflection and informed adjudication can be likened to the traditional "spiritual practice" of "discerning the Spirit." But whereas malestream spirituality requires obedience to "spiritual direction," a feminist wisdom spirituality insists on justice. Like malestream spirituality it presupposes that we cannot see reality and ourselves clearly but that we need the light and guidance of divine Wisdom-Spirit. However, it does not assume that we need a spiritual director, spiritual "father" or spiritual "master"

---

13. Jill M. Bystydzienski and Joti Sekhon, eds., *Democratization and Women's Grassroots Movements* (Bloomington: Indiana University Press, 1999), 9. This book analyzes the variety of ways in which wo/men from sixteen different countries struggle "for more control over their daily lives while simultaneously creating and extending opportunities for greater participation" (18).

to escape self-deception and the "snares" of the evil One. Rather, a feminist spirituality replaces the kyriarchal discipline of "spiritual direction" with the practice of a systemic analysis of domination and subordination.

Whether we are able to recognize the structural patterns and mechanisms of domination and dehumanization depends on the lenses or analytic categories we use. Social analytic categories offer "lenses" with which we can approach the sociohistorical rhetorical situations and contexts of our own lives. Such lenses of spiritual interpretation in the "open house" of Wisdom seek to tear down the walls and patterns that dehumanize and divide us from creation and from each other.

The patterns of domination can be seen as functioning like the choreographic design that determines the steps and movements of a dance, although often such designs are not conscious to the dancers. Some kind of a sociopolitical and religious "choreography" of domination is always at work not only in biblical texts and interpretations but also in our own experience and rhetorical situation, even though such patterns are often not conscious or critically reflected.

To take an example from my own religious background, in order to understand Roman Catholic patterns of domination one must ask: What kind of the*logical and ecclesial self-understanding comes to the fore for instance in the banning of condoms or in the prohibition of wo/men's ordination? How is the Roman discourse of power and sexuality constituted and what is its motivating force? What is the social location of these categorical prohibitions and what are its the*logical ramifications? Why does Rome resort to strategies of censure and repression instead of argument and persuasion? What are the fears that continue to motivate wo/men's exclusion from the sacred or their control of procreation?

In order to make conscious the "choreography" of domination we need to use feminist social analytic tools that also can identify an alternative "choreography." Such an analytic is an assemblage of critical concepts and categories that are necessary for critically naming the "choreography" or patterns of domination. Different sociocultural analytics have been developed by liberalism, Marxism, colonialism, socialism, fascism, capitalism, feminism, postmodernism, and other sociopolitical theories.

Since malestream theories, however, generally do not focus on the situation of wo/men but take elite men—or better, gentlemen—as the paradigm for being human, critical liberationist feminists have developed a sociocultural, socioreligious analytic that can provide an interpretation of ourselves and the world in which wo/men no longer are exploited, marginal, and subordinate. In order to be able to adequately "decode" situations of wo/men's oppression and to engage in the ongoing process of transformation, we need to internalize categories of analysis that can help us to recognize malestream sociopolitical and religious-cultural kyriarchal identity formations and discourses of dehumanization.

The ability of subordinated and oppressed people to imagine a complete overthrow of relations of domination and situations of injustice depends on the articulation, circulation, radicalization, and institutionalization of radical egalitarian democratic wisdom/Wisdom discourses. Once people have cultivated the spirit and legitimacy of the principle of justice and equality, they will seek to extend it to all spheres of life.

In and through cultural, political, and religious discourses the social structures in which we are positioned are interpreted. Since we cannot stand outside of the interpretive frameworks available in our society and time, we "make sense" out of life with their help. For instance, one wo/man might be influenced by neo-conservatism and believe that her social position results from the fact that she worked harder in life than the wo/man on welfare who lives down the street. Another wo/man shaped by right-wing religious fundamentalism might explain her situation by the fact that she is blessed by G*d because of her virtuous life, whereas the unmarried mother on welfare has gravely sinned and therefore is punished. Again another wo/man might believe that her success as a wife and mother is due to her feminine attractiveness and selfless dedication to her husband and children, and that the fate of the wo/man on welfare is due to her lack thereof.

A Wisdom Spirituality of Resurrection

If we always have to resort to existing interpretive discourses for making sense of our lives, then the importance of a wisdom discourse and a Wisdom spirituality of justice becomes obvious. Since hegemonic the*logical discourses provide the frameworks in which we "make meaning" in oppressive situations, feminist the*logical works are challenged to provide discourses that illuminate not only the choreography of oppression but also the possibilities for a radical democratic society and religion.

A Christian feminist Wisdom spirituality of justice has rediscovered Jesus as Sophia-Wisdom's prophet, who was executed as the Messiah/Christ, vindicated by G*d as the Living One, and who is always ahead of us. Such a Wisdom spirituality is to be articulated and proven "right" again and again and in variegated ways, within the continuing struggles of the *ekklēsia* of wo/men for survival, justice, and well-being. Such a spirituality derives its life-enhancing powers from our engagement in struggles for justice in society and church. It inspires the *ekklēsia* of wo/men gathered around the table of divine Wisdom. Instead of looking to authorities for solutions and answers, a critical Wisdom spirituality of justice insists that G*d and the resurrected One can only be experienced among us, the Living Ones. The Living One is not to be found among the dead.

The stories of the "empty tomb" are ambiguous and open ended.[14] They invite us to cultivate a Wisdom spirituality of justice that is inspired rather than

---

14. See my book *Jesus: Miriam's Child and Sophia's Prophet* for the elaboration of the significance of the wo/men's witness to the "empty tomb."

threatened by such openness. In the face of the empty tomb the search for ortho-dox control and scientific certainty becomes questionable. Instead the spirituality of the empty tomb valorizes a compassionate practice of honoring those who are unjustly killed in body or spirit. The empty tomb stories of the Gospels celebrate wo/men as faithful witnesses who do not relinquish their commitment and soli-darity with those who fall victim in the struggle against dehumanizing powers. Most importantly, they affirm that Jesus' struggle and all struggles for justice have not ended in execution and death. The tomb is empty!

The Living One is not going "away," to live in heavenly glory, not leaving us to struggle on our own. The "empty tomb" does not signify absence but presence: it announces the presence of *Wisdom-Sophia* on the road ahead, in a particular space of struggles such as Galilee was. According to the Gospel of Matthew Jesus as the Living One, as the embodiment of divine Wisdom, is pres-ent in the "little ones," in the survival struggles of those who are impoverished, hungry, imprisoned, tortured, and killed today. The "empty tomb" proclaims the Living one as present in the faces of our grandmothers who have struggled for survival and dignity, in the *ekklēsia* of wo/men gathered around the table of divine Wisdom.

To sum up my argument here and in the whole book: A feminist wisdom/Wisdom spirituality of justice challenges us to create wisdom/Wisdom the*logies and spiritualities rooted in movements of Wisdom's friends. Feminist the*logy and spirituality need to serve such Wisdom movements for justice and transfor-mation. Such a wisdom/Wisdom spirituality involves moving out of internalized relations of kyriarchal domination and into the radical democratic space of divine Wisdom, the *ekklēsia* of wo/men; it means to nurture multicultural and multi-religious grassroots democratic movements for the well-being of all; it means to initiate and get involved in consciousness-raising wisdom/Wisdom groups. It means to become engaged in the *ekklēsia* of wo/men, which all over the world envisions, debates, and puts into practice such a radical democratic future of well-being for everybody without exception. The primary task of feminist the*logies and studies in religion, I have argued in these pages, is to nurture such move-ments for change and to articulate religious visions of hope and transformation.